Praise for *Dealing with Dilemmas*

"Frank excels in taking a broader view on performance management, and in being able to formulate his inspiring ideas and observations in a clear and understandable way. A formidable combination."

—Dr. Carsten Bange, Founder and Managing
Director of Business Application Research Center (BARC)

"Buytendijk challenges best practices and offers a new view on decision making in business and public sector."

—Dr. Edmund Stoiber, former Minister-President,
Bavaria, Germany

"Dealing with dilemmas is an integrated and perpetual challenge when developing an international business. This book takes an interesting and thought provoking deep dive into the intricacies lying behind all the important decisions we have to make every day."

—Steen Riisgaard, CEO & President, Novozymes A/S

"All executives face dilemmas. Frank Buytendijk, a performance management expert, does a terrific job of combining research, executive perspectives, and a practical view to improve our leadership skills and help us reconcile dilemmas."

—Heidi Melin, Chief Marketing Officer, Polycom

"*Dealing with Dilemmas* is important reading for anyone involved in the development and implementation of corporate strategy. This book explains why most companies, using a purely analytical approach, fail in these endeavors. It provides keen insight into how to identify, understand, and address the dilemmas companies face. By following the innovative framework presented in this book, a company can increase its chances of success."

—Dr. Raef Lawson, Vice President of Research and
Professor Emeritus, Institute of Management Accountants

"Frank Buytendijk's new book takes us on a personal, cultural, and organizational journey into the nature and art of decision making and strategic planning. Rather than reiterate time-worn treatises on these subjects, truly out-of-the-box thinker Buytendijk takes a different perspective, borrowing from philosophy, psychology, economics, and strategy management, and in the process shakes up our preconceptions until we see things in a new light."

—Wayne Eckerson, Director of TDWI Research

Dealing with Dilemmas

Dealing with Dilemmas

Where Business Analytics Fall Short

FRANK BUYTENDIJK

WILEY

John Wiley & Sons, Inc.

Published by John Wiley & Sons, Inc., Hoboken, New Jersey.
Published simultaneously in Canada.

For general information on our other products and services or for technical support, please contact our Customer Care Department within the United States at (800) 762–2974, outside the United States at (317) 572–3993 or fax (317) 572–4002.

Wiley also publishes its books in a variety of electronic formats. Some content that appears in print may not be available in electronic books. For more information about Wiley products, visit our web site at www.wiley.com.

Library of Congress Cataloging-in-Publication Data
Buytendijk, Frank.
   Dealing with dilemmas: where business analytics fall short / Frank Buytendijk.
      p. cm.
   Includes bibliographical references and index.
   ISBN 978-0-470-63031-0 (cloth), ISBN 978-0-470-76846-4 (ebk);
   ISBN 978-0-470-76847-1 (ebk); ISBN 978-0-470-76848-8 (ebk)
   1. Strategic planning.   I. Title.
   HD30.28.B898 2010
   658.4'012—dc22

                                                                    2010007799

Printed in the United States of America

10 9 8 7 6 5 4 3 2 1

Dedicated to Henry Mintzberg

Being confronted with the traditional view of
strategy being a purely analytical, well-defined process,
I always felt intimidated.

Henry Mintzberg's work taught me that, instead,
strategy is messy and mixed up. You learn as you go
along, interpreting ambiguous information and trying to
cope with conflicting requirements. I feel much
more comfortable with this view.

Contents

Foreword

By Dr. David P. Norton
Co-creator, the Balanced Scorecard, and
Founder and Director, Palladium Group, Inc.

Organizations exist to create value for their stakeholders. Strategies describe how they intend to create that value. Mastering the formulation and execution of strategy must be viewed as a central competency of every organization. Research shows this to be an elusive goal: 80 to 90% of organizations fail to execute their strategies. There are two basic reasons for these paltry results. First, there is no generally accepted way to *describe* a strategy. Unlike the financial domain where frameworks like income statements and balance sheets exist to support measurement and communication, the description of business strategies becomes a set of sound bites developed by inspirational leaders. Second, management systems are not linked to the strategy. Personal goals, budgets, investments and compensation are linked to short-term operational and financial goals. If you can't describe a strategy, you can't link it to the management system. You can't manage what you can't measure. And you can't measure what you can't describe. It should not be surprising that 80 to 90% of organizations fail to execute their strategies.

When Bob Kaplan and I developed the concept of a Balanced Scorecard nearly 20 years ago, we were faced with this dilemma. Intellectually, all agreed that organization performance must be looked at in the long term. Accountants used the term "going concern" to convey this. Yet measurement systems intended to motivate performance were focused on the short term, generally measuring financial lag indicators. We developed a simple tool called a *strategy map* to address this problem. The map hypothesized that while financial value for shareholders was the ultimate measure of organization performance, this value was created by building satisfied customers. Customer satisfaction, in turn, was created through internal processes such as quality supply chains, product development and relationship management. Excellence in these processes was, in turn, derived from intangible assets like human capital, culture and technology. The strategy map created a framework of cause and effect that allowed us to deal with the performance dilemma of long term versus short term.

In this excellent book, *Dealing with Dilemmas: Where Business Analytics Fall Short*, author Frank Buytendijk extends the logic of the strategy map to explore several additional dilemmas that frustrate those responsible for executing strategy. Is performance to be managed top-down or bottom-up? Inside-out or outside-in? Do we listen to the customer or do we lead them? Do we optimize today's organization or innovate tomorrow's?

There are no simple answers to these questions. That is the nature of a dilemma. Yet we must develop approaches to deal with them. The answer, in my experience is captured in the work "balanced." Business strategies are a mixture of short-term and long-term, top-down and bottom-up, listening and leading, and so on. The art of the successful executive is to find the balance that is appropriate at different points of time.

Frank Buytendijk is to be commended for the insights and awareness that this book brings to the market. It is an important work that will enhance the effectiveness of your organization.

Preface

"Synthesis is the essence of managing: putting things together, in the form of coherent strategies, unified organizations, and integrated systems. This is what makes managing so difficult—and so interesting. It's not that managers don't need analysis; it's that they need it as input to synthesis. Where to find synthesis in a world so decomposed by analysis?"

Henry Mintzberg, *Managing*, 2009

We are obsessed with analysis. We believe that if we have all the data, and are smart enough, we can solve any problem. In looking for smart people, we test their analytical skills. We invest millions in computer software to analyze customer behavior and business performance. Many professional people even call themselves *analysts* (I was one for many years at industry analyst firm Gartner).

Why is everyone so obsessed with analysis? Analysis is only one style of solving problems. Analysis means taking one big thing (like a problem) and breaking it apart into separate pieces to understand the whole thing. We seem to have forgotten all about *synthesis*, the opposite approach. Take two or more ideas and combine them into a larger new idea. Tackling a problem in this way might lead to entirely new insights, where problems of the "old world" (before the synthesis) do not even occur anymore. Where analysis focuses on working within the boundaries of a certain domain (breaking one big thing into smaller pieces—inside the box), synthesis connects various domains—out of the box.

Why are there no people calling themselves *synthesists*?

Synthesis is particularly useful when one is confronted with something more fundamental than a straightforward problem—such as a dilemma. Dilemmas in strategic decision making is a subject that has fascinated me for years. It seems that many managers are struggling with it. This is probably because straightforward analysis does not help that much. And it is hardly an obscure problem. Many management gurus have pointed out the importance of reconciling dilemmas, and have identified *high-performance organizations* that apparently have found ways of doing so. But how do they do it?

The problem in answering the *how* question is not the lack of research. Research has been extensive and exhaustive in this field, dating back to the old Greek philosophers. But within three mouse clicks you will find philosophers discussing *meta-ethics* while contrasting the *deontological* and the *teleological* view on *moral dissensus* according to *modernist rationality*. That is hardly helpful. You will find economists arguing that making projections as part of business strategy is *stochastic* in nature, and they will advise you to calculate the portfolio variance as $\sigma_p^2 = w_A^2 \sigma_A^2 + w_B^2 \sigma_B^2 + 2w_A w_B \sigma_A \sigma_B \rho_{AB}$. Great, I am sure we have people for that. And while one strategist would offer the advice to let solutions emerge from the bottom, the next strategist will argue that you should adopt a methodical top-down process. Thank you; please agree among yourselves first, and once you have figured it out, do let us know.

Clearly, you can spend a lifetime studying dilemmas and still have no practical answers. What I have tried to achieve with this book is to make some fairly complex concepts accessible and readable, in order to ignite a spark of inspiration and enable a better understanding that dilemmas are not something to be scared about. Doing the research for this book has been quite an experience, broadening my own horizon. The book contains insights from the fields of philosophy, social psychology, intercultural management, mathematics, economics, performance management, innovation, and operations, and a very wide range of strategy topics. I also conducted a survey, the Global Dealing with Dilemmas (DwD) Survey, with a total of 580 respondents. I asked them about the strategic dilemmas in their business, but also about their own personal choices and ways they deal with a dilemma. Finally, throughout the book I share what I have learned through various interviews with top managers around the world. As dealing with dilemmas is what they struggle with every day, these interviews were surprisingly open and engaging.

In my previous book, *Performance Leadership*, I ended by answering a very fundamental question: What is an organization? Most would define it as a group of people sharing the same goals. However, rarely is this the case. In fact, in many cases the parties involved have conflicting requirements. Employees may look for job security, whereas shareholders value the flexibility of a quick reduction in force to save costs. Your customers want a good product at low cost, whereas suppliers try to maximize their profits in selling their products to you. In fact, an organization is better defined as a unique collaboration of stakeholders that reach goals and objectives through the organization that none of them could have reached by themselves. For that, they need to reconcile their differences, facing some stakeholder dilemmas. This thought was a good start for *Dealing*

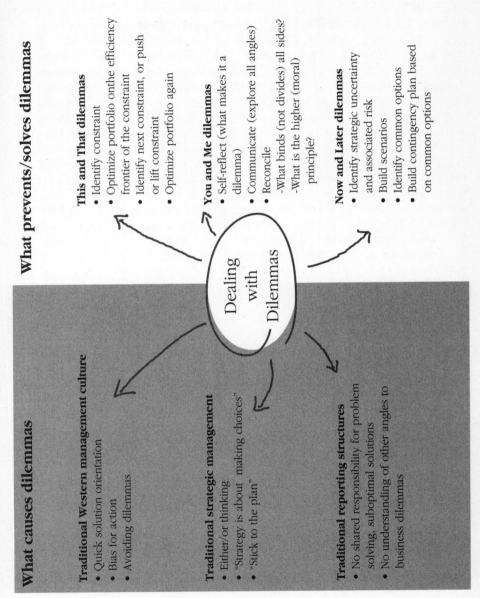

What causes dilemmas

Traditional Western management culture
- Quick solution orientation
- Bias for action
- Avoiding dilemmas

Traditional strategic management
- Either/or thinking
- "Strategy is about making choices"
- "Stick to the plan"

Traditional reporting structures
- No shared responsibility for problem solving, suboptimal solutions
- No understanding of other angles to business dilemmas

What prevents/solves dilemmas

This and That dilemmas
- Identify constraint
- Optimize portfolio onthe efficiency frontier of the constraint
- Identify next constraint, or push or lift constraint
- Optimize portfolio again

You and Me dilemmas
- Self-reflect (what makes it a dilemma)
- Communicate (explore all angles)
- Reconcile
  - What binds (not divides) all sides?
  - What is the higher (moral) principle?

Now and Later dilemmas
- Identify strategic uncertainty and associated risk
- Build scenarios
- Identify common options
- Build contingency plan based on common options

Dealing with Dilemmas

FIGURE 0.1 Dealing with Dilemmas

with Dilemmas: How do we reconcile these various (sometimes even con-flicting) requirements?

While writing this book, I returned to explore another fundamental question: What is strategy? Everyone seems to have his or her own answer. "A plan of action to achieve a particular goal" is the simplest definition of *strategy*, and "making those big choices" would describe *strategic man-agement* very well. I subscribe to a different school of thought that defines strategic management as the art of *creating options*. We cannot predict the future; we can merely be ready for it. The more we can shape our plan of action while going forward, the better it is. And as far as this concerns making big choices, it should be the choice that creates the most options.

There are so many angles to the subject of dilemmas, it is easy to get lost. There are different things that cause dilemmas in strategic decision mak-ing, and if you understand those causes, you can work to prevent them—or sometimes even better—embrace them. There are also multiple types of dilemmas, and each type requires its own toolbox. The graphic shown here provides a high-level mindmap of what causes dilemmas, and what you can do to tackle them. This mindmap also serves as the structure of the book.

Summing it up, *creating options* and *finding synthesis* are the two cor-ner pillars of this book. They opened up a world of creativity for me, and I hope this book does the same for you.

Acknowledgments

There have been many people who have graciously offered their help, and their contributions have made this book what it is. First, I would like to thank Toby Hatch, who was a coauthor of an article on "scenario-based strategy maps" that has become the larger part of Chapter 9. Furthermore, Toby has been a great help in designing the DwD survey and doing the analysis. My gratitude to Claudette Kints, who also helped with the survey design. I would further like to thank Dr. Pietro Micheli of Cranfield University School of Management, who was also a coauthor of the "scenario-based strategy maps" article, for his guidance throughout this book project. He has provided a listening ear and has kept me on track on many occasions. Thank you, Jim Franklin, Steve Hoye, and Dr. Ziggy MacDonald, for your help on Chapter 7, which discusses portfolio management and operations research.

Of course, I would like to express my great gratitude to all who have been so kind as to donate their time, and allow me to speak with them. In alphabetical order of the companies they represent (see the Appendix for all company profiles): Jeroen van Breda Vriesman, member of the Board, Achmea; Bill Fitzsimmons, chief accounting officer, Cox Communications; Nirmal Hansra, former chief financial officer, Fujitsu Australia Pty. Limited; Steen Riisgaard, chief executive officer, Novozymes; Heidi Melin, chief marketing officer, Polycom; Jack de Kreij, member of the board and chief financial officer and Ton van Dijk, chief information officer, Vopak. Special thanks go to General (ret.) Dick Berlijn, former Commander Dutch Armed Forces, and Dr. Edmund Stoiber, former prime minister of Bavaria, the largest state in Germany. Furthermore, I would like to thank the executives who were willing to talk with me but who preferred their companies to stay anonymous.

Then there are 580 thank-yous to all respondents to the DwD Survey. I would also like to acknowledge the help of the Chartered Institute of Management Accountants in the United Kingdom (www.cimaglobal.com), the Institute of Management Accountants in the United States (www.imanet .org), and Cranfield University School of Management (www.som.cranfield .ac.uk) for supporting the DwD Survey and sending it out to their members and students. My reviewers spent many hours going through the manuscript and providing me with feedback, and I am deeply in their debt. Thank you, Ivo Bauermann and Jim Franklin of Oracle Corp., Randy Russell of Palladium Group, and most of all my good friend, Tess Rutgers van Rozenburg. I would especially like to thank the members of my family, who helped by entering the countless copies of the paper version of the DwD Survey into the survey system. Last but not least, I would like to thank Tim Burgard and Stacey Rivera at John Wiley & Sons for believing in this project from the beginning and Dexter Gasque for keeping the project on track.

Most of all, I would like to thank you for picking up this book. I hope you will enjoy it. Please also visit the web site, www.frankbuytendijk.com, for more information.

FRANK BUYTENDIJK
The Netherlands, 2010
f.a.buytendijk@planet.nl
www.frankbuytendijk.com

CHAPTER 1

What Is the Problem?

The test of a first-rate intelligence is the ability to hold two opposing ideas in the mind at the same time and still retain the ability to function.

F. Scott Fitzgerald

"If you are not part of the solution, you are part of the problem," and "Don't bring me problems, bring me solutions" are executive mantras that can be heard all over the Western world. Western management culture has a solution-oriented view on problems. *Oops*, sorry; I am not even allowed to say "problem." I should refer to it in a more positive way and call it a *challenge*.

We live the *80/20 rule*, where we realize that 80% of a solution can be realized in 20% of the time, while the remaining 20% of the solution would cost 80% of the time. We state that "*better* is the biggest enemy of *good*." We are action-oriented. Time is money. Any decision is better than no decision. Keep it short and simple.[i]

I find this type of management culture worrying, if not downright scary. If we jump to conclusions and implement the first solution we think of, do we really understand the problem (not *challenge*!) at hand? Are we not trading in one problem for the next, which we then quick-fix, too? You may argue that there is a well-known rule here: the *law of conservation of misery*. It says that for each problem you solve, at least one new problem is created, or as many new problems that together equal the trouble

---

[i]Granted, there are cases where it is better to focus on the future, and not to dwell on the past. There is always the danger of "analysis paralysis," where we spend too much time analyzing an issue, until the window of opportunity has closed. And as the cliché goes, "the pace of business is increasing"; we cannot always afford a perfect solution.

1

caused by the original problem. The best you can do is create a situation where problems hurt the least, and preferably under someone else's jurisdiction. Problem moved = problem solved. Partly, this is true. Einstein already said no problem can be solved from the same level of consciousness that created it. So the people who caused problems are usually not the ones who solve them. And as long as the situation that created the problem still occurs, all we can do is move the problem elsewhere.

For instance, the corporate scandals in the early 2000s were based on companies evading rules—accounting rules and legal rules. But more rules, like the Sarbanes-Oxley regulations in the United States, did not solve the problem. On the contrary, organizations found different ways of creatively dealing with business ethics, leading to the credit crunch a few years later. The breach of trust of the corporate scandals was replaced by a breach of trust due to the excessive banking bonuses, immediately leading to a demand for even more regulations.

Or consider large multinationals that often have special curricula for high-potentials—a small group of young employees who have the potential to make it to the board level. For decades it was seen as the task of the company to run its executives' development. They were told which trainings to take, and which expat assignments to accept. People's own leadership was not accepted. Times changed, and the opposite approach was adopted. People should be responsible for their own education, and true talent would surface, anyway. But part of being a leader is also learning to take on less popular assignments, such as a project in a remote country. Now it is clear that neither of these opposites work. Truth is in the middle. Corporate objectives should lead the direction of executive development, but the way it is filled in can best be left to people themselves. Different people have different ways of learning the same lesson.

In your personal life, think about repressive medication. If you have a headache, you can take painkillers. Painkillers can cause drowsiness, for which you can take a different medication. As a side-effect this may cause blood pressure problems, for which . . . , and so on. And somewhere down the line you can bet the side-effect of a certain pill is having headaches. One problem causes the next; in this case, it is a vicious circle.

Trying to solve a problem without a true understanding of it leads to "solutions" that are *reactions*. Reactions tend to magnify the problem (by throwing more money at it, or imposing even more regulations), or lead to exchanging one problem for the opposite problem, or create a vicious circle. Only if you do see the true cause of the problem, you can move to a higher level of understanding.

At the core of many thorny problems—personal problems, business problems, or social problems—that somehow keep repeating themselves lies a *dilemma*—a difficult choice of some sort. If you delve deep enough, it becomes apparent that there is no simple solution. This is not a popular thought in Western management culture. Dilemmas put you on the spot. Whatever decision you take, there is an unacceptable downside. Dilemmas make managers grumpy; there is no way out, no way you can win. Dilemmas cause what psychologists call *cognitive dissonance*. This is what happens if two processes of thought (cognitions) clash. This dissonance is an unpleasant experience, leading to negative emotions such as anger or frustration if the dissonance cannot be lifted. It is perfectly understandable that dilemmas cause strong emotional reactions.

But not understanding, seeing, or acknowledging a fundamental dilemma underlying your problem will not make it go away. At least a dilemma forces you to stop and think about the consequences of what you are going to decide, and equally important, the consequences of what you are deciding against. Studies of human cognition show that when people grapple with opposing insights, they understand the different aspects of an issue and come up with effective solutions.[1] This is true for individuals as well as teams. Particularly in teams with a strong culture, being faced with a problem can easily lead to "groupthink." One person with formal or informal power suggests a solution, and we all start implementing it, happy that there is a way forward. A dilemma does not allow groupthink to happen. It requires every individual involved to discover where he or she really stands.

I think managers should be happy facing a dilemma—it is a sign they actually have developed an understanding of the problem at hand. Derived from what Einstein said, a dilemma is an opportunity to fundamentally solve a problem, as understanding the dilemma lifts you to another dimension of insight. And there are ways of doing that. Dealing with dilemmas does not have to be a threat.

What Is a Dilemma?

There are many ways to describe the difficult choices that we face.[ii] A *dilemma* can be defined as a situation requiring a choice between equally undesirable or unfavorable alternatives. It is a state of things in which evils or obstacles present themselves on every side, and it is difficult to determine what course to pursue. It comes from the Greek terms, *di-* (two) and *lemma* (premise). If there are three options to choose from, this would be called a *trilemma*, and more than three options would lead to a *polylemma*.

[ii] Definitions of *dilemma* and *paradox* are drawn from New Oxford American Dictionary, second edition, 2005, Oxford University Press.

In practice, however, *dilemma* can be used in the case of more than two options as well.

Although it means something entirely different, the term *paradox* is often used in relation to dilemmas. A paradox is a self-contradicting statement or proposition that may have some truth anyway. "I always lie" would be a paradox, or "One must sometimes be cruel to be kind." This term also has a Greek background. *Para* means "contrary to" and *doxa* means "opinion"; in other words, a paradox represents something other than what you would think. Contrary to a dilemma, a paradox does not force you to choose; it is more of a conceptual exercise.

A *catch-22*,[2] from a military regulation in a novel of the same name by U.S. novelist Joseph Heller, is a frustrating situation in which one is trapped by contradictory regulations or conditions. For instance, safety regulations may require the use of certain materials in the kitchen of a restaurant, while health regulations clearly forbid this. Or think of needing a physical address to open up a bank account, while the landlady requires you to show you have a bank account before she accepts you as a tenant. Although not correct, a catch-22 is often referred to as a dilemma as well. Close to the term *catch-22* is a *Mexican standoff*, a strategic deadlock in which no party can ensure victory. In the Western-movie cliché, it is portrayed as several people each pointing a gun at each other. The dilemma that it poses is *what to do*. Doing nothing does not resolve the situation; lowering the gun creates vulnerability while shooting leads to likely being shot as well.

Executive View

Heidi Melin, chief marketing officer at Polycom, emphasizes the difficulty of choice. A dilemma is a problem that makes you stop and think. This can be on the personal level or professional level. A dilemma represents a fork in the road, and the decision you are going to take has a large impact.

Dilemmas can be found in any complex organization, Bill Fitzsimmons, chief accounting officer of Cox Communications, observes. He has a very straightforward description: A dilemma is a multidimensional problem, like most issues that reach the executive level. If it had not had multiple angles, it would not have—or should not have—reached the executive level. It is the task of top management to deal with dilemmas. In Mr. Fitzsimmons' view, dilemmas should not be seen as a nuisance, but should be understood. Avoiding dilemmas does not make them go away. Treating them as a nuisance leads to merely passing the problem along instead of tackling it. And the buck stops in the executive offices.

Dr. Edmund Stoiber, former prime minister of Bavaria, the largest state in Germany, stresses a different point: Dilemmas can also appear through bad decision making. Dilemmas can be the consequence of decisions that are not well thought through. When making far-reaching decisions, the consequences for all involved stakeholders should be clear. If this is not done correctly, irreversible damage may be done. You need to be very careful and conscientious in decision making.

Perhaps the best-known dilemma of all is the *prisoner's dilemma*,[3] which comes from a mathematical field called *game theory*. In this dilemma, two criminals are being caught for a serious crime. It is clear they are guilty, but there is no definitive evidence. They are put in separate jail cells and cannot communicate with each other. The police make the criminals a proposal. If they both remain silent, there is nothing the police can prove other than illegal possession of a firearm, and both will go to jail for six months. If one testifies against the other, while the other remains silent, the betrayer walks, while the other receives a ten-year sentence. If they betray each other, both get a five-year sentence. It is clear that the best course of action is to remain silent, but you cannot be sure the other will make the same decision. Most likely each will consider what is good for himself first, and turn the other in.

Dilemmas such as the prisoner's dilemma can be a stimulating intellectual exercise. But once confronted with a pressing dilemma yourself, you would probably feel differently.

Many dilemmas exist only in the mind. We have to make a difficult decision, and no matter what decision we make, it has negative consequences. Suppose a dear aunt, at whose home you eat regularly, cannot cook very well. Do you tell her this, as you want to be honest and because your sense of integrity suggests this? The negative consequence will be that your aunt will feel hurt. Or do you simply say dinner was delicious out of empathy, making your aunt feel good? The drawback will be that nothing changes in terms of her cooking.[iii] This dilemma is based on

---

[iii] This dilemma is fairly simple to solve. For instance, suggest to your aunt that you cook together, as you enjoy being with her so much, and over time, teach her some cooking tricks—provided *you* can cook, of course.

a conflict of two positive values both of which you hold dear: truth and empathy. Whatever the choice, you violate your values. Another example: You are in a conversation and you have forgotten the other person's name (and there is no one around you can ask inconspicuously). The longer you wait to ask, the more awkward it becomes. You cannot ask anymore, as it has become embarrassing. But not asking, and not being able to address the other person by her name when saying goodbye, is equally embarrassing.[iv]

Other dilemmas are more serious. For instance, you need to fire an employee as the company is downsizing. The logical choice may be a senior manager, who is doing very well in his job, but whose area of responsibility is not core to the business. The problem is that your senior manager is 55 years old, is the sole provider of income in his household, and likely will not find another job. Another option would be to fire a young high-potential who came into your department a few months ago. He or she might easily find another job, but the excellent work of this person was just starting to pay off. What would be your decision? Or take a lawyer who learns about an upcoming liquidation of a police informer. The rules prohibit the lawyer from reporting this, but what if the police informer is a friend of a friend? And consider a doctor who is confronted with two immediate cases in the emergency room: a famous older person (a government official) and a nine-year-old child. Only one can be treated at a time, and there is a good chance the other will not make it.

Global Survey

In the Dealing with Dilemmas survey, I asked respondents what they would decide, being the doctor in the emergency room. Of all respondents who chose one of the options I provided, 85% would save the child, 6% the government official, 3% whichever one had family in the waiting room to avoid difficult decisions, and 6% would flip a coin. Respondents were also able to provide their own answers. The most common answer people came up with themselves was to treat the one that came in first. One respondent tried to

---

[iv] This dilemma is also easy to deal with. Ask the person for her business card and e-mail address, promising to send something. But I bet you were sweating a bit before you came up with this gentle way out.

reconcile with the politician, telling him there is a nine-year-old kid, and trying to get agreement from the politician to treat the child first. One respondent found a higher moral ground. He would consider the religion of both people. If the politician were religious, he would treat the child first, knowing that if the politician were to die, he at least would know he would be going to a better place. I am not sure how to interpret the responses of a few others. One suggests treating the politician first, because of the ramifications for the hospital, while the parents can always have another child. And someone else added he would treat the one that had family in the waiting room first, assuming that the other would have no caring family or friends. The reality, of course, is that you cannot expect doctors to make calls like this. There are protocols that doctors follow. In this particular case the protocol is called *triage*.

In another question, I asked the respondents to imagine they were the CEO of a small company ('you') and had been working on a large deal for almost a year. If you win the multimillion-dollar deal on the table, you could expand the business. If you lose the contract, you would have to fire 20% of the employees, some of them in their fifties, and others having families with small children. The dilemma is clear, a choice between integrity and responsibility. Your contact is indicating that if you would pay him $10,000, the contract is yours. Forty percent of respondents would expose the employee of the prospect to his boss, 48% would not pay, 9% would actually pay, and 3% would even resort to blackmail ("If you don't give us the deal now, I will report you to your boss"). Some respondents were very creative in their schemes, including establishing a bank transfer, and then exposing it to the prospect's employee's boss, or even spending the same amount of money to hire a private detective to find something with which to blackmail the contact. Some respondents place themselves outside of the dilemma. It is simply "cost of sales" in certain countries. Others make it depend on the circumstances. One person—I guess with a sales background—asks if it is a transactional deal (deliver the goods and move on) or a relational deal (service delivery and repeat sales opportunity). In the former case, he would pay; in the latter case, he would not. Others ask themselves what are the chances it would come out publicly. They define the dilemma differently, namely between the chance of success or of being exposed themselves. One wonderful answer came from someone who wanted to know

(continued)

(continued)

what the prospect's employee would use the money for—it could be for a good purpose.[v] One person found a moral middle ground for himself: Pay the bribe out of his own pocket. This is one of those dilemmas that can be easily avoided—it appears only if you do not think through your customer-interaction process. In case you feel there is a chance of ethical issues arising in a deal, make sure there are always several people in the meeting and involved in any decision. Involve other stakeholders at the customer level, and make sure several people of your own company attend.

Other dilemmas may appear among people, between you and someone else, or between two other people who turn to you for a decision or input. In dealing with dilemmas like this, we can learn from the field of negotiations. Successful negotiations are based on a win-win situation, where parties focus on what binds them, instead of what divides them. Dilemmas between people are often based on strong mutually exclusive desires. For instance, in a personal relationship, one partner may want to have a child, while the other does not want that at all. That is a pretty binary choice that has to be made, with not much middle ground. In business terms, two executives may have a strong disagreement about the strategic direction to take. Making a certain acquisition or not is also a clear and binary choice—it is either yes or no. Colleagues from different cultural backgrounds may have completely opposing views on what it means to respectfully treat each other, and may even play the "either he is leaving or I am" card.

Dilemmas between people can be full of emotion, indeed. And in the heat of the fight, we forget that the choices presented might constitute a false dilemma, often called a *sucker's dilemma*.[4] The choices presented are not at all the only options on the table. "Either he is leaving or I am" is narrowing down an argument to an escalation path only—an ultimatum. "Clean up your room now, or go to bed early," "my way or the highway," "now or never," "either you're with us or against us," or "if you don't listen, the consequences will be yours" are sucker's dilemmas we have

---

[v] Later we will see that philosophers call this style of decision making *consequentialist*, making a decision depend on the context, instead of its being fundamentally right or wrong.

all heard.[vi] Who says it is one or the other? There might be many different ways to deal with the issue. The moment you get sucked into such a dilemma, you do not think about solving the matter at hand, but feel you have to make a choice. You are thinking *or*, and not *and* anymore. How could I satisfy my mother and clean up my room, while first finishing the videogame I am playing? How can his way be combined with my way, so there is a mutual way instead of a highway? Is it possible to delay "now" a bit while satisfying the other person's sense of urgency, so that "never" never comes?

Fortunately, most daily dilemmas are small and not of cardinal importance. In fact, most dilemmas are not even real. They are what I call "chicken-or-beef" dilemmas, based on a psychological phenomenon called *loss aversion*. People prefer avoiding losses over acquiring gains, or in other words, when facing a choice, they focus more on what they do not get than what they will. The biggest problem in choosing between chicken or beef for dinner is that if you choose chicken, you will not have beef, and vice versa. Despite how good the chicken looks, the idea of not having beef is stronger. The only loss in this dilemma is the loss of the *option* of beef, not even the beef itself.[vii] If you truly examine everything you would call a dilemma, the majority of them would be in this category.

A *Short* Overview of History

The basis of a dilemma is a contradiction—often the contradiction between good and bad. Doing the right thing might lead to bad results; for instance, helping one person in the emergency room does not improve the chances of the other. Doing something bad might lead to good results, such as saving the company by winning a large order involving a bribe. The idea that everything consists of opposites goes back to the concept of *yin and yang*[5] in ancient China. Originally meaning the shadowy and sunny side of the mountains, yin and yang came to represent all dual or polar aspects of the world: dark and bright, good and bad, noisy and silent, soft and hard, slow and fast, feminine and masculine. Yin and yang are opposites,

---

[vi] My favorite one came from a bumper sticker: "Would you like to have sex, or do you want a cookie? By the way, we're out of cookies." But this is so politically incorrect, I could not write that down in a business book.

[vii] As the chicken-or-beef dilemma is deeply rooted in human behavior, the easiest way to deal with this dilemma is to appeal to the same feeling your table companion may have. One orders the chicken, the other the beef, and you share. On an airplane this may work only if you actually know the person sitting next to you.

FIGURE 1.1 Yin and Yang

but part of a mutual whole. (See Figure 1.1.) There cannot be one without
the other. Yin and yang also interact; they transform each other. After high
comes low, after day comes night. In the traditional yin-yang symbol, this
is represented by the small dot of white in the black part of the symbol,
and vice versa.

The Greeks adopted similar thinking; however, they used the idea of
opposites to find truth, through a rational and logical discussion. This concept is called *dialectical inquiry*, or *Socratic reasoning*.[6] The Socratic way
is based on formulating hypotheses ("So, if A is the case, logically B must
follow") and asking questions ("And what would it look like if we add C
to the mix?"). Philosophers have used Socratic reasoning to ask themselves
the big questions, for instance, about what is right or wrong, or what is
good or bad. Can something bad lead to something good? For instance, "If
we agree that killing a person is bad, is it also bad to kill a person who is
about to kill several other people, in order to prevent those killings?" Or
can something good lead to something bad? For instance, "If marriage is a
holy institution, should one be encouraged to get married to a person with
a history of domestic violence?" In the modern age and in business terms,
we can use dialectic inquiry to challenge assumptions and best practices.

In his books, Mintzberg is known for his Socratic style, challenging
what we believe is true about management sciences. For instance:

> *It has become a popular adage in some quarters that if you can't
> measure it, you can't manage it. That's strange, because who has
> ever really measured the performance of management itself? I guess
> this means that management cannot be managed. Indeed, who
> has ever tried to measure the performance of measurement? Accept
> this adage, therefore, and you have to conclude that measurement
> cannot be managed either. Apparently we shall have to get rid of
> both management and measurement—thanks to measurement.[7]*

The Socratic method is still in use today—for instance, in law schools, where the teacher continues to ask questions and solicit answers from the students. The aim of the approach is to explore different sides to a complex legal matter. Many *what-if* style questions are being asked to explore how tiny circumstantial differences can lead to entirely different outcomes. But in most business educations, dialectic inquiry is not taught and not understood.

For centuries, no new philosophical developments in this area occur, until the German philosopher Georg Wilhelm Friedrich Hegel (1770–1831) comes along with a breakthrough, trying to explain the evolution of philosophy. Hegel's dialectic consists of a three-step process: thesis-antithesis-synthesis.[viii] The process starts with a current situation or common wisdom, called the *thesis*. The situation usually has a strong disadvantage, such as an unexplainable phenomenon in a theory, or needs of people not being met. This at one moment leads to people adopting the opposite belief, approach, or situation. This reaction is called the *antithesis*. It solves the previous disadvantage, but brings new disadvantages as well. We are now in the stage of a dilemma: Both thesis and antithesis present dominant disadvantages. So far, this is nothing new, as yin and yang provided the same insight. But where with yin and yang the pendulum keeps swinging between opposites, Hegel offers a way out. He introduces the idea of *synthesis*, where over time the two opposites will fuse, or reconcile, creating the best of both worlds. And then, interestingly enough, the synthesis becomes the new thesis, what is believed to be true, to be eventually challenged by an antithesis once again. The pendulum swings after all, but on a higher plane.

In our own time, for instance, self-regulation in a free market was deemed unacceptable after the corporate scandals in the early 2000s. It led to a strong reaction, with strict regulations, such as Sarbanes-Oxley, consisting of many specific rules with which to comply. It introduced a huge bureaucracy in large enterprises and, although certain fraud attempts may have been prevented, discussions around executive compensation and risk management were still prolonged, into the economic recession of 2009. The synthesis? Regulations should not be based on strict rules, but based on principles, where organizations need to *explain* how they adhere to the principles of good corporate governance. Or think of the development of Western society itself, starting out as a tribal environment where every

---

[viii]Although this model is often named after Hegel, he himself never used that specific formulation. Hegel ascribed that terminology to Immanuel Kant. Carrying on Kant's work, Johann Gottlieb Fichte greatly elaborated on the synthesis model and popularized it.

tribe was self-sufficient. The antithesis to this became the feudal society, with kings and emperors ruling their countries. These were more efficient, but were taking the needs of only the few into account. The synthesis between the tribal and feudal societies is the democracy. We are ruled by elected leaders, but the key to a democratic society is that the government aims to take the needs of all stakeholders into account. Closer to business, think of competition. The thesis of business was collaboration— entrepreneurs in a certain trade in a certain city would be part of a guild. This led to the antithesis of all entrepreneurs competing with each other, as that would be better for the price of goods and quality of service. Today, many organizations engage in "coopetition," where they compete and cooperate at the same time. Think of airline alliances, or automobile manufacturers sharing certain parts to create economies of scale.

Recently, dealing with dilemmas as part of leadership has got the attention of management thinkers in multiple disciplines. Trompenaars, widely recognized as a leading thinker in intercultural management, even defines leadership as the ability to reconcile dilemmas[8]—to be able to inspire as well as listen, be strategic as well as have an eye for detail, and centralize your organization around local responsibilities. Called one of the most influential psychologists of his generation, Howard Gardner defined the synthesizing mind as one of the five important mindsets for the future. Management guru Jim Collins speaks of the tyranny of the *or* and of embracing the genius of the *and*.[9] The tyranny of the *or* makes proclamations such as "you can have low cost *or* high quality," and "you can have change *or* stability." Collins describes visionary companies as the ones that can embrace both extremes. He specifically points out that this is not about balance or compromise, but about doing *both* to an extreme— yin and yang.

Although I will borrow from multiple sources, such as psychology, intercultural management, ethics, economy, and other areas, this book will focus on strategy management, ranging from strategy formulation to strategy implementation and strategic performance measurement.

CHAPTER 2

Strategy Is about Making Choices, or Is It?

No battle plan survives first contact with the enemy.
Field Marshal Helmuth von Moltke, 1848–1916

S trategy formulation is often seen as a somewhat mystic process. Heroic stories in the business press do not make it easier. They typically like to portray business leaders as geniuses with brains the size of a basketball who can see things that others cannot. At a crucial moment in time, they make a strategic call that turns out to make all the difference in business performance ever after, leading the competition by years. But the higher these leaders rise in the eyes of the public, the harder they can fall, in case their prediction did not come true. And there are severe consequences for the share price.

The press loves to write about brilliant CEOs such as Steve Jobs of Apple (although in earlier times this was very different), Wendelin Wiedeking of Porsche (until the debt grew out of control), and Fred Goodwin of Royal Bank of Scotland (until the credit crunch came along). And we love to hear and believe these stories. Even managers and leaders working within an organization find the strategy formulation process nebulous. Once a year, the executives organize an off-site and gather for a few days. To the rest of the organization it is unclear what they are doing. Perhaps they sing secret songs around the campfire. And once the off-site is over, the executives communicate the new strategy to the organization. As it is unclear where it comes from, and even more opaque as to how to implement the new strategy, business as usual goes on. Eighty-five percent of leadership teams spend less than one hour per month discussing strategy, so it is no wonder that 90% of well-formulated strategies fail due to poor execution.[1]

13

Strategy formulation is not a very well understood process. In fact, strategy is not a very well understood term. It is amazing to see how such a foundational concept is not clearly defined. Most people would intuitively define strategy as making the big choices that matter, the decisions that set the direction of the company.

With this idea of strategy in mind, perhaps the perception that strategy is about "bet-the-farm" choices and decisions actually *create* many of the strategic dilemmas. And perhaps the traditional processes to formulate strategy add to that perception. Possibly, strategic thinking itself may lead to what Jim Collins calls the "tyranny of the *or*." A different vision on what constitutes strategy might prevent many dilemmas from even appearing.

What Is Strategy?

In short, a *strategy* is an action plan to achieve the organization's long-term goals. More formally, it is a pattern of decisions in a company that determines and reveals its objectives, purposes, or goals, produces the principal policies and plans for achieving those goals, and defines the range of business the company is to pursue.[2] The three key questions that need to be answered for such a plan are: where your company is today, where you would like it to be, and how you think you will get there.

Peter Drucker refers to the *theory of the business*, which consists of the assumptions about the environment of the organization (society, the market, the customer, and, for instance, technology), the assumptions about the specific mission of the company (how it achieves meaningful results and makes a difference), and the assumptions about the core competencies (where the organization must excel to achieve and maintain leadership).[3] This definition is also fairly straightforward: What does my environment expect, what are we good at, and how do we match up those two? From here it becomes fuzzy. Mintzberg even introduces multiple definitions of strategy, the five *P*s.[4] So we know already that strategy is about a *plan*, which is considered the way forward. For instance, it can be our strategy to become the cost leader in our market, to reach our goal of sustained business performance. Mintzberg adds strategy as a *pattern*, which is consistency in behavior over time. Think of Rolls-Royce, which has been known for many years for its high-end luxury cars. Strategy is also a *position*, introducing and maintaining particular products in particular markets, like Nike entering and dominating the market in various sports, such as soccer and golf. Strategy is also a *perspective*, the understanding of the executives of the market and their organization (like in Drucker's definition). Mintzberg ends with strategy as a *ploy*, a specific maneuver to outwit a competitor, such as acquiring a certain company, or even lobbying for a law that favors your company.

None of these definitions imply that strategy is about making big choices. All these definitions simply suggest views on how to make market demand and supply meet in the most favorable circumstances for your company. It is Michael Porter, one of the world's most recognized strategy experts, who stresses the importance of making choices. Porter defines strategy as the creation of a unique and valuable position, involving a set of activities that is different from rivals.[5] Two elements are critical to this definition. First, a strategy needs to differentiate a company from others. Second, strategy involves making choices. Strategy is very much about what *not* to do, and requires trade-offs. Porter elaborately describes these trade-offs. Companies should choose a consistent set of activities that fit their image and credibility. For instance, Unilever's reputation would be damaged if it were to go into the tobacco business. Different activities also require different resources and competencies that may be hard to build up. For instance, extending your position as upper-class kitchen supplier to being a leader in interior design requires different skills, different suppliers, a different sales approach, and so forth. But most important, companies that avoid choices and lack trade-offs become stuck in the middle, do not differentiate, and cannot sustain.

Porter even warns against "popular management thinkers" claiming trade-offs are not needed, and dismisses the thought as a half-truth. The bit that is half true is that trade-offs are not necessary when the company is behind in the "productivity frontier" or when the frontier is pushed out. According to Porter, the productivity frontier is the sum of all existing best practices at any given time or the maximum value that a company can create at a given cost, using the best available technologies, skills, management techniques, and purchased inputs. Not operating on the productivity frontier means you are not leveraging your assets well enough. For instance, if the cost structure has not been optimized, if there is room for improvement in the quality of products and services, and if the business pace is below par, indeed all three can be optimized at the same time, and no choices between cost, quality, and speed have to be made. That situation is to be avoided, anyway. As many organizations have not reached their productivity frontier yet, it is easier to simply follow the market and copy what the competition is doing. In these situations, making no choices may even be preferred to risking blame for a bad decision.

This all may sound logical, but let us argue with Porter a bit. "Stuck in the middle" sounds like a compromise. A compromise means meeting in the middle. Arguably, this is where most companies are, as per definition there can be only a few leaders. However, it is not a desirable place for those who want to outperform their competition. Dealing with opposites does not always have to lead to either a compromise or an either/or choice. Jim Collins referred to this as the tyranny of the *or*, and pointed to the genius of the *and* as a better approach, embracing both extremes. If you want to move from "good" to "great," Collins points out, you should not too quickly accept that avoiding making choices leads to being stuck in the middle. There might be less linear and analytical and more lateral and creative ways of thinking.

Further, it is generally accepted that strategy should ensure a company's future success, plotting the steps toward the goal. And if there is one thing we know about the future, it is that it will most likely be different from today. How are we supposed to make the right choices today that impact tomorrow's performance? And is it wise to make choices that will limit our flexibility to respond to tomorrow's needs? Do we *really* believe that with analytical rigor we can foresee the future? That if we have all the data and are smart enough, we can crack the code? Of course not; that is not the question. The real issue is how to deal with the unknown future. Sure, to a certain extent we are the architects of our own future, but strategic uncertainty is a given, and your choices will either turn out to have been effective, or not. Strategy has to align itself to the fluid nature of the external environment. It must be flexible enough to change constantly and to adapt to outside and internal conditions.[6]

What happens if we do not think of strategy as making choices and commitments, but rather as creating a portfolio of options?[7] Options, as opposed to choices, do not limit our flexibility in the future; they create strategic flexibility. You can compare strategic options to stock options. Stock options give you the opportunity to buy shares at a certain price, but you can choose when this is (within a period of time), and you do not have to. Strategy as a portfolio of options behaves the same. It gives you the opportunity to exercise these options in the future, but you do not have to. Options allow you to make a relatively small investment now, with the opportunity to make bigger investments later, when you have more or better information. In short, options enable you to wait until the moment is right. Obviously these options should not be random—they should be structured around strategic themes, such as growth based on acquisitions, or organic growth, or themes such as creating a greener way of working, entering or retreating from certain markets, or specific go-to-market strategies.

The concept of options in the real world, as opposed to options as a financial instrument, is called, not surprisingly, *real options*.[8] Examples could include investing in university relationships, having a finger on the pulse of possible future innovation. Or it may consist of implementing an open IT architecture, to be ready for future software requirements. Or think of not immediately terminating a nonprofitable customer relationship and invest in it for a while, there might be alternative ways of improving profitability.

In the traditional view, risk and uncertainty depress the value of an investment. If you focus, not on making bet-the-farm choices, but on creating managerial flexibility, risk actually becomes an instrument for value creation. Uncertainty, seen this way, does not depress the value of any investment, but may amplify the value of investments. Strategy, with its focus on the future, is characterized by uncertainty. The more uncertain a future is, the more having flexibility and adaptiveness as a core strategic competence is worth. Defining strategy as creating options for the future allows you to take on riskier investments that have a potentially higher upside, for the same risk appetite an organization may have. Or alternatively, they allow you to lower the risk of your current profile, as you can still opt-out from subsequent investments.

If you see strategy as creating a portfolio of options, there is no "single best strategy." Let us use the metaphor of a puzzle. Strategy is often seen as a traditional puzzle. Each puzzle piece is a part of the strategy. External factors, such as competition, market conditions, regulations, and value chain constraints, are puzzle pieces, as well as internal factors such as resources, capabilities, culture, and expectations. And the idea is to find out how to combine all the puzzle pieces into one single "big picture."

The alternative view, strategy as a portfolio of options, looks much more like a *tangram*,[9] a Chinese puzzle. It consists of seven pieces—five triangles, one square, and one parallelogram—and it can be used to create many pictures. The right-hand side of Figure 2.1 shows some examples, such as a dancer, a cat, and a rabbit.

Traditional view
Strategy as a puzzle with
one optimal solution

Alternative view
Strategy as a chinese puzzle (tangram)
with many solutions

FIGURE 2.1 **Strategy as a Puzzle**

The idea is not as esoteric as it sounds. In fact, it is already practiced in a number of areas. Financial institutions are moving to a strategy of product components and half-products, instead of off-the-shelf standard products. Based on the customer risk profile or specific customer requirements, financial product components can be combined into a uniquely tailored product. Some mortgages may involve investment components, and others not. Financing objects may be a combination of leasing, loans, and other instruments. And in an ideal case, not all components even have to come from the same financial services institution. A platform of compatible product components has been created to construct product configurations that you had not even thought of before. Because of the upfront investment in a portfolio of product options, there are no dilemmas as to which products to introduce and which not. The idea of having a platform is very common also in the automotive industry. A single car chassis is often shared among multiple models, sometimes even spanning multiple brands. An extreme case involves the Toyota Aygo, Citroen C1, and Peugeot 107, all of which share not only the same chassis, but also the same engine.

Using the principles of a portfolio of options, the software industry is currently undergoing a paradigm shift, adopting what is called *service-oriented architectures*. In these architectures, pieces with a well-described set of single functionality are called *components*. Systems can be constructed, deconstructed, and reconstructed using multiple components. An example of a component could be a piece of functionality that supplies all address details when it is called by a system that "knows" only the customer number. Or think of a component that assesses the risk of a claim in an insurance company and returns a recommendation whether to involve a damage assessor or not. All of these components have to be built only once, and can be used many different times. As long as they fit in the same "component-based framework," components can come from different developers and different firms. The idea of a service-oriented architecture has a huge impact on how to build a systems landscape. Moreover, it has an equal or even bigger impact on organizational strategy. Systems are all too often barriers to change, and traditionally may not even support the organizational agility implied by a portfolio of strategic options.

The idea of strategy creating options does not conflict at all with the established definitions of strategy. It supports the definition of strategy as a plan of action designed to achieve a particular goal. The goal stays the same; the plan of action just becomes clearer over time. It is the same with the definition of strategy as understanding where you are now, where you would like to be, and how you will get there. The details will unfold while on the road, avoiding unexpected roadblocks and discovering previously unknown shortcuts. In fact, the idea of strategic options even supports

Executive View

Oil products move around the world 24 hours a day. Exploration, refining, and consumption usually occur in very different places. At first glance, value chain integration, trying to offer complete logistical services, seems the best strategy for a company such as Vopak. It would seem this would create the greatest number of options for growth. And until 2002, this was the track the company was on, trying to expand its footprint throughout the different steps in the value chain. However, the company was experiencing disappointing synergies, leading to disappointed shareholders. Somehow, value chain integration was not working for the company. For each step in the value chain there are so many different ways of achieving excellence, it is hard to define a single attractive concept.

When a new management team was appointed in 2003, it was decided to drastically change the strategy. Not only did the company decide to specialize in storage and transshipment only, but the company was even split up (only a few years after a merger) as the ultimate consequence of such a strategic choice, to create complete focus. Vopak now focuses on storage and transshipment, Univar takes on chemical distribution. This could be seen as a hallmark of classical strategic management: making clear choices and focusing on core activities. But how does that fuel growth? On closer examination, Vopak's strategy actually creates many more new options for growth, compared to the old strategy.

In the old strategy, new growth options each required large investments, with limited synergies. Every step in the value chain required different skills, expensive equipment and facilities, each with a long-term focus—a capital-intensive industry, in other words.

In the new strategy, given capital constraints, growth options are sought within the investments in storage and transshipment. Next to oil and chemical products, with the same set of skills and facilities, other bulk liquids, such as LNG, vegetable oils, and all kinds of biofuels, can be handled as well. The investment leverage of this strategy is much higher.

The risk of such a strategy in the logistics industry seems very high: being pushed out by others who do offer the complete stack of services. However, this would be true only if storage and transshipment were commodity services. With increasing regulations, for instance, around safety, storage and transshipment is a very specialized business,

(continued)

(continued)

and the large investment needed in terminals makes for significant barriers to entry in the market. Furthermore, with the emergence of different types of bulk liquids, such as biofuels, the company actually lowers its risk profile—it does not depend on the traditional oil value chain alone anymore.

Almost paradoxically, it is the focus that Vopak has that enables the company to create the most and the best options for growth.

Porter's definition by turning his thought about the productivity frontier around. Porter states that the only situation in which you are not required to make choices is when you are not operating on the productivity border, in other words, when you are below par on cost, quality, and speed. What if you find ways to continuously push out that border, so that you are not required to make choices that others would have to make? That would be a source of competitive advantage. In addition, your superior ability to create options and utilize opportunities can also be a source of differentiation.

This does not mean you do not have to have a strategy, and you jump on every opportunity. Creating options does not equal opportunistic behavior, jumping on every profit-making activity that comes along. The strategic goals still need to be clear. We need to ensure we make it to our goal, and at the same time do this in an efficient manner. Some options help us reach the goal; others detract from that focus. It is merely the way the strategy formulation process is structured and how the strategy is described that are different. Traditionally, formal strategy and planning implies setting positions, targets, and measures. Alignment means *follow the leader*. Assets are allocated based on forecasts that are expected to hit their targets. Instead, I would like to propose a different view on alignment, where organizational learning is emphasized as well as being prepared for whatever conditions may arise. Alignment means *learn and collaborate*.

Does all this sound too much like "postponing thinking," going with the flow, and being reactive to change? On the contrary; I would say it requires much deeper thinking than traditional strategy formulation, as it requires uncovering the deeper truth of what Drucker called the *theory of the business*. The theory of the business is a strategic framework. The strategic framework describes our assumptions about the environment of the organization (society, the market, the customer, and, for instance, technology), the assumptions about the specific mission of the company (how it achieves meaningful results and makes a difference), and the assumptions about the core competencies (where the organization must excel to achieve and maintain leadership). In laymen's terms, the word *theory* perhaps sounds static, but theory means nothing else than "the best possible understanding of reality we have." And in business that is a highly dynamic process.

In the traditional sense, once choices are made and a strategy is implemented to move forward, usually the assumptions are forgotten. The choices and the strategy become hard truths. "We aim to be an operationally excellent company" or "we differentiate based on superior service" make us forget to look outside and see if this is still what is expected from us, or what we are recognized for, or if by industry standards we still live up to our claim. By investing the time to create a strategic framework describing the theory of the business, we keep track of our assumptions and can road-test them continuously. While the goal (that we chose) remains intact, and the assumptions remain in place as long as they match reality, we can travel toward our goal, assessing whether options that we create and opportunities that we see fit into the framework. If so, we capitalize on them; if not, we let them go. And the moment assumptions change, we can immediately see which activities do not lead us to the goal anymore, or which activities are lacking in making it to the goal. Choices do not turn into dilemmas.

Still, the idea of strategy being about making tough choices is deeply entrenched in today's best practices. We will further explore this, and what to do about it, examining three dimensions: strategy content, strategy process, and strategy context.[10]

Strategy Content

"Strategy is about making choices, and there are only so many choices you can make." This is what the strategy textbooks teach. "The number of ways you can differentiate is limited and you cannot have it all." I recall seeing a sign in a shoemaker's shop, "We can do things quick, cheap, and well. Pick two." (See Figure 2.2.)

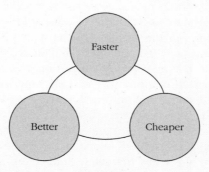

FIGURE 2.2 Pick Two: You Cannot Have the Third

This seems to make perfect sense. If the shoemaker is asked to mend a pair of shoes quickly and well, it will not be cheap since he will have to drop everything else in order to repair that one pair of shoes. The shoemaker can then charge a premium. If the work needs to be done quickly and cheaply, the shoemaker will ask his apprentice to do the job, and thus the repair will not cost as much. The third option is for the shoes to be done well and cheap, which means it will have to wait. But you cannot have all three at the same time. This thought is also deeply embedded in strategy best practices. Again, we need to look at Porter, who defined three generic strategies: cost leadership, differentiation, and market segmentation (or focus).[11] The work that Treacy and Wiersema did regarding what they call *value disciplines* is very similar.[12] They speak of operational excellence, product leadership or product innovation, and customer intimacy. Organizations need to be sufficient in all disciplines, but excel in one.

Cost leadership, or more broadly defined, operational excellence, emphasizes efficiency and convenience. The aim is to attract customers by having the lowest price in the market while offering at least sufficient quality. Usually the products are not very differentiated, but come in one or just a few configurations. Mass production is a good way to create economies of scale, and there may a limited number of ways of interacting with customers. There should be no barriers for customers to order and use the product or service. Good examples of companies with this strategy would be EasyJet (or other low-cost carriers), ING Direct (offering standard products interacting through the Internet and call centers), and the Tata Nano car (offering a car for $2,500, which is about half the price of the cheapest alternative).

A differentiation or product innovation strategy focuses on having a unique offering, which allows the company to charge a premium. Keeping the lead in the market is a competitive differentiator; it requires the competition to follow, and keeps the barriers to entry into the market for others high. Organizations adopting this strategy invest heavily in research and development. As products and services are usually positioned in more exclusive market segments, the amount of units sold is usually lower compared to cost leaders, but the margin (and cost of sales) is much higher. Think of Apple (Macintosh computers and iPods), BMW (offering superior performance and cutting-edge new technology), and investment funds (seeking higher returns through creative and risky investment constructions). A variation on this theme would be brand mastery, creating loyalty because people care about the brand experience, such as with Nike or Coca-Cola.

Porter's definition of market segmentation is slightly different from Treacy and Wiersema's customer intimacy discipline. Market segmentation means focus on just a few market segments and know these markets inside out. Think of software vendors offering software for the telecom industry, or pharmaceutical companies focusing on various types of medication for cancer treatment. Products and services are tailored to the specific needs of that market. Customer intimacy is another type of focus, trying to understand the changing needs of different customer segments, and creating long-term relationships. Good examples would be all-round banks using database marketing to predict customer demand across a complete set of different products, retailers that differentiate product assortment per store and provide personalized discount coupons to customers, and airline loyalty programs that take personal preferences into account and provide special services for loyal customers. Whereas in product innovation people care about the brand, in customer intimacy and market segmentation, the brand cares about the people.

Traditional strategy says you cannot excel in each area. If your company focuses on operational excellence and cost leadership, you cannot afford the cost of sales and the R&D budget associated with a product innovation strategy or the extensive investments in customer relationship management that fit with customer intimacy. And a product innovation company usually has a culture that cares deeply about engineering and brand management, which is at odds with the cultural characteristics that fit customer intimacy.

However, others argue with that. Companies need to go beyond competing with existing competitors in existing markets, which is the basis of both Porter's generic strategies and Treacy and Wiersema's value disciplines. New profit and growth come from "blue oceans."[13] Blue oceans are new markets, where new demand is created. In existing markets, referred to as "red oceans," the structure of the industry, the business model, and market conditions are largely a given, or cannot be influenced directly. Markets may grow, but are basically a zero-sum game. Market share gained by one competitor is lost by another. In a blue ocean, competition is irrelevant as the first mover sets the rules of the market. In this view, innovation seldom comes from concrete market demand, but is always created on the supply side, based on inventions. Think of e-mail. No one ever asked for it—it was simply suddenly there.

Today, there are many blue ocean examples coming from co-innovation initiatives. Co-innovation happens when organizations, often in entirely different industries, collaborate to create new products or services, based on sharing complementary and unique resources and skills. For instance, Senseo is a one-touch-button machine for espresso coffee, based on the collaboration between Philips and Douwe Egberts. Philips created the appliance; Douwe Egberts a special blend of coffee. The Heineken Beertender is based on the same principle, where the beer comes from Heineken and the hometap from Krupp. Or think of the Nike+ system, a collaboration between Nike and Apple, where a Bluetooth sensor that fits in your Nike running shoe sends running statistics to your iPod.

Although the idea of blue oceans is mostly connected to creating new markets or new types of demand, we can also apply the same principles to the creation of new business models. These would be applied in existing markets, but lead to an entirely different way of producing goods and selling them. Mass customization and customer self-service models have transformed many industries. Mass customization means products and services are produced based on the principles of mass production, aiming for low unit costs while at the same time offering flexibility of individual customization. Every single unit in the production process can have its own configuration. Or in terms of administrative systems, every transaction looks different. For instance, banks move from defining financial products to financial components that can be combined based on individual preferences and risk profiles. Pharmaceutical companies envision a future with personalized medication, where different active ingredients are combined based on the specifics of a patient's DNA. The number of options on a car nowadays is virtually unlimited. Mass customization is an example of breaking the idea of either/or strategy. You cannot start with mass customization without being operationally excellent; mass customization is a rather complex concept to implement. With operational excellence as the basis, the production process itself becomes the innovation. Keeping track of all customized orders also gives you deep insight into customer behavior, and you may even be able to predict customer preference—three birds with one stone.

Consider another example. Self-service models offer customers access to the organization's business systems, allowing customers to specify and alter their requirements themselves, and to monitor progress of their order. Think of airline booking systems, and online check-in. Often mass customization is combined with customer self-service. Dell builds computers based on specific customer requirements, entered through the web site. Insurance companies offer customers the opportunity to compose their own general insurance. Build-a-Bear is a retail chain that offers children the chance to put together their own Teddy-bear. There are web sites that connect consumers looking for a second-hand car to whatever car dealers have to offer. The twist on some of these sites is that the data about the age and origin of the car do not come from the dealer, but from the car registry office, which offers a much higher level of reliability than a traditional market web site. And, of course, web sites such as amazon.com not only offer a much more efficient and innovative ordering experience; they even recommend books, DVDs, or music that you might like based on "market-basket analysis" (customers who bought X also bought Y).

These blue ocean business models defy the idea of strategic choice. The innovation strategy focuses on the business model, which is part of the product experience. It leads to an entirely new form of operational excellence, where the customer takes over quite a bit of the work. At the same time, the organization is collecting a wealth of customer information through the web-based systems, enabling a longer-term relationship. Which strategic choice was made? The bar was raised significantly on all three levels—a *strategic synthesis* has taken place.

You could argue that this is simply extending the productivity border by using new technology, forcing a new optimum within the same strategic choices you have made, but I do not think this is the case. The way Porter described it, pushing the productivity border is an incremental and evolutionary process. The efficiency of existing processes is improved. Mass customization and customer self-service models are nothing less than a paradigm shift. Ironically, though, this synthesis becomes the new thesis and over time it becomes the new norm. Mass customization and customer self-service will lead to a reaction, the antithesis. And then a new jump forward is needed again.

Strategy Process

Strategy is a highly confusing discipline. First, there is no established definition of the term; second, there are no clear best practices on what process to follow. Figure 2.3 describes 10 schools of thought, each of which

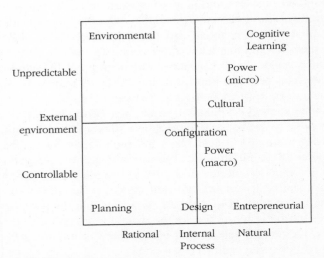

FIGURE 2.3 Ten Strategy Schools of Thought
Adapted from: Henry Mintzberg et al., *Strategy Safari*, Free Press, 1998.

concerns itself with strategy and the strategy process.[14] Sometimes these schools of thought are complementary, but more often they flat-out contradict each other.

These schools of thought can be classified using two dimensions. Some schools of thought focus on a very rational, structured process, others on a more natural, organic process. Some schools of thought see the organizational environment as controllable, to be analyzed and understood. Others see the external environment as highly unpredictable. The more stable a market is, the more classical strategy processes work. The more volatile the environment, the more another approach is needed. I think we all agree that most markets are volatile, and that the markets that seem stable compared to others are certainly less stable than they used to be. It is all the more astonishing that strategy processes are still viewed in such a traditional way, defining strategy in terms of planning, design, or power.

Common wisdom is that strategic management consists of three deliberate steps or phases: strategy formulation, strategy implementation, and strategy evaluation. In each, usually different people are involved, and each step has its own methodologies. According to today's best practices, strategy formulation consists of an internal and external analysis. For an external analysis, for instance, Porter's five forces model[15] is used, examining the competition in the market, the power of suppliers and customers, the threat posed by new entrants, and the threat of substitute products. The optimal corporate strategy is set to counterbalance those forces. The internal analysis looks at the resources available in and to the organization, the capabilities, strengths and weaknesses, and in more modern processes, the organizational culture. In the classical view this process is owned by top management, and is based on thorough analysis, and the success of the implementation is based on the rigor and the detail of the complete analysis. At the end of the analysis, all scenarios are evaluated and a choice for the single best strategy is made. This new-and-improved strategy is then handed over to middle management to be implemented, based on clear objectives.

Following strategy formulation, strategy needs to be implemented too. As in the classical view, "structure follows strategy," a reorganization may have to take place, putting in place the right hierarchy to deal with the various elements of the strategy. Through a top-down budgeting process, resources in terms of money and people are allocated. Several strategic projects are started to set up the right systems. The aim is to come to a focused and aligned organization. *Focus* means that the strategic goals are clear in everyone's mind. We know what to do and what not to do. *Alignment* traditionally means that we all share those strategic goals, and we all know our own specific contribution.

Strategy evaluation, then, is the feedback process, often also referred to as *performance measurement* or *performance management*. Performance indicators report to what extent the organization is reaching its goal. Based on where underperformance or overachievement is reported, additional analysis needs to take place to find out which corrective action needs to take place, or which lessons learned can be copied to improve performance elsewhere. It is a continuous process, traditionally called the *PDCA* cycle[16] (Plan-Do-Check-Adjust). Usually the focus of the process is on internal management control; it does not take external factors such as change in markets into account. We plan, execute, analyze the outcome, and see how we need to adjust our actions based on the outcomes so far.

In a more visual way, we can look at strategic management as "loops of management," as shown in Figure 2.4.[17] The loops of management illustrate how strategy needs to be managed. The first, inner loop of management concentrates on monitoring the current state of things, in other words, strategy evaluation. Activities on the operational level are being monitored and the results are being measured against the targets. The moment the targets are not met or the measurements go in the direction of critical thresholds, adjustments need to be made. In the first loop of

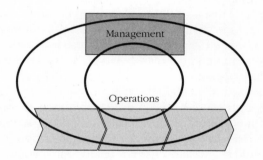

Donut Shaped Loops of Management

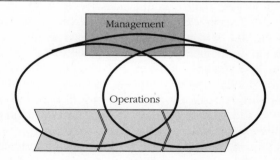

Pretzel Shaped Loops of Management

FIGURE 2.4 Loops of Management

management, we generally let the decisions follow the facts; the decision-making process tends to be rather rational. We operate within the rules and confines of a predefined control environment and seek to protect that from discontinuities. Actions tend to be reactive and defensive. The second loop of management, or outer loop, represents strategy formulation. In the second loop of management, we seek improvement through change, not through control. The first loop of management focuses on measuring how the performance compares to the targets; the second loop of management focuses on whether we are still running the right processes, and whether we are measuring the right thing. Strategy implementation, then, is putting together a new set of loops in case of strategy changes.

Because of the explicit, disconnected nature of the phases of strategic management, the loops of management often look like a donut; the cycles go around independently. This creates a serious strategic dilemma that we can all recognize in the many organizations that work this way. Creating a new strategy is, in this line of thinking, considerable work. It requires reorganization, new systems, and new ways of working, so strategic changes will not happen very much. Only a few, big changes are possible; the organization does not have the agility to cope with more frequent, smaller changes. So, what if reality changes? That is a dilemma. If you choose to change before the natural due date of the strategy, it—again—will be an enormous amount of work. And if you do not change, well, you are out of touch—that is, if you even *notice* the changes in the outside world in time, as they tend to be picked up first in daily operations.

There is another school of thought that proposes a very different way of structuring strategy processes, called the *learning school*. This is where strategy is seen as much more of an evolutionary process. Proponents of this school believe that the environment of an organization is simply too complex to fully understand, and changes too often to control (and who can disagree with that?). Could Apple have known upfront that its iPod would be such a success that it would later decide to change the name of the company from Apple Computer to Apple? Would the German conglomerate Preussag AG, which decided to diversify after it became clear that coal mining did not have a future, have known that its travel business, TUI, would actually overtake Preussag and eliminate the original name of the company? Honda Motors definitely did not know that the 50cc motorcycles that early U.S.-based employees used to run errands would become the key to successfully entering the U.S. market. Honda's strategy was about positioning its heavier motor bikes, which on face value fit the American market much better. Cynics would be quick to add another definition of strategy: "the story you tell afterwards." In more neutral terms, *serendipity*—accidentally discovering something fortunate, especially while looking for something else entirely[18]—is often part of strategic success.

In short, uncertainty makes it impossible to come up with the single optimal strategy. The speed of change means you do not even have time to collect, interpret, and decide upon the information needed to come to such an optimum, should such information even exist.[19]

Deliberate strategies focus on control; the learning school of thought is more aimed at letting ideas emerge. The interaction between established daily routines and new situations is an important source of learning—the first moment a new phenomenon or a change in the market is experienced.

Moreover, allowing strategies to emerge taps into the creativity of the complete organization, instead of just the top management team. This does not mean that top management should sit back and wait for innovative things to happen. On the contrary; top management is there to guide the process and make sure that ideas that fit the theory of the business are tested based on conducting experiments. Strangely enough, this does not contradict the traditional strategists' appetite for structure and numbers at all. In fact, a "test-and-learn" approach to prove the value of an idea is one of the key characteristics of analytical firms.[20] Using a controlled environment and a test group can show the value of an idea before rolling it out on a global scale. With multiple experiments testing multiple variations of the idea, a good feel for the effectiveness of an idea can be tested before it is vetted as strategy. You could argue that the idea of "test-and-learn" is the strategic process in reverse. We start out by evaluating an idea, then implement and copy it on a wider scale, so that it becomes part of the corporate strategy. Moreover, the three phases of strategy—formulation, implementation, and evaluation— become a single process. It is a continuous cycle, where changes are picked up in daily operations, through a process of escalation evaluated on their strategic impact, and course corrections are immediately implemented. The loops of management form a pretzel, as shown in Figure 2.4.[21]

There are two pathways to higher business performance.[21] In one, you can invent your way to success. Unfortunately, you cannot count on that. The second path is to exploit some change in your environment—in tech- nology, consumer tastes, laws, resource prices, or competitive behavior— and ride that change with quickness and skill. This second path is how most successful companies make it.

Of course, you can criticize this way of thinking. In emerging strate- gies, ideas come from within existing structures. In other words, strategy follows structure, which is constraining. If structures need to change, this needs to come from the top. Another danger is what is called *strategic drift*. Slowly but surely, with each little increment, the organization drifts away from its intended direction. Emerging strategies may lack focus. Many wonderful small strategies do not make an effective overall strategy. There may be gaps, things that no one happened to think of. It may very well lead to a lack of alignment.

Clearly this is a dilemma in itself. Both a deliberate strategy process and strategy according to the learning school have dominant and unacceptable disadvantages. A synthesis is needed, combining the best of both worlds, fusing both approaches. The answer lies in organizing strategy according to the principles of *strategic intent*.[22]

Strategic intent starts with having a true understanding of the theory of the business, understanding the assumptions that form the foundation of the strategy. Every decision that is taken in the business, on the corporate level or in a certain business unit, needs to fit into that framework. If not, the decision should not be taken immediately, but further evaluated. Furthermore, there should be a very clear understanding of the goals— one clear picture that is easy to convey and instantly remembered, such as "Beat Competitor X," "Grow to 10 billion dollars," or "Do whatever is realistically needed to create a happy customer." Understanding the goal provides a clear sense of direction, and the strategic framework provides the guardrails to make sure the emerging strategies do not go astray. How? That is a question to which the answers unfold while we are on the road. There might be roadblocks, weather conditions may change, we may have to deal with fatigue while driving. All of these unforeseeable conditions will be dealt with once they arise, but we will never take our eyes off the goal.

Strategic intent also describes modern army doctrine. The field general describes the goal to his commanders in clear terms—there can be no misunderstanding about the focus. Which installations or other targets need to be destroyed? The alignment between the various army units is clear as well; each unit understands its own task and the tasks of others. Deadlines, handover points, and dependencies are perfectly clear, too. But how each unit moves through enemy territory, dealing with the landscape and unpredictable enemy movement, is up to each single unit. Translated to business, management is not defined as sticking to the plan, but as continuously looking for new ways to make it to the goal in a better, quicker, or more cost-efficient way. Structure and strategy go hand in hand; they are interdependent. Top management creates a structure fitting its strategic intent, and the organization comes up with new strategies within the boundaries of the structure. The structure is not limiting flexibility, but providing direction.

The biggest strategic dilemma occurs when strategy is out of sync with reality. It took too much time making a decision, leading to unfavorable circumstances, or the decisions were made too early, not taking critical circumstances into account. For example, we waited too long with creating an efficient business, and when times are tough we are forced to lay off large numbers of people. If we do not, we will suffer heavy losses, and if we do, we will suffer a severe brain drain in better times ahead. This dilemma is typically created by not making critical decisions in time, and sticking to the original plan too long. Conversely, if we bet the farm on a strategic direction a while ago and it cannot be reversed due to unforeseen market circumstances, we have an equally fundamental dilemma. If we change course, we may not survive as we do not have the resources and capability; if we do not change course, the ship sinks anyway as the tides have changed. Applying the principles of strategic intent prevents many instances of this dilemma from even appearing. We have eliminated the gap between changing circumstances and putting a change into place. And who knows? If we are skillful enough, we can drive a few changing circumstances ourselves. Remember, certainty is not found by avoiding uncertainty. Certainty is better defined as a process, coming to resolution of conflicting positions, applying Socratic reasoning as part of a continuous process of learning.

Strategy Context

The third dimension of strategy, next to the content and the process, is the strategic context. No organization (or its strategies) stands alone. In the Porter point of view, the context is even the centerpiece of the strategy. Strategy is about positioning the company in the market, differentiating it from its competitors. This is in essence an interactive process. Every move from a competitor leads to a counteraction from other competitors; even sitting still can be a strong reaction. Although each change in strategy may be disruptive for the company plotting that new course, from a total market perspective it is incremental. Reaction follows reaction follows reaction. It is not all that dissimilar from the learning school of strategy. It is interesting that there is no such term as *market drift*, comparable to the *strategic drift* a company can display. The market is always right, and no one is in charge of the market, so how could it drift?[i] With one reaction leading to another reaction, and strategies being a response to competitive moves, the chances of strategic synthesis happening are pretty small. Thesis then only leads to antithesis, and antithesis will then lead to anti-antithesis—which is some kind of thesis again. Creating the synthesis requires seeing and understanding the thesis and antithesis, which is notoriously hard when you are part of the actual thesis or antithesis happening in the market. Synthesis comes from creating a new context, redefining the rules of the game—a blue ocean, if you will. Within existing markets,

---

[i]Perhaps the 2009 recession, caused by the 2008 credit crunch, can be seen as a market drift. Collectively, all financial institutions invested in a bubble of subprime mortgages and other overly complex financial constructions, slowly moving astray from the real business.

creating a truly new context happens only once in a while. And even less often does the change come from one of the established parties in the market, as they tend to have deeply entrenched and fortified positions.

Specific markets may each have their own dilemmas, within the context of that market. Take, for instance, the pharmaceutical market. Pharmaceutical companies need to be profitable, like any other company, if not for the good of the shareholders, then at least as a means to invest in the next round of the development of new medication. This sometimes requires high prices. At the same time, it is the task of pharmaceutical companies to improve the health of their customers, and from a wider point of view, of the general public at large. This would require prices as low as possible.

Or consider the oil industry, where business success has an opposite effect on the environment. During the 1990s, Shell needed to close down its Brent Spar oil storage installation off the coast of Norway. It did a thorough analysis and decided that the most economical, and technologically and environmentally safe solution would be to sink it. Unfortunately, pressure groups did not agree with this, and public opinion turned against Shell, leading to a customer boycott. It would have been better if Shell had sought a dialogue, which could have precluded these opposite positions.

Doing business in multiple countries provides a wide variety of cultural contexts as well, leading to interesting dilemmas. Should an American firm that acquires a French manufacturing plant abolish drinking wine during lunch in the cafeteria? Trying this might easily lead to a strike. Should a multinational bank allow a local branch to finance perfectly legal activities that are illegal or frowned upon in other countries? These dilemmas start with a discussion on corporate structure (how dependent or independent are legal entities), touch on competitive issues, and end with a moral debate.

Many strategic dilemmas can simply be prevented, as they are actually caused by "best practice" strategic thinking. "Strategy is about choices." "Strategy formulation is a discrete process that needs to be separated from implementation and evaluation." "Strategy is about competitive positioning." Understanding the theory of the business is the key to a different approach. What are your most important business assumptions? Do these assumptions still work or are they past their due date? Which likely events could invalidate your assumptions? What would be your strategic response?

Make the Choices that Create Options

As much as I have argued for creating options, there is nothing wrong with making choices. You cannot have a contingency plan for every possible future; not making any choices at all, while trying to go along with everything that passes by, leaves you unfocused and most probably unsuccessful.

The trick is to make the strategic choices that create the right options. That sounds like a paradox. If you make a strategic choice, you close the other options. However, it opens up the options that come with the choice you made. For instance, if you need to choose whether to open up a store in New York or in Boston first, only one can be the first. Assuming you choose Boston, this choice opens up all the options associated with being successful in Boston, like marketing to the local university, and making use of Boston-specific programs. You open up the choices of the "next level." The key to solving this paradox is to focus on the intention of the strategic choice. If the intention is to come to the single best strategy, this is the wrong intention. If the intention of the choice is to open up a maximum portfolio of options, this is the right intention. Strategy defined as creating options does not exclude strategic choice.

CHAPTER 3

All Kinds of Dilemmas, but Just a Few Types

There is a theory which states that if ever anyone discovers exactly what the Universe is for and why it is here, it will instantly disappear and be replaced by something even more bizarre and inexplicable. There is another theory which states that this has already happened.
Douglas Adams, author of *Hitchhiker's Guide to the Galaxy*

Dilemmas are all around us. We encounter them in daily life and they are part of every business. In fact, as we live in the globalized world and our societies become more heterogeneous, we are facing more dilemmas now than, say, 50 years ago. Life is less predictable, and we are confronted with more people who have different views. Managers from different generations can be peers in the same company. Different subcultures, each with their own identity, put their mark on the corporate culture. Companies operating in multiple countries have to deal with different national cultures. These can all lead to important dilemmas to deal with.

Functional disciplines each have their own typical dilemmas. For instance, in sales, people often have to weigh the certainty of a small, tactical deal now, versus the opportunity of a more strategic deal later. Or should we sell to a customer directly and keep all the margin, versus selling through a partner, which may lead to reciprocal business, but also leads to lower margins due to partner commissions. Or, more fundamentally, do we focus on value, and advise a customer not to buy a certain high-end product but to go for good-enough, versus focusing on the revenue and trying to upsell to a customer regardless his or her particular need? A typical marketing dilemma would be disassociating yourself from the competition to differentiate, while associating yourself with the competition to have a market. Or consider the world of information technology

(IT), where managers and professionals struggle for many years with the dilemma of building systems based on a long-term architectural vision versus quick-and-dirty solutions that provide a tactical return on investment.

Dilemmas are all around us. *Harvard Business Review* (*HBR*), the renowned journal for managers and professionals, every month publishes a case study that, while fictional, presents common managerial dilemmas, and offers competing points of view from various experts. The idea is for the reader to make up his or her own mind. These *HBR* dilemmas are a great sign of the times as they reflect current issues. Some dilemmas are people oriented, and other dilemmas are subject oriented. People-oriented dilemmas deal with human resource (HR) issues, such as taking a promotion that requires a relocation, or hiring a very experienced person versus bringing in some fresh blood. They may also cover leadership issues, such as how to deal with a very friendly and competent manager who drives people crazy by micromanaging. Or they describe moral dilemmas, for instance, what the CEO should do when uncovering evidence about patent fraud involving one of his predecessors.

From a sample of more than 60 issues of *HBR* over the past few years, about 50% of the dilemmas were people oriented, while 10% were moral dilemmas. The other 40% were subject oriented; they described a difficult strategic choice a leader needed to make. Think of deciding whether you would want to make a private-label product for one of your largest customers, going forward with an acquisition that may have a negative impact on your profitability in the short term, or how to deal with an activist group that criticizes you on the choice of raw materials in your product. Further examination of those case studies reveals that some take place within the organizations, while other dilemmas play between the organization and (one of) its stakeholders, or among stakeholders of the organization—in other words, intraorganizational and interorganizational dilemmas.

People and organizations are not that different.[i] Intraorganizational dilemmas resemble the dilemmas within someone's mind (as introduced in Chapter 1). They represent cognitive dissonance on the organizational level. Interorganizational dilemmas are like the ones between people. The dilemmas people and organizations experience are fundamentally the same.

---

[i] Both are living organisms (A. de Geus, *The Living Organization: Habits for Survival in a Turbulent Business Environment*, Longview Publishing, 1997). Like people, organizations are born, grow up, and die. Some barely grow up; they die young and irresponsible. Other organizations mature and grow old and wise. Over time, organizations expand and sometimes contract, like people who gain weight and diet when necessary. Organizations, like people, create children in the shape of new activities and business units that sometimes spin off into other activities and units. People can understand who they are only by understanding their place in society. Equally, organizations do not operate as islands; they interact with their stakeholder environment all the time. They affect their environment and their environment

Like personal dilemmas, intraorganizational dilemmas make you examine your motives. Like dilemmas between people, stakeholders with conflicting requirements may put you on the spot. Studying people-oriented and subject-oriented dilemmas, for instance, the case studies described in *HBR*, forces you to think. And reflecting on the often-conflicting advice of the experts who comment on those cases makes you take a position. But can you predict which dilemmas you will face, based on your strategy?

Identifying Dilemmas Using the Balanced Scorecard

Douglas Adams put it eloquently in this chapter's opening quote: Once you have cracked the problem, something else will come in its place. True as this may be, it does not have to be inexplicable and bizarre. In fact, the strategic dilemmas you will face are quite predictable, using a framework that many organizations already have in place. The *balanced scorecard*, developed by Kaplan and Norton, is a framework to describe an organization's strategy and to provide feedback as to its effectiveness.[1] The key message of the balanced scorecard is that the performance of an organization should be structurally viewed from four perspectives: financial, customer, business process, and learning/growth (see Figure 3.1).

- **Financial perspective**. How are we perceived by our shareholders? Without profits, there is no supply of capital and no sustainable business models. Having sound insight in finance is important for every single economic entity.
- **Customer perspective**. How do our customers look at us? The customer perspective ensures not only that we measure an internal view, but that the metrics also show how the organization is viewed by the customers.
- **Business process perspective**. How effective and efficient are our processes? Processes need to be efficient so that the costs can be managed. Equally important, processes need to be effective so that the customers' needs are served. Proper management of day-to-day operations ensures the short-term health of an organization.
- **Learning/growth perspective**. How able are we to learn and adapt? Investing in human capital (skills), information capital (insight), and organizational capital (ability to change) is necessary in order to be successful in the long-term.

---

affects their behavior. Organizations have a responsibility toward their environment. Organizations build partnerships and alliances, just as people have friends. Some of these relationships last a long time and cross various phases in the organization's existence; some belong specifically to a particular phase in time, as friendships do.

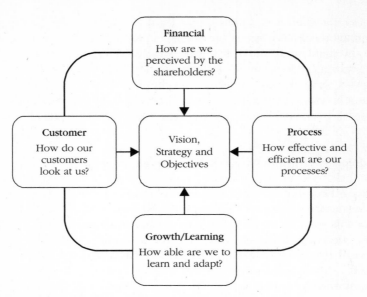

FIGURE 3.1 The Four Perspectives of the Balanced Scorecard

Some even called the balanced scorecard one of the most influential management concepts of the twentieth century. This might be slightly overstated, but it is clear that the balanced scorecard has established itself as a core management instrument. According to the Dealing with Dilemmas (DwD) Survey, roughly 70% of respondents indicated the balanced scorecard is used in their organization. Either it is used elsewhere in the organization (20% of cases), people use it themselves (25% of cases), or it is a company standard (the remaining 25%). Since its inception in 1992, the balanced scorecard concept has significantly evolved.[2] It started out as a performance measurement system to bring together financial and nonfinancial information in a single report.[ii] Quickly, Kaplan and Norton realized there was strategic value in this style of reporting. Limiting yourself on the key performance

---

[ii] I was not in the room during the workshops that led to defining the four perspectives, but I have a hypothesis as to how it could have happened. In figuring out which nonfinancial areas to pick, someone may have mentioned the three value disciplines from Treacy and Wiersema that I described in Chapter 2: operational excellence, product innovation, and customer intimacy. These map process, growth/learning (innovation), and customer exactly. The fourth perspective had to be the financial outcome. From this point of view, you could see the first version of the balanced scorecard as a first attempt to solve strategic dilemmas—to see how to balance all. If it did not happen this way, at least it shows the logic of the four perspectives, as they align with other established management theory.

indicators that drive value creates strategic focus and alignment. Managers throughout the company all know which strategic objectives matter, and how to evaluate the results. The concept of the strategy map turned the balanced scorecard into a complete framework for implementing and executing strategy—a strategic management system to drive future financial performance. A *strategy map* is an illustration of an organization's strategy. Its main purposes are to facilitate the translation of strategy into operational terms and to communicate to employees how their jobs relate to the organization's overall objectives.[3] Strategy maps are intended to help organizations focus on their strategies in a comprehensive, yet concise and systematic way.[4]

In the strategy map, the four perspectives, the associated strategic objectives, and the key performance indicators are linked as cause-and-effect relationships[5]. Figure 3.2 shows a stylized strategy map of a fictive company called Tier 1 Talent (also discussed in Chapter 9).

The idea behind the cause-and-effect relationships within the balanced scorecard describes something fundamental. In order to be successful and have a healthy bottom line, you need to have your shop in order and keep your customers happy. And to make sure it stays that way, you need to adapt to changes in your environment. Conversely, if you do not invest in learning and growth, people will start making mistakes in existing and new processes, upsetting customers, who will stay away and negatively affect the bottom line. In a strategy map, the cause-and-effect relationships depict a one-way, linear approach starting with the "learning and growth" perspective and culminating in financial results. You can argue that if those relationships are linear, the idea of cause-and-effect relationships between strategic objectives is extremely powerful.

But let us return to the original visualization of the balanced scorecard, as it reveals an important new insight. Grouping the four perspectives around the strategic objectives, as in Figure 3.1, shows how each of the perspectives not only represents a different angle to business performance, but also poses conflicting requirements. Financial results and the growth and learning perspective live at odds with each other. And optimizing business processes does not necessarily match with a customer orientation. In fact, the perspectives of the balanced scorecard help in predicting which strategic dilemmas will present themselves in devising, testing, implementing, and evaluating new strategies.

Figure 3.3 shows six dilemmas that can be found in every business:

1. Value or profit?
2. Long term or short term?
3. Top down or bottom up?
4. Listen or lead?
5. Inside out or outside in?
6. Optimize or innovate?

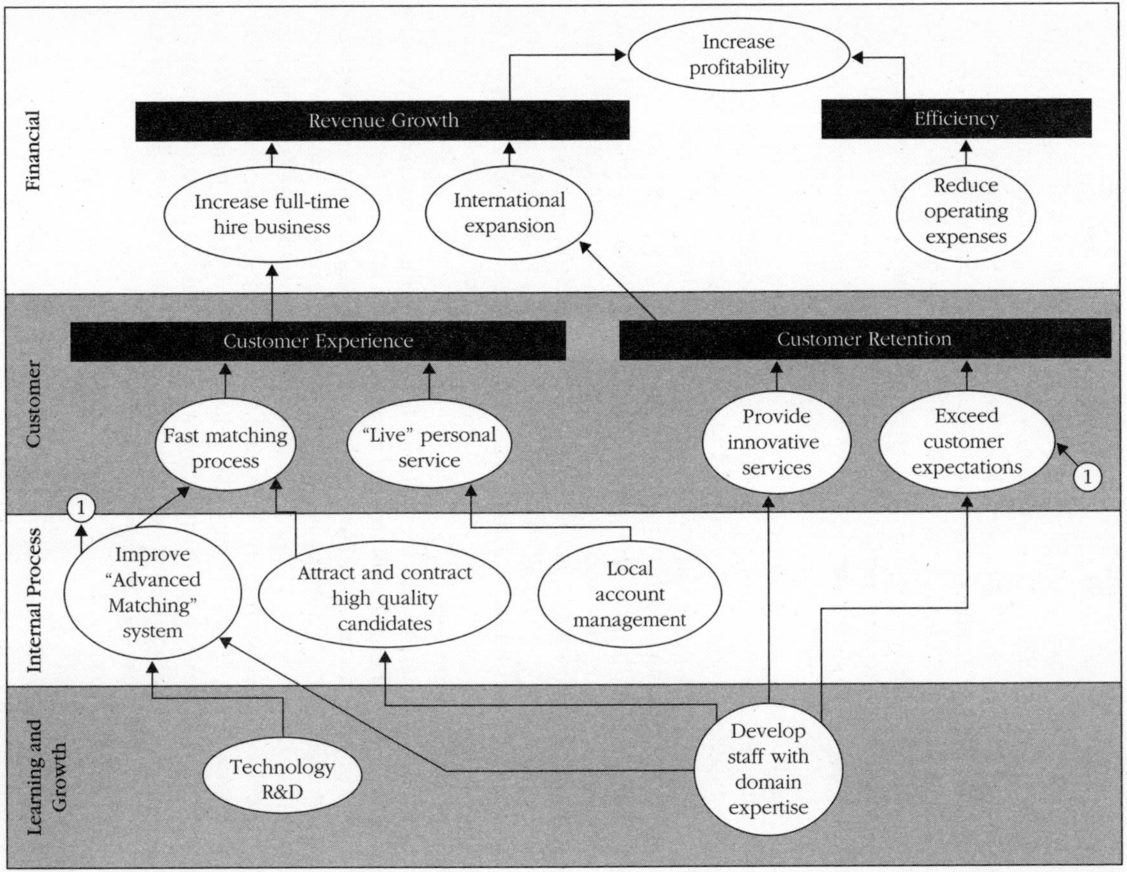

FIGURE 3.2 Strategy Map of Tear 1 Talent

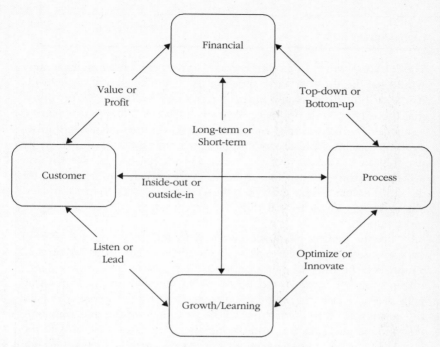

FIGURE 3.3 Six Dilemmas that Can Be Found in Any Business

Value or Profit?

In markets driven by intense competition—and that seems to be the case in most markets today—it is natural to see business as a zero-sum game. In other words, what I win must be your loss. There is only so much market share and market growth, and my share needs to be protected and preferably expanded. Business success is expressed in terms of shareholder value. Market share is based on revenue. Profit is the bottom line, and sales to customers are the means to that goal. Perhaps, at some stages, you may be even busier competing with your competitors than minding the actual driver of performance, looking to serve customers well.

Earlier in this chapter, I discussed a few sales-specific dilemmas that would be very visible here. Do you sell the product that best meets the customer's needs or the one that brings the highest profit? Should you focus on the quarterly results and go for the tactical sale now, or do you develop the relationship and aim for a much larger deal later?

Customers are looking for a good deal, or at least value for money, when considering your products or services. Customers are willing to pay

Global Survey

The Dealing with Dilemmas survey asked respondents how they would handle the following situation. A customer is very clear in his desire to buy from your company a certain photocopier. You know that there is another photocopier your company offers that will have a much lower total cost of ownership based on the actual need; however, the commission you would earn is much lower. You can really use this deal to make your quarterly target. What do you do? Do you sell the customer the photocopier he very specifically asked for, or do you explain to the customer the concept of total cost of ownership (TCO) and try to sell him the product that will bring him the most value?

Seventy percent of respondents who felt they had to make a choice stated they would explain the concept of TCO, and 30% would simply sell the photocopier requested. "The customer is always right," one respondent says. Another respondent simply reframes the issue and does not see the dilemma: "You work for the company, not for the customer"—a clear bias toward the profit side of the dilemma. One respondent lets it depend on how agreeable the conversation with the customer is, and another wants to know whether it is a one-time-only sales opportunity, or whether there is a longer-term relationship.[iii] Most respondents who make use of the option to fill in their own answer successfully reconcile the two: Explain the TCO concept, but let the customer decide between the two. Others come to a more proactive reconciliation: Look at any criteria other than cost the customer might have. If cost is the overriding issue, actively sell the cheaper machine, but sweeten the deal by cross-selling a number of optional add-ons or services.

for service. They understand you need to make a fair profit and they may even consider paying a premium for the brand. But your profit maximization is not their goal. Looking back to their early days, most organizations did not have this "profit-versus-value" dilemma. The whole mission of the organization consisted of creating value for the customer. It is when ownership of the business becomes more distant, and shareholder value enters the game, that objectives start to differ and to conflict.

[iii] In Chapter 8 we see that this way of thinking is *consequentialist* in nature.

A good test to see how organizations deal with profit versus value is too see how transparent their product specifications and pricing structure really are. Have you ever noticed that on closer examination consumer insurances often have overlapping coverage? Have you ever tried to compare the subscription costs and prices of a mobile telephone provider with its direct competitors? The lack of transparency cannot be a coincidence; it is done on purpose. The prices of some products or services cannot be explained merely by fair profit and brand value. The gap between the price and the value is based on market intransparencies—that is, customers not knowing that the same product or service can be obtained elsewhere at a better price. Lack of information, limited market access, or even price cartels all cause murkiness in the market. Although organizations may profit from that, the profit is not sustainable.[6] Once a competitor pushes for transparency, this becomes a source of competitive advantage.

The good news is that the value-versus-profit dilemma is entirely self-inflicted, by allowing conflicting requirements to distort the business model. A sustainable business model is not based on the idea of a zero-sum game, but is based on win-win situations, in which the dilemma does not even exist. If you truly add value to the business or personal lives of your customers, then profits represent the reward. These profits can be used to invest in additional added value, and the company will be rewarded with additional profits. Business has become a virtuous circle. Profits should be seen as a reward, not as a goal.

Long Term or Short Term?

A long-term versus short-term focus is one of the most fundamental management dilemmas. From a sales perspective, should you focus on the quarterly results and go for the tactical sale now, or do you develop the relationship and aim for a much larger deal later? From a marketing angle, should you allocate more budget to lead generation or invest in brand awareness? Do you stress more marketing of emerging products, or choose the certain payback of investing in the best-selling products? From a financial perspective, what is an acceptable period to reach return on investment? Short periods create lower return, but more certainty. Longer periods create higher returns, but with higher risks as well. And in the IT world, how much time, money, and effort can be invested in long-term IT architecture versus immediate user benefits?

If you do not invest in new approaches, products, and services, at some point, business will dry up. Tomorrow's business will suffer. But if you do not invest in today's *performance*, there will be no tomorrow's business to worry about. The answer is clear: Choice is not an option here. You simply

Executive View

Novozymes' business, biotechnology, is full of innovation. The company's culture is very much geared toward this as well. But being on the edge of innovation is not always easy. In 2007, the company had to decide whether to enter a new business area within biopharmaceuticals. It offered great opportunity, but what if this new area did not work out? What if the technology was not mature enough? What if the company did not deliver? It was a classic dilemma between performance and risk, between long-term and short-term thinking. Clearly, innovation is needed in this market to keep up with new developments. Cash cows have a limited lifespan, and long-term growth, profit, and success needs to be minded too. At the same time, a risky investment could hurt the company's profitability in the short term. After careful deliberation, the company decided to enter this new segment, for two reasons. First, because of its culture; the need for innovation is deeply engrained in everyone's way of working. Second, the decision was not just a one-off. Earlier, the company had decided it wanted to adjust its risk appetite, and over the years it had created a portfolio of initiatives that would allow for a few more risky activities. Also, the innovation did fit the competences and specialized knowledge available within the company. Portfolio management is not about jumping on just any opportunity. Lastly, earlier experiments had led to confidence in the technology involved. The main constraint in this dilemma, risk, was successfully pushed out.

In another case, in the late 1980s, Novozymes missed a significant trend within an important market segment. With hindsight, the company could have avoided this and should have seen it coming. The current executive team reflects that in those days the company was too self-confident, and interestingly enough, was suffering from not enough competition. As a result, Novozymes in this case missed out on gaining initial advantage on an important intellectual property, which again resulted in the company having to struggle unnecessarily hard to gain market power.

have to find a way to do both at the same time. Part of the answer is in product lifecycle management. Products and services each have certain stages of maturity. In terms of the Boston Consulting Group (BCG) portfolio matrix, as shown in Figure 3.4, products move from question mark to star, and via cash

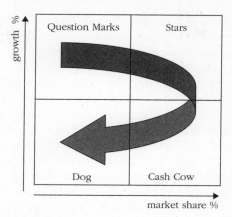

FIGURE 3.4 BCG Portfolio Matrix

cow to poor dog. Products and services start off with high growth and low market share, then build market share, then growth slows down, and at the end of the lifecycle market share shrinks as well. Question marks represent strategic options that materialize (or not) over time.

The real dilemma is in how to *organize* for dealing with the long term versus the short term. Within the standing organization, innovation has a hard time succeeding. The hurdle rate, the standard return on investment the organization is demanding, is too high. Return on investment may be too low, may take too long, or is too uncertain. The overhead of the overall business presses too much on the innovative project and the initial tests that need to be as inexpensive as possible. Standard processes and systems do not allow the innovation team to explore different ways of working. And in general, innovation areas may not be seen as very attractive; the small size of the potential market may not satisfy the growth needs.[7] In many cases, organizations decide to create a new organization around the innovation. IBM did so when developing the personal computer. Most large companies did so when starting their e-business units in the 1990s—nimble, effective businesses, far away from the efficiency-driven main organization. But it should not be a surprise that there is an opposite school of thought as well. Organizations should embrace the concept of *creative destruction*. This term, introduced by Joseph Schumpeter in 1942, describes a "process of industrial mutation that incessantly revolutionizes the economic structure from within, incessantly destroying the old one, incessantly creating a new one."[8] *Creative destruction* originally described the forces of the market, such as cars replacing horse carriages, downloading music succeeding physical music carriers such as CDs, and e-mail obsoleting fax machines, but the term is sometimes also used to describe how organizations must redesign themselves from top to bottom based on the assumption of discontinuity.[9]

Organizations that have organized in a way that enables them to think for the long and the short term at the same time are often called *ambidextrous*.[iv] How do you develop radical innovations that shape the future of your business, while at the same time protecting your traditional business? Ambidextrous organizations combine the two schools of thought: They create separate businesses under the same roof.[10] Strategy and structure are interdependent. Existing organizations tend to create strategies to protect existing business. New strategies may require new structures, so innovations are put into a new structure. Doing this within the same organization allows business units to share capital, talent, customers, and so on, whereas making them separate business units at the same time allows them to adopt different working styles and have a different culture. Some organizations combine this with the concept of *internal venture capital*. Emerging businesses within the organization can compete for capital, while top management invests in multiple initiatives to spread risks, creating a portfolio of options.

Top Down or Bottom Up?

In the traditional best practices of strategy formulation, strategy is a top-down process. It starts with understanding the market, and how to differentiate to create competitive advantage. Then the optimal strategy can be created, and through a planning process that strategy cascades down into the organization. In the top-down process, the creation of shareholder value is the bottom line. The return on capital employed needs to be as high as possible. One popular way of aligning the organization around shareholder value today is the *economic value added* (EVA) methodology. EVA aims to capture the true economic profit of an enterprise and to describe creation of shareholder wealth over time. The EVA formula equals net operating profit after taxes (NOPAT) minus the required return times capital invested.[11] EVA explains to business managers on all levels that capital is not for free and should be applied to activities that at least provide a higher return than the cost of capital. Managers are forced to focus on creating value. Business unit plans, investment proposals, and

---

[iv] *Ambidextrous* means being equally skillful with both the left and right hand. For instance, an ambidextrous tennis player can always play a forehand. In the context of business, unfortunately, nowhere is it clear whether the left hand stands for long term and the right hand for short term, or vice versa.

even some projects can be evaluated on their return in the EVA formula as to their contribution to the net operating profit and their expected return. In short, organizations should deploy the initiatives that bring the highest returns.

The opposite view, to create competitive advantage in a bottom-up style, is called the *resource-based view* of the firm.[12] Resources can be tangible or intangible. *Tangible* resources include, for instance, access to certain raw materials, as in mining industries. Or think of labor that is particularly skilled, or resides in low-cost countries. Capital is an important resource as well, as are facilities that are needed to produce products and buildings. But in today's globalized economy, *intangible* resources are perhaps a more deciding factor in gaining competitive advantage. Intangible resources can include specific knowledge, perhaps protected by patents. Or think of having access to certain distribution channels and market segments through partnerships, or a database with consumer information. Cultural attributes such as organizational resilience, perseverance, and entrepreneurialism are resources you can draw from as well. Resources need to be valuable, rare, inimitable, and non-substitutable (VRIN). If you single out any one resource, it might not pass all elements of the VRIN test. A collection of tangible and particularly intangible resources, however, may be a solid basis for a differentiating strategy.

In the top-down approach, the financial results are leading. Based on the desired outcomes, the organization needs to look for and deploy the resources that are needed to fulfill those requirements. The opposite approach, bottom up, takes the resources as the starting point and aims to maximize the output.

To be successful, the bottom-up and top-down approaches need to be fused. Strategy as a learning process is about continuously tweaking the alignment between resources and financial outcomes. The more you can invest in dynamic capabilities and resources, being able to reconfigure the use of resources, the more effective this process of alignment can be. Figure 3.5 shows the levers in this process of alignment.[13]

The objective of continuously aligning resources and financial results is a sustainable, profitable business. Financial results are achieved by selling products and services that are produced through certain activities. Activities in turn are fueled by resources. If the products and services are not providing the right results, on the financial side you can either adjust the price (increasing it for a higher margin, or decreasing it for lower margins but higher turnover), or adjust the resource cost by renegotiating contracts or switching to a supplier that delivers the same for a lower price. But not all controls are price related. If the demand requirements change, the right amount of increase or decrease of resources

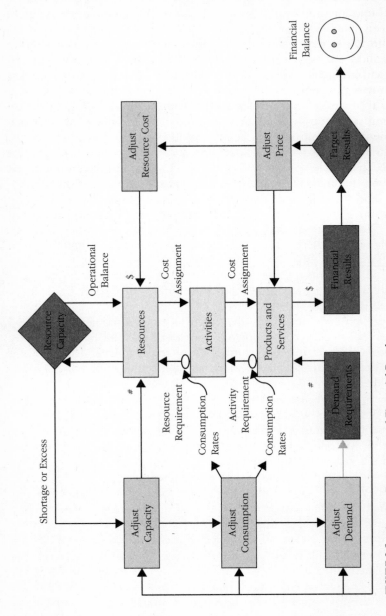

FIGURE 3.5 Aligning Resources and Financial Results
Source: CAM-I (www.cam-i.org).

may be needed. A deep insight into the relationship between products, activities, and resources means that the right resource can be adjusted by the right amount (adding, for instance, a new machine, or a new hire). Alternatively, the resource consumption can be changed. Perhaps it is possible to use people's time more efficiently. Or maybe a new product design reduces the number of parts, leading to a lower cost and a speedier production process. Further, demand can be influenced by marketing, as in a "buy two, get one free" campaign.

Both the top-down and bottom-up approaches try to achieve the same thing: to prevent local optimizations. In a bottom-up approach, the decentralized resources are aligned with the corporate goals, and the goal is to contribute as much as you can. From a top-down point of view, the centralized goals are the starting point. Many organizations continuously struggle with the balance between centralization and decentralization.

Executive View

Publishing Corp. is a federated organization. Its various divisions, including newspapers, magazines, books, digital, and print, are in different markets, each with a different dynamic. At the same time, they are all part of the same organization. Publishing Corp. reviews on a regular basis the merits of centralizing or decentralizing business functions, often leading to intense debate. At the same time, centralizing or decentralizing functions should not lead to continuous structural change and business instability.

Most federated organizations are in the same situation. The answer will never come from viewing a federated organization as a financial portfolio of businesses. Other than a certain profitability, the businesses do not really have to have anything in common. Creation of centralized services is always an issue because of its impact on autonomy of the business units. However, if the federation is defined as a *brand* portfolio, it becomes easier to craft a successful organization. Each business unit needs to add to the authenticity of the brand. No matter how profitable a unit is, if it does not contribute to the brand experience, it should be divested, as it dilutes the brand. Shared services in a brand portfolio are easier to set up as well, as people staffing the shared services have a common understanding of the overall brand experience.

(continued)

(continued)

Publishing Corp. has come up with a very original solution to deal with the independent units within the larger organization. All divisions are headquartered in the same building, in the city center. The building is clearly recognizable as the Publishing Corp. building. However, each floor in the building looks entirely different. Each division has a different layout, uses different colors, has a different style of art on the walls, and has a very different culture. In this way, the building itself, as a metaphor for the Publishing Corp. organization, celebrates cultural diversity.

Inside Out or Outside In?

Larger organizations have a natural tension between the front office and the back office. The front office represents most customer-facing activities, such as sales, service, and large parts of marketing. The back office represents administration, manufacturing, or other types of production, procurement, logistics, and support functions such as Finance, Legal, and Human Resources. The front office, being market driven, is looking for ways to cater to the specific needs of customers. "There is always an opportunity to jump on, if only the back office would understand," they say. The back office has an eye on standardization, looking for ways to create a lean-and-mean operation. "There simply must be some rules to comply with, if the front office would only grasp that," they argue. In short, the front office has an outside-in approach, whereas the back office works from the inside out. There are different angles to this dilemma. Flexibility is battling with scalability; agility is at odds with manageability. In short, the need for both effectiveness and efficiency may pose conflicting requirements.

In entrepreneurial organizations, the front office clearly has the lead. Senior management adopts *first-mover* strategies to beat the competition. There is always an opportunity. Business is operating at the bleeding edge. The complete organization is built around agility, the ability to respond quickly to change in the market. The company is willing to make big bets, and if they turn out to be the wrong ones, the decision is reversed and the company changes course. These outside-in-driven organizations can be extremely effective, but are usually not very efficient. The back office has to "pick up the pieces," and needs to make significant investments in reorganizations, business processes, and IT systems to do so.

In more bureaucratic environments, the back office has the lead. The strategy is about economies of scale, standardization, and cost control. New ideas tend to focus on more efficient ways to do business. The business is a master in adopting and fine-tuning best practices. As a competitive strategy, the firm is not particularly nimble, but may have a good level of absorption.[14] Its lean-and-mean structure can endure good and bad times, and when the time is right, it will strike and claim its market share. The inside-out-driven organization is very efficient, manageable, and scalable, but, as a side effect, not very flexible. Sometimes it seems the most important job of salespeople is to explain to customers the ordering process, and Legal is nicknamed the "sales-prevention department."

Of course, these are black-and-white caricatures. In fact, organizations may find it surprisingly hard to tell "who is in charge." Is sales selling what manufacturing has produced, or is manufacturing producing what sales has sold?

Common belief says you should not address this dilemma at all; instead you should *nurture* it. Organizations need to be both effective and efficient. Equally strong back-office and front-office forces may keep the company balanced. However, technology innovation has at least moved the border for this dilemma. Many business models have adopted mass customization principles, where every single transaction can be tailored to the customer's specific needs. Consider the pharmaceutical industry's move toward personalized medicine, the configuration options car makers offer buyers, and commercial web sites offering personalized homepages. These business models are often self-service in nature. The customer-order-decoupling point[v] has shifted dramatically. Customers can compose their own insurance or mortgage based on financial components, check themselves in for a flight via the Internet, and make changes to the configuration of their PC minutes before it gets produced. In processes like this, where does the front office stop and the back office start? There is no difference anymore. Both back office and front office contribute equally to the customer experience. Real-time monitoring has changed the dynamics in the value chain. The value chain can be supply driven (inside out) based on iron discipline in product delivery, and event driven (outside in) based on a good grasp on inventory turnover, at the same time.

---

[v] The customer-order-decoupling point is the moment in a process where customers can no longer make any changes in specifications. For instance, in terms of producing an automobile, specifying the color can be done at any time from the moment the order is submitted, to seconds before the actual moment of painting the nearly finished car.

Executive View

Recently I bought one of those fancy outdoor kitchens, and it runs on gas bottles. I got one bottle as part of the BBQ, and off we went. After a while, the bottle was empty, and I wanted to exchange it, getting my deposit back. I found a garden center in the neighborhood that sells that brand. My wife was surprised to see me come back to the car with two bottles: a full one and an empty one. I had not been successful in trading it in. The garden center explained to me that I needed a special deposit form, and the original receipt. The special deposit form could be obtained by sending in yet another form to the supplier's headquarters, and they would send the deposit form back—*within three weeks*. (Excuse me? Are we in the twenty-first century?)

A short call to the call center proved them right. Indeed, it was a complete circus of administration that would make most "red tape" look pale pink. And I did not have the original receipt anymore. I sent an angry e-mail to the contact center, with the request to pass it to management. I pointed out that both our interests were aligned: I have their bottle that they want back, and they have my deposit that I want back. Dysfunctional processes like this can lead to serious consequences. People might give up and simply dump the bottle in the trash, which would not be in line with the "green image" the gas company wants to portray. There is also reputation risk. It would take only one person to set fire to the bottle, and make a funny video out of it that is posted on YouTube.

The next day I got an e-mail from the company's marketing director. I had caused a dilemma, she said. Either help an angry customer, but run the risk of fraud (no paper trail), or keep a tight process and lose a customer once in a while. Then she asked, "What would you do in this case, Mr. Buytendijk?" That was the most wonderful response you can think of—showing strength by opening up, turning a complaint into an opportunity, using my negative energy in a positive way. "Service recovery," customer representative management (CRM) specialists call this. It means that complaints properly dealt with often lead to higher customer satisfaction, even compared to before the incident.

Over the next few days we had an interesting e-mail conversation about lean and Six Sigma. The starting point is that processes need to add to customer value. If they do not, they should be abolished or changed. This process clearly does not add value; in fact, it destroys customer value. Although I did not see the need for such a

process (in fact, I reasoned, all you need is to track the serial number on the gas bottle), if the company would insist, first move it to
the Internet, and second, make it a worthwhile process by supplying customers with BBQ tips generated by the community of users,
while they are registering their bottles. However, what I found out
was that these bottles do not have a serial number. That is odd; it
is a basic principle in auditing that wherever there is a chance for
fraud, the flow of goods needs to be monitored. Without identification, there is no monitoring. The lesson we can learn from that
is that if the basics fail, no process and no technology is capable
of adding customer value anymore. Unless you get the basics right,
all you can do is damage control. And, reasoned the other way
around, if you get the basics right, the problems the company has
between balancing the needs of the back office (fraud prevention)
and the front office (smooth customer interactions) would completely disappear.

Optimize or Innovate?

The *production dilemma*[15] is foundational to manufacturing environments,
and has become very apparent in administrative processes as well. Some
refer to it as *exploration versus exploitation*, where exploration includes
things captured by terms such as *search, variation, risk taking, experimentation, play, flexibility, discovery, innovation*. Exploitation includes
such things as *refinement, choice, production, efficiency, selection,
implementation*, and *execution*.[16] Exploration enables the creation of new
knowledge, whereas exploitation supports the refinement and use of existing knowledge.[17] In the context of strategic dilemmas, I prefer to use a
more generic description: *optimization versus innovation*. Optimization
means tailoring an environment toward a specific goal. All waste must be
eliminated. Waste would be defined as everything not directly contributing
to reaching that goal. But what happens when the goal changes? Was all
the waste that was eliminated really waste? Or did we throw the baby out
with the bathwater and lose all the capabilities to be agile and change the
process as well? Some organizations complain that they have become so
good at efficiency, they cannot innovate anymore. The bias toward optimization is logical. There is less risk involved, the returns are realized in
the short term, and the gains are relatively easy to measure. The disadvantage is too much focus on internal control, and losing sight of the changes
in the market. And the more you optimize toward a certain goal, the more

you hardwire your processes toward that particular goal. The question is whether the efficiency gains outweigh the (potential) costs of change.

This does not mean that manufacturing environments have no attention for change. In fact, the dominant school of thought in this field, called *lean*,[18] counts on continuous improvement as one of its corner pillars. The best-known method for that is *Six Sigma*,[19] which utilizes data and statistical analysis to measure and improve a company's operational performance, practices, and systems. Six Sigma identifies and prevents defects in manufacturing and service-related processes, and represents a measure of quality that strives for near perfection. *Sigma* (the lowercase Greek letter σ) is used to represent the *standard deviation* (a measure of variation) of a statistical population. The phrase *six-sigma process* means that if you measure six times the standard deviation between the mean outcome of the process and the nearest critical threshold, there is a minimal chance of failure. Six Sigma is not a project, but a process aimed at continuous improvement. Processes are continuously monitored, analyzed, improved, and controlled to ensure that any deviations from target are corrected before they result in defects. There is continuous improvement, indeed, but within the existing paradigm prescribed by the strategic objectives, instead of improvement toward facilitating change based on new goals.

Executive View

Achmea, a large insurance conglomerate, uses *lean* to optimize and innovate its processes. Lean is a methodology aimed at continuous improvement, and it originally comes from the manufacturing world. Obviously, it can also be used for administrative processes.

One of the key elements of lean is to define the customer value that the organization needs to deliver, and then to eliminate everything that does not contribute to that goal. The problem with that could be that you stop innovating. Customers usually do not ask for innovation; they just want to do business hassle-free. This insurance company took a different approach. The company did not simply ask customers; it did not merely analyze data. The company *observed* customers closely.

One example of what Achmea improved was the process around customers moving to a different house. Optimizing that process is simple: Once you know the customer's old and new address, you can immediately change that in the system, and send out a confirmation letter or e-mail. Process optimized, costs saved, unnecessary steps eliminated, and on to the next process. But let us think this through: How do we add customer value? Moving to a new house from a health-care insurance point of view is quite impactful. If you move to another city, you may need a new dentist, a new general practitioner, new specialists, and so on. Why not offer customers the chance to register with a new doctor, and point them to the web site where other customers rate their doctors, dentists, and so on? Customers become a community. This actually represents the core business model of an insurer: collecting a community of people to create economies of scale, with the purpose of eliminating the risk of the individual. Achmea, understanding the basics of its own business model, applied this concept in multiple ways.

Lean and Six Sigma do not always have to be "within the box," merely about cost savings and operational excellence. Really thinking through what adds customer value is the key to bridging the gap between innovation and optimization. Not only are the customers happier with a process more aimed at delivering service, but it creates a huge cost-saving opportunity in the back office as well.

The Toyota Production System (TPS) is geared towards mastering the dilemma between optimization and innovation. The company actually succeeds *because* it creates contradictions within the organization.[20] Employees on all levels need to constantly grapple with challenges, and must come up with fresh ideas. For many years, Toyota moved slowly, expanding production capacity only step-by-step, yet making big leaps forward, such as with the Prius, a revolutionary hybrid engine[vi]. Toyota is known to be a very cost-conscious organization, like IKEA or Wal-Mart, but is equally known for investing heavily in manufacturing facilities, dealer networks, and human resources. Finally, Toyota is a very hierarchical company, but has a culture in which strong and candid pushback is encouraged.

[vi] It seems this touches the core of the problem that Toyota experienced with its 2010 recalls. It can be traced back to the principles of TPS. Part of the success also was the slow but steady speed of growth. When Toyota worked towards the goal of becoming the largest car manufacturer in the world, it found out (the hard way) that growth was a constraint in its formula for success. Another dilemma emerged, growth versus stability. Given Toyota's ability to handle the optimization versus innovation dilemma so far, I have all the faith it will find a way to deal with growth versus stability as well.

Many have commented that the innovation versus optimization dilemma is eternal. You cannot optimize and innovate at the same time; the forces each push in a different direction. However, as I argued in Chapter 2, when discussing emerging strategies, there is interaction between established daily routines and new situations. The combination is an important source of learning, as hitting a transaction or activity that the process cannot cope with represents the first moment a new phenomenon or a change in the market is experienced. What would happen if you deliberately allow or bring perturbation, disturbance, or confusion[21] into processes, such as ambiguous goals, errors, or strange requests? This would shake things up, and force managers and processes to deal with discontinuity. Little shakeups take a process into unknown territory, where no precedents exist to guide organizational action. No one knows for certain what process should be executed next. Shakeups can be accidental, the kinds the organization did not seek and did nothing to prompt. Think of natural disasters. At the other end of the spectrum there is induced confusion, purposefully provoked by the organization, for instance, to conduct experiments. Induced or accidental, the key to reconciling optimization and innovation is how you deal with those shakeups and turn them into additional options for the process to address.

Listen or Lead?

What are you looking for from your customers? By doing good business, you hope they bring you profit and growth. You hope they trust you, so they come back for more business. But you would also be interested in their opinion, to make sure you are on the right path with your innovations. Conversely, customers are looking for products and services that fit their needs. These need to be reasonably priced. Interactions with the supplier need to be fast and it should be easy to do business.[vii]

It is interesting to see that in this list of customer requirements, there is no such thing as innovation. Typically, if at all, customers express their opinion on current needs, not their future needs. Innovation does take place; things move in an evolutionary way. The moment a customer needs change, products and services evolve with those changing needs. It is vital to stay in touch with market demand; otherwise, a business loses its relevance.

But breakthroughs rarely come from *listening* to customers. Who ever asked for e-mail, spreadsheets, or the Nintendo Wii? Did anyone express

---

[vii]This list of customer contributions and requirements is drawn from a methodology called *Performance Prism*, which will be further discussed in Chapter 10.

the need for matches or a lighter? And what about options such as power steering and park distance control in your car? Or soda drinks, the telephone, Monopoly (the game), collector soccer cards, roller-skates, or the paper clip? Someone simply came up with them, and—after perhaps a few generations of product improvement—this created a new need and demand altogether. Successful breakthrough innovation comes from *leading* your customers.

Both listening and leading are needed, in order to protect both current business and new business over time. There are multiple ways to connecting listening and leading.

No one says you need to have a single strategy for the complete organization, that constraint is caused only by taking too much of a classical top-down approach to strategy. Different business units need different strategies. Think of a construction company, offering both prefab houses and bespoke construction work. In the prefab housing business, it may make sense to listen to your customers. Profit comes from reselling a certain model many times, and there are certain trends that everyone seems to like in a certain timeframe. Customers see finished products and in their buying decision judge whether they like it. Being well in touch with customer perception is a good recipe for success. In offering bespoke construction work, the construction company is the expert, knowing specific regulations and the right constructions. Specific customer requirements may not be practical, or may lead to excessive cost. It is important to provide your expert opinion—in other words, to lead the customer.

However, there is a time where one of the approaches is more important than others. In times of *paradigm shift*, leading the customer is more important. In the IT world, that would be the shift toward service-oriented architectures. In the automotive industry, that would be the switch from gasoline-driven cars to electric cars or cars driving on hydrogen fuel cells. In the telecom industry, providers have been switching from gsm to "third generation," experimenting with umts, gprs, hsdpa, edge, and other standards. The idea of switching modes, from stability and continuity to disruption and change—and back again—is a premise of a strategic management school of thought called *configuration*. Strategy is a process of configuring the organization, its resources and processes and other important elements, and *reconfiguring* them if the market evolves or the organization itself matures. The goal is to sustain stability most of the time, but periodically to recognize the need for transformation, and to be able to manage that disruptive change without destroying the organization.[22]

In the true spirit of synthesis, you can also try to fuse both leading and listening. You could be the leader in listening to customers, picking up signals before your competition does, and extrapolating what you learn far beyond the customer's own imagination. For instance, chip manufacturer

Intel made use of ethnographic research techniques.[23] By directly observing households, researchers created a better understanding of how people are making use of technology in their daily lives. By observing obstacles in using technology, or by discovering practical but unintended uses of technology, Intel can create products that serve the customer needs in a better and innovative way. And by using techniques that create a much deeper insight than traditional market and consumer research, Intel positions itself as a leader in the market.

Executive View

Novozymes' mission statement, "to change the world, together with our customers," describes an interesting dynamic. Usually companies that aim for world-changing innovation are not very customer focused. Customers who are attracted to strong innovation will find their own way to the company themselves. Innovation also seldom comes from customers; there is demand for a new product or service only after it has been invented. True and disruptive innovation usually comes from organizations that do not listen to their customers at all; their customers listen to them. They lead their customers.

Novozymes aims to do both at the same time. First, Novozymes does not sell directly to the end consumer. It has a business-to-business sales model, selling to other companies who use the enzymes and biopharmaceutical ingredients in their products. Novozymes, however, does not define its success in terms of what it achieves for its customers, but rather for the customers of the customer, which is the consumer. With the consumer in mind, it is clear that Novozymes alone cannot guarantee success; it needs its customers to reach its goals. Defining success in terms of the customers of your customer is an excellent start to reconciling the listen-versus-lead dilemma.

At the same time, Novozymes tries to detect the real question behind the customer question. Often, a customer will formulate its requirements in terms of its own solution, which is not necessarily the best solution. By finding out what the customer is trying to achieve and offering an even better solution, Novozymes exceeds customer expectations.

In one case, a customer asked to remove a certain biochemical element from a product. It would have been perfectly fine to comply with that request, make it a special order, and ask for a special price.

The customer would have been happy and the transaction would have been profitable. However, further investigation revealed that it would be much better to remove the enzyme that caused the biochemical element to be part of the product. Novozymes offered to eliminate the cause, instead of the outcome. Interestingly enough, this solution came from a team member specialized in an entirely different area. Sometimes, solutions to a difficult matter come from a different field where, under different circumstances, the problem has been solved already. Novozymes leads by listening just a little bit better than the competition.

Two Types

On closer examination, the dilemmas that we have examined both within the organization and between organizations can be classified in two types: the ones that highlight conflicts between parties (you versus me) and the ones that separate the long term from the short term (now versus later). Figure 3.6 shows an overview of how to classify the dilemmas.

Each type of dilemma has its own way of being addressed. You-versus-me dilemmas require synthesis, looking not for what divides the conflicting sides, but for what binds them. Organizations that take a stakeholder approach seek to add value to their stakeholders as a means to maximize profit, and profits are a means to create stakeholder value. Organizations that have broken down the walls between the front office and the back

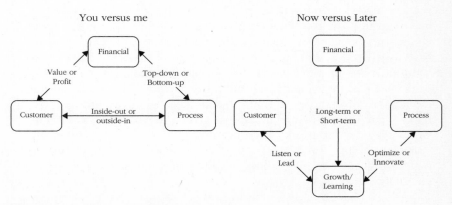

FIGURE 3.6 Two Types of Dilemmas

office have raised the bar on customer experience. The back office is even more efficient while customers do part of the work in a self-service business model, and the front office has the benefit of higher customer satisfaction. Organizations that have aligned a top-down financial focus with a bottom-up resource-based view of the firm have overcome the dilemma. Every change in both financial means and operational resources and activities can immediately be translated into an overall new picture. The complete value chain is optimized instead of each functional domain in itself. In terms of Jim Collins, you-versus-me dilemmas benefit from having the genius of the *and*.

Executive View

NCB (a National Central Bank in one of the European countries) has a unique perspective across all financial institutions in the country. But this broad perspective continuously creates dilemmas for the bank. For instance, one institution requests approval for hedging a certain risk. This is no problem, as long as not all of the banks try to hedge the same risk at the same moment (which could create a vicious circle where prices decrease and more banks will hedge the risk, which will decrease prices even further). There also is the risk that too many institutions could develop a similar risk profile, which makes them all vulnerable to the same events.

For NCB, this is a difficulty; approval would clearly improve the individual institution's risk profile. However, if NCB approves, it sets a precedent for other banks as well, ultimately creating a systemic risk. As always, communication is key to solving you-and-me dilemmas. Through stress-testing, NCB can simulate various scenarios and familiarize the banking sector with system-wide risk. One scenario NCB tested was a liquidity crunch: What would happen if banks were short of cash? In playing out this scenario, virtually every financial institution that participated indicated they would attract more savings money. However, if most of the banks have to cope with that scenario, there is no savings money to attract, as the effect is system-wide. Playing out those scenarios not only helps NCB safeguard financial stability, but helps each of the regulated institutions build a better insight into the overall market dynamic, and broaden its strategic toolbox.

A key challenge is time consistency of policy. This holds for monetary policy, but also for banking supervision. It is better to make clear beforehand that failing banks will not be rescued or saved through regulatory forbearance. Otherwise, there is a clear incentive for excessive risk taking by the industry: Benefits of risk taking accrue to the managers and owners of the banks, whereas the costs are socialized (society would pay the cost of failing banks). When a bank fails, however, the costs of saving the bank may well be lower than the costs of letting it fail. The problem is that rescuing a bank makes the threat that failing banks will not be rescued not credible and increases moral hazard. However, the local picture looks different. It consists of individuals not getting all their savings back and losing their pensions. Which perspective is more important? Both have an equal social impact.

NCB is looking for solutions to such challenges. One elegant solution is education. The bank facilitates schools in teaching financial planning and management by offering teaching materials. This enables citizens to guard themselves against financial constructions that do not fit an individual citizen's risk profile. Other solutions under investigation are contingent capital and additional capital requirements for banks that are most subject to moral hazard.

A dilemma of central banking in general and banking supervision in particular is how to deal with the transparency society demands. Financial stability gains by diplomacy in the background, to avoid causing a self-fulfilling prophecy when NCB has concerns. At the same time, citizens got in an uproar when they found out that NCB knew about problems at a certain bank that folded. NCB's culture can best be described as judicious, prudent, self-restrained, and extremely discreet. A consequence is that the general public does not always perceive NCB as particularly strong and actionable, especially in times when that is needed. But there is no either/or choice here. NCB should create a *transparency portfolio*. For some areas of the business it is crucial to be opaque; indeed the bank would not want to start a self-fulfilling prophecy when it starts an investigation. However, there are many areas where transparency is not damaging. In fact it would strengthen the bank's position. For instance, the bank could open up a web site that shares macroeconomic information, that allows citizens to assess the risk profile of their investments, that teaches financial management and planning, and that shares some fun facts like amount of money in circulation, amount of pre-euro currency still being exchanged, and so on. When confronted with criticism on the bank's practices of working behind closed doors, it can respond in a positive way by pointing out the popularity of the web site and the social goals the bank tries to reach, while adding that indeed some activities are better performed behind the scenes. That would make a world of difference.

Now-versus-later dilemmas require a different approach. They are about creating options. It means making sure that whatever the future brings, you can flexibly deal with it and still reach your goals. Organizations need to be ambidextrous in nature, minding both the short and the long term at the same time. With only a long-term view, the organization might not actually realize its long-term vision, while short-termism alone endangers future success. Fueling innovation creates future options. Although listen or lead certainly has you-or-me aspects, it is mainly a now-versus-later dilemma. Listening to customers is important in times of evolution, when once in a while strategies need to be reconfigured and taking the lead to reach a new level is required. Taking the lead opens up new doors and new options. Finally, optimize versus innovate can be addressed by creating confusion and ambiguity. If people can handle this, they will be able to handle unplanned shakeups as well. Their toolkit is able to handle more options than a hardwired and optimized process.

Executive View

National cultures differ in risk tolerance. The United States tends to be more risk tolerant than continental Europe. This could well be an explanation for the higher number of bank failures in the United States as compared to Europe. Every year, a few regional savings and loans banks fold. As strange as this may sound, there is an advantage to this. Other banks and consumers then always remain diligent, as there is a certain risk associated with the banking business. There is less risk of "moral hazard," where banks that are or feel overly protected from risk ("too big to fail") may take more risks than they would if they were fully exposed to the risk. Similarly, consumers have greater incentives to monitor the soundness of deposit-taking institutions. In most European countries, bank failures occur with very low frequency. Consumers are not used to a system with continuous ups and downs. Financial institutions are supposed be rock-solid, and full of checks and balances. There is an implicit or explicit expectation that if things go wrong the government at the end of the day will pick up the bill. But in such a context, once something goes wrong, the psychological impact of failure is high. The immediate impact on consumer confidence can be stronger than that of a failure in an economy where consumers are more familiar with bank failure.

The situation in Europe has not always been as stable as it is nowadays. Especially before World War II, bank failures occurred relatively frequently. Better risk management (thanks to advances in finance), better regulation, and better supervision (supervision was not embedded in law before World war II) have helped to make the system more stable and make bank failures infrequent. The costs of infrequent failure, however, are twofold. First, the price to pay for increased stability may be that when the system breaks down the impact is larger than it would have otherwise been: Risks have built up over a longer period of time. Second, in a society that is not used to bank failures, the perceived impact of a failure (on the sense of wellbeing) may be larger than would be the case in a society in which bank failures are a familiar event. However, on average, the benefits of the lower frequency of failure outweigh the costs of increased severity of events. On a cumulative basis, a system with smaller but more frequent failures leads to more value destruction.

Which system is better? The system of smaller but more frequent failures makes an emotional appeal (trying to prevent society-wide shocks; preventing moral hazard), while the system with occasional hiccups is clearly more rational, as there is less value destruction over time.

NCB is trying to achieve both. NCB prefers the system with a low frequency of failure and, through macro-prudential analysis, tries to find the reasons these occasional failures spin out of control, as we have lately seen in 2008. For instance, certain financial constructions can be made more costly by imposing higher capital requirements, which gives banks an incentive to improve their risk profile (i.e., reduce certain undesirable risk exposures). This is something that is currently done for securitization and proprietary trading. Or NCB can change the system of how banks are interconnected. Instead of all banks being connected to all other banks (which would invoke a chain reaction instead of checks and balances), NCB could require banks to operate via a central clearing system that enables more intervention. There would still be failures, as these are inherent to all markets, but NCB would be better equipped at "smoothing" them.

Now that we understand how to recognize the typical strategic dilemmas, and we understand that there are ways of dealing with them, they are not that scary, anymore. With that concern taken away, now is the time for a self-assessment.

CHAPTER 4

The Strategy Elastic

No man was ever so much deceived by another as by himself.

Fulke Greville

Improvement is driven by three questions: Where am I now, where do I want to be, and how do I get there? So if we want to improve the way we deal with dilemmas, we should start with a *self-assessment*. A true assessment requires reflection, the ability to take a hard and honest look at your organization, and not kid yourself. Moving from an either/or approach to an and/and attitude requires deep understanding not only of the organization's strengths, but also its weaknesses.

The Global Dealing with Dilemmas Survey (DwD survey) reveals the self-assessment of 580 respondents from 55 countries (see Figure 4.1). The majority of responses came from commercial companies, although 9% of respondents represented public sector organizations. The three most prominent sectors in the survey were professional services, high technology, and financial services. However, almost every other industry was represented, too, such as telecom, oil and gas, retail, aerospace, pharmaceuticals, automotive, and utilities.

These self-assessments were collected during interviews, workshops, presentations, and through a web survey. In the survey, I asked respondents to score themselves and their organizations on a number of things. I asked how well they think they deal with strategic dilemmas, and then asked a number of questions to verify that self-assessment. I also inquired as to what extent respondents were familiar with a number of management methodologies, and asked them questions on how they would solve particular dilemmas.

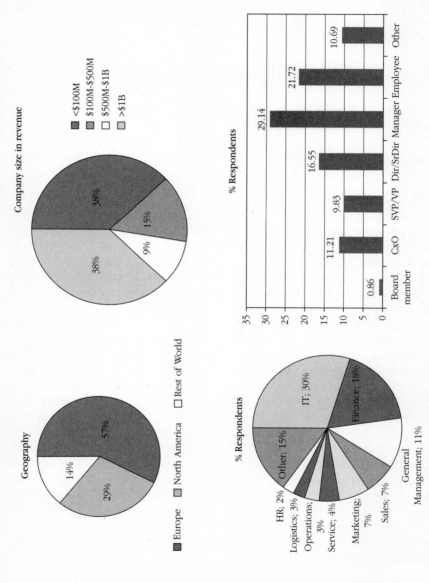

FIGURE 4.1 Dealing with Dilemmas Survey

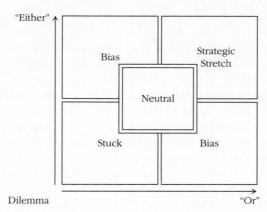

FIGURE 4.2 Five States in Dealing with Dilemmas

I have found a total of five possible "states" an organization can be in when assessing its capability of handling the six fundamental dilemmas defined in Chapter 3: (1 and 2) Organizations can have a strategic bias (to one side of the spectrum or to the opposite side); (3) they can have a neutral view; (4) they can be strategically stuck; or (5) they can have achieved strategic stretch (see Figure 4.2).

Strategic Bias

In many cases organizations will have a *strategic bias*. This means that they typically approach a dilemma from one side. For instance, they tend to be more inside-out driven than outside in, which means that the needs of the back office usually come first. Customer processes are defined to satisfy the back office first. Or their bias goes the other way: The front office is always in the lead, and it is the task of the back office to make it all work. This strategic bias, to one side or the other, can appear in each business dilemma. You have an either/or attitude, and it is usually *either* that is chosen. The consequences can be predicted, the need for addressing the opposite side is clear, but it takes the organization out of its comfort zone. It takes extraordinary effort to deal with issues caused by the other side of the dilemma.

Neutral Zone

If you score neither high nor low on both sides of the dilemma, you are operating in the *neutral zone*. You deal with the dilemma by looking for a trade-off; you are trying to strike a balance or find a reasonable compromise. You optimize processes a little, and once in a while, within the existing processes, you consider how you can incrementally improve and innovate. Or, as another example, you make sure you are profitable, but do not try to maximize profitability, as that would be at the expense of the value you deliver to customers. In essence, there is nothing wrong with this state, as long as it is in an area where you feel you do not have to differentiate from the competition. Simply seeking a compromise between two opposites requires the least management attention, and it can be a sustainable state.

Strategically Stuck

If you score low on both sides of the dilemma, this means you are *strategically stuck*. You are good in neither one nor the other side of the dilemma. You do not listen and you do not lead. You do not optimize and do not innovate. You neither plan for the long term, nor are successful managing the short term. It seems every problem you encounter takes you out of your comfort zone. This, of course, is an undesirable situation, whether it is a strategic dilemma or not. Being strategically stuck is a strong wakeup call. In areas where you should have competitive differentiation, your competition is probably already overtaking you. And in areas that are not strategically important, you are simply not very efficient, draining resources that could be better used elsewhere.

Strategic Stretch

If you score high on both sides of the dilemma, you have found a way to reconcile both sides of it, through synthesis. You have achieved *strategic stretch*. You have found a way to listen *and* lead, for instance, by leading the competition in being a better listener to customers, or—the other way around—involving customers heavily in groundbreaking innovation. You have found a way of maximizing profits, *because* you offer the most value to customers. Or you know how every short-term decision and tactical program contributes to the long-term strategic objectives. For dilemmas you deem crucial in your business, this is the desired state where you have found "the genius of the *and*."

Strategy Elastic

A good way to visualize how you are doing with the six dilemmas is to create what I call a *strategy elastic.*[i] Creating strategic stretch is very much like working with an elastic band. If you pull it from only one side, the other side will move along in the same direction. You can stretch it only if you pull it from *both* sides. And the harder you pull in multiple directions at the same time, the more space you create, which is the objective of strategic management. The metaphor of an elastic band is particularly appropriate because it implies you cannot stop pulling; otherwise, the elastic band goes back to its neutral position. Strategy management is the same. You need to keep working on creating strategic stretch—otherwise, the organization will fall back to average results. Execution is a continuous process.

Consider the strategy elastic of a U.S.-based media and entertainment company[ii] with over $1 billion in revenue, as shown in Figure 4.3. Its results are not extreme, but they do tell an interesting story. The one thing the company is good at is the listen-and-lead dilemma. It has found a way to innovate beyond direct customer requirements, while at the same time listening to customers very well. The company does so by spotting trends, even before the customers have spotted them. However, the

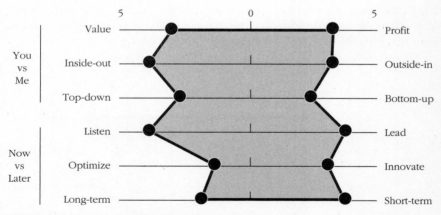

FIGURE 4.3 Strategy Elastic of U.S.-Based Media and Entertainment Company

---

[i]Strategy Elastic™ is trademarked by Frank Buytendijk.
[ii]All survey entries were anonymous. I only asked only for industry, size, geography, and a few other characteristics.

company has mostly a short-term focus. It probably jumps from one trend to another. This is not very good for creating a long-term vision. As a media and entertainment company, it is very much focused at translating trends into new products and pushing those products out. There is a bias toward inside-out thinking. The company scores slightly below neutral, and toward being strategically stuck on the top-versus-bottom and the optimize-versus-innovate dilemmas. It does not pay a lot of attention to processes, and alignment is a problem as well. It seems margins are relatively high in this market, as the company can afford to be in the neutral zone, trading off customer value and profitability.

Let us look at a small financial services firm, based in Western Europe. Its strategy elastic is shown in Figure 4.4. Perhaps it is the economy (the survey was held during the latter part of 2009), but the short-term focus on the company is relatively extreme. However, the focus and alignment in this company is very high. The strategic objectives of the company (top down) are known to everyone, and it is clear to everyone how their daily work contributes to those strategic objectives. The alignment between creating customer value while maximizing profitability is also remarkable. For a small financial institution, such as an upscale private bank, this actually should be the basis of the business model—having transparent fees and commissions, while increasing the wealth of its customers. As a small organization, it does not pay a lot of attention to its processes. It borders on being strategically stuck here. It is probable that the optimization that takes place is based on regulations and compliance. The products that the firm offers are not particularly innovative, but the company distinguishes itself by being close to its customers. Its strategic bias here is clear.

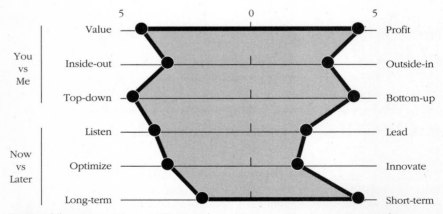

FIGURE 4.4 **Strategy Elastic of Small Western-European Financial Services Firm**

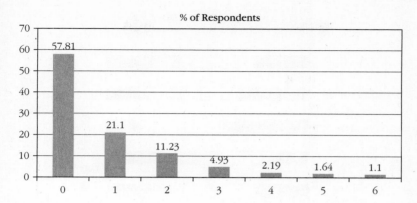

FIGURE 4.5 Distribution of Respondents on the Number of Stretch Dilemmas

Being able to reach strategic stretch on a certain dilemma is not a trivial thing. More than half of the respondents in the DwD survey do not score any strategic stretch across the six dilemmas. Only 20% of respondents achieve strategic stretch on one dilemma, and less than 5% are able to stretch on three dilemmas.[iii] Figure 4.5 shows the overall distribution. Although strategic stretch is a good thing, and organizations should work toward strategic stretch on as many dilemmas as they can manage, it is not necessary to score stretch on all dilemmas. It takes energy to stretch an elastic, and once you stop, it goes back to its old shape. Organizations do not have the energy to be perfect on all fronts. It is better to choose which dilemmas contribute most to the organization's competitive profile and focus on those.

Profiles in Performance

Each company has its own profile. In fact, the survey data did not suggest there were profiles that were significantly more common than others. However, when examining how organizations are doing on the level of individual dilemmas, a clear pattern emerges. Not all dilemmas are equal. Figure 4.6 shows which dilemmas are more prominent than others.

[iii]One percent of respondents report they score strategic stretch on all six dilemmas. In other words, they have scored themselves five points on all questions on strategy, operations, and culture. I do not think these are reliable answers, and they should be ignored.

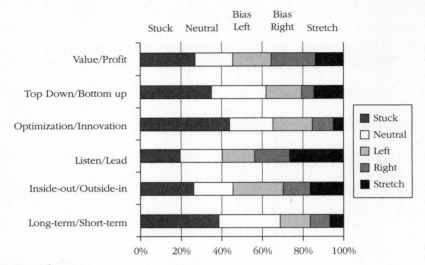

FIGURE 4.6 Most Common States per Dilemma

Some dilemmas are harder to deal with than others. Close to 40% of all respondents state they are strategically stuck in the long-term-versus-short-term dilemma, and over 40% of all respondents feel the same about innovation versus optimization. Even if you look at the companies that score very high (the top 4% that stretch four or five dilemmas), it is typically long term versus short term and innovation versus optimization that score the lowest. These two dilemmas seem to be the two thorniest ones. Chapter 9 extensively addresses long-term versus short-term dilemmas, discussing options-based strategies and scenario planning.

The biggest area of strategic bias can be found in the value-versus-profit dilemma. Some organizations focus on the customer, following the philosophy that profits follow as a logical consequence. But this is not always true. Most customer profitability analyses show that a certain percentage of large and respected customers are simply not profitable. Having large account teams, offering quantity discounts, and other measures to keep and grow large customers also add to the cost of sales, which is not always considered in the customer relationship. However, more organizations have a strategic bias for the profit side, even to the detriment of providing customer value. This cannot be a sustainable situation for the long term. At one point, customers will find out or will find alternatives, and will defect.

Listen and lead is the dilemma that organizations have mastered most. Around 25% of respondents report they have a strategic stretch. The U.S.-based media and entertainment company reported strategic stretch on this front. Leading customers with innovation is usually called *product innovation*, whereas listening to customers is called *customer intimacy*. As discussed in Chapter 2, traditional strategic management advocates that you have to choose. However, most companies report that they do both equally well.

If you break down the scores into three buckets, the 33% worst-scoring companies, the 33% average-scoring ones, and the 33% best-scoring ones, some very interesting conclusions emerge.

- Those that are at the bottom one-third, and are stuck or neutral in four or five of the dilemmas, are much more likely to have a bias toward value, leading customers, and preferring an outside-in approach. These are the three biases connected to the customer perspective in the balanced scorecard. What this means is that "putting the customer first" is not automatically the right thing to do. The key to success is to reconcile *both* customer focus and a focus on your own strategic objectives.
- Organizations with average scores and that are neutral or stuck in three or four dilemmas tend to have a bias for inside-out thinking and leading the customer, and a profit orientation. These are the companies that are driven from the inside, with a focus on their own objectives. They change when needed by absorbing it, but do not really drive change.
- In the top one-third of companies, which score stuck or neutral in two dilemmas or less, where they score a bias, it seems to be toward innovation, a long-term view, and an outside-in approach. These are largely connected with the growth/learning perspective—worrying about tomorrow's performance. This seems to be a good starting point for getting strategic stretch all over.

Time to Look in the Mirror

A quick way to get your own strategy elastic self-assessment started is scoring your organization on the questions in Table 4.1. If you decide to use the survey for others within your organization, I recommend that you randomize the order of the questions. This way the structure of the six dilemmas does not reveal itself so easily, which would otherwise bias the answers.

A score of 1 means you tend to disregard the subject; scoring a 3 means you do an average job, nothing spectacular. If you score yourself a 5, that means you consider your organization to excel in that respect and it constitutes a strategic differentiator. For each side of the dilemma,

TABLE 4.1 Assessing Your Strategy Elastic

Create Your Strategy Elastic

Value

S1: Do you involve key external stake-holders, other than investors (such as partners and customers) in making strategic decisions?
O1: To what extent do you hire sales representatives who are long-term relationship builders, and measure customer satisfaction and repeat business?
C1: When making decisions, to what extent does your organization truly focus on what is best for the customer?
Average score:

Profit

S7: Is the creation of shareholder value central to strategic decision making?
O7: To what extent do you hire sales representatives who hunt until they close a deal, and then measure them on revenue?
C7: When making decisions, does your company focus mostly on the question "What is in it for us?"
Average score:

Inside Out

S2: To what extent can your strategy be characterized as "focusing on the core business"?
O2: How would you score the quality of your product marketing?
C2: To what extent can your culture be described as seeking conformity and consensus throughout the organization?
Average score:

Outside In

S8: To what extent does the organization know how to recognize sudden new opportunities in the market and seize them?
O8: How would you rate the quality of your relationship marketing?
C8: To what extent are employees encouraged to behave entrepreneurially, for instance, being empowered to make immediate decisions?
Average score:

Top Down

S3: When there is a strategic change, to what extent can you translate new financial goals into updated operational plans?
O3: Are most people in your organization informed about financial performance indicators, such as profit, cost, and EVA?
C3: Do you and your colleagues know exactly what top management expects from you?
Average score:

Bottom Up

S9: To what extent can you measure the financial impact of changes in operational company resources (capital, people, systems, materials)?
O9: Are operational performance indicators, such as production, waste, speed, and quality, shared broadly in your company?
C9: Do you know exactly what your colleagues in other business domains expect from you, and vice versa?
Average score:

TABLE 4.1 *(continued)*

Create Your Strategy Elastic

Listen

S4: To what extent is your strategy based on being very close to the needs of your customer, in other words, "customer intimacy"?

O4: To what extent is your organization structured around customer interaction processes and channels?

C4: To what extent is your organization looking to jump on the bandwagon of new customer trends?

Average score:

Lead

S10: To what extent is your strategy based on product or service innovation to differentiate from the competition?

O10: To what extent is your organization structured around the products you produce and sell?

C10: To what extent is your organization always on the forefront in setting new trends?

Average score:

Optimize

S5: Do you agree with the following statement: "For us, innovation and improvement is a process of continuously taking small steps forward"?

O5: Have you embraced lean, Six Sigma, or related concepts?

C5: Are the people who drill down into issues deeper than anyone else seen as the "heroes" in your organization?

Average score:

Innovate

S11: Do you agree with the following statement: "For us, innovation is about making dramatic moves in the market, like large acquisitions or revolutionary new products and services"?

O11: How would you characterize reorganization processes in your organization?

C11: Are "out-of-the-box" thinkers recognized most in your organization?

Average score:

Long Term

S6: Is it clear to all employees what the long-term vision of the organization is and the road ahead?

O6: How would you rate your product lifecycle management?

C6: Does your organization agree with the statement: "You need to fix the roof during summer" (meaning, reorganize and save money when times are still good, to be able to weather bad times)?

Average score:

Short Term

S12: To what extent is it clear to everyone how and how much their daily activities contribute to the everyday success of the company?

O12: How would you rate your level of insight into customer and product profitability?

C12: Does your organization agree with the statement: "We will cross that bridge when we get there" (meaning, better to wait until bad times are here and we understand them, so we can take the appropriate action to save cost and reorganize)?

Average score:

there are three questions. One question is about the strategy of your organization (S). Another question deals with operational aspects, such as processes, methodologies, and measures of success (O). The third question addresses cultural aspects (C). In case the specific question does not relate to the reality of your business, answer in the spirit of the question.

Misalignment

With these scores, you can plot your strategy elastic, and discover your strategic biases, strategic stretch, and where you are strategically stuck. Particularly in areas where you score only average, it is important to look at the distribution of the three scores. You may, for instance, score high on strategy, but low on culture. This result may indicate a misalignment in your organization, and probably a continuous source of struggle.

We can distinguish the following types of misalignment:

- If you score high on strategy, but not on the others, you may have an execution issue in the organization. You have the right ideas, but somehow they do not make it to the execution phase, or it is hard to cascade them down into the organization.
- If you score high on operations/processes, but not on the others, the organization probably is "cruising." Your organization is ready for it, but the right ideas are not coming, and if the right ideas are there, the people in the organization do not have the passion or drive to make a change. It means you are vulnerable in economically stressful times.
- If you score high on culture, but not on the others, there is certainly intent and ingredients for success, but they are not pulled together. The organization is a hotbed for talent, but it is not turned into results. Most likely, staff turnover, particularly among the high potentials, is high. At first, people are enthused by the vibes in the organization, but they get disappointed quickly, as nothing really happens. Some very innovative organizations are actually known for this. They provide the basis of many inventions, but others turn them into profitable businesses.

The DwD survey shows that on average organizations score the weakest in the area of operations and processes (see Figure 4.7). This confirms most of the research that states that strategy execution usually is the weakest link. Ninety percent of well-formulated strategies fail in the execution. It also highlights an important shortcoming in traditional strategic thinking that separates strategy formulation, strategy implementation and execution, and strategy feedback. Making strategy a continuous process puts

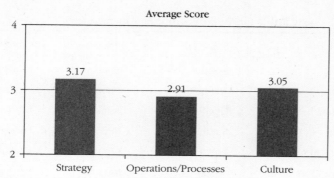

FIGURE 4.7 Average Scores on Strategy, Operations, and Culture

TABLE 4.2 Strategy Elastic for South African Education and Research Organization

	Strategic	Operational	Cultural
Value/Profit	Stuck	Profit-bias	Neutral
Top/Bottom	Stuck	Stuck	Neutral
Optimization/Innovation	Opt. bias	Stuck	Neutral
Listen/Lead	Stuck	Neutral	Listen bias
Inside Out/Outside In	Neutral	Stretch	Outside-in bias
Long Term/Short Term	Short-term bias	Stuck	Long-term bias

execution at the center of successful strategy management. Conversely, the results show that the organizations that score well on the operations-related questions also do well on the strategic and cultural level.

The area where you score high, for instance, on the cultural level, may be a good starting point to improve scores in the other areas as well, like strategy and operations.

Let us analyze a few examples from the DwD survey, looking at their specific scores for strategy, operations, and culture. Take, for instance, this education and research organization in South Africa that seems to be experiencing some issues. Its strategy elastic looks like Table 4.2.

As with so many academic cultures, the staff has a strong long-term focus, and an entirely different sense of urgency compared to the management of the organization. No wonder the organization is stuck in a number of places. Management and staff are on completely different paths. As a result, it is stuck between delivering value in the form of excellent research

TABLE 4.3 Strategy Elastic for Western European Manufacturer

	Strategic	Operational	Cultural
Value/Profit	Neutral	Stuck	Profit bias
Top/Bottom	Neutral	Neutral	Neutral
Optimization/Innovation	Opt. bias	Stuck	Innovation bias
Listen/Lead	Stretch	Neutral	Listen bias
Inside Out/Outside In	Inside-out bias	Neutral	Outside-in bias
Long Term/Short Term	Stuck	Neutral	Long-term bias

and education, and a healthy financial bottom line. There is definitely no alignment in the organization—it is strategically stuck in the top-versus-bottom dilemma. However, this organization is mostly on the operational level. Given that for half the dilemmas the organization reports being stuck on the operational level, it seems the organization and its processes need to be fixed. There is passion in the culture, but not for the dilemmas that are aimed at running an efficient organization. The staff cares deeply for listening to its customers, taking an outside-in approach, and minding the long term. The staff's culture is fairly neutral toward issues of management in the first three dilemmas in the table. Organizational change may not be resisted too much, which means there is hope for this organization.

Or consider this mid-sized Western European manufacturer, as shown in Table 4.3. It must be very frustrating for the people working there because although they have a strong bias for innovation, the management is mainly concerned with optimizing current operations. New ideas do not get a chance on the strategic level. Even worse, there is a strong entrepreneurial spirit, but management is more interested in simply running the core business. As a result, the company is stuck or at best scoring neutral on all dilemmas from an operational point of view. It is no wonder, with such misalignment between culture and strategy.

With an assessment of current results on the table, and your own strategy elastic defined, the next logical question is: How do we create strategic stretch for the dilemmas that matter most to us? Different dilemmas need different approaches. Now-or-later dilemmas benefit most from creating a portfolio of options, whereas you-or-me dilemmas should be addressed by seeking synthesis. The concept of synthesis was introduced in Chapter 1, and defining the goal of strategy management as creating a portfolio of options was the subject of Chapter 2. I will address techniques for creating such a portfolio and how to achieve synthesis in the chapters ahead.

CHAPTER 5

Dealing with Dilemmas, or Not?

Ever notice that "what the hell" is always the right decision?

Marilyn Monroe

Strategic dilemmas can be predicted; they are deeply rooted in most organization's business models. In fact, we can even classify a number of them. Long term or short term, listen or lead, and optimize or innovate are all "now-versus-later" dilemmas that require creating options. Value or profit, inside out or outside in, and top down or bottom up are "you-versus-me" dilemmas and you should seek synthesis. These dilemmas are universal. Next to these predictable dilemmas, there are always one-time strategic "this-or-that" decisions to be taken that require a clear choice or a certain trade-off.

But how? Everyone seems to agree that the genius of the *and* is important. However, how can that genius be embraced? We all understand that conflicting requirements need to be reconciled to create a win-win situation, but that seems to be more art than science. Or is it? What is the right course of action? There are many ways to deal with dilemmas.

How *Not* to Deal with Dilemmas

"What the hell" may have worked for Marilyn Monroe. Sir Richard Branson of Virgin preaches, "Screw it, let's do it."[1] The famous Peters and Waterman describe a "bias for action" as one of the key principles of successful management in *In Search of Excellence*.[2] These are all examples of the current Western management culture not really helping in recognizing and dealing with dilemmas. This way of thinking emphasizes the need to make a decision, to make either/or choices. "A decision is better than no decision," "Flip a coin," "Take a deep breath, and choose between the two evils," "Make the tough decisions, make the hard calls," "Be the great decider."

In these cases, problems are usually not fundamentally resolved. The chosen solutions are a reaction to the old situation. Or you make a choice for negative reasons, to simply avoid the consequences of the other option. The pendulum swings. Reorganization follows after reorganization. From centralization to decentralization back to centralization. From product-oriented organizations to process-oriented organizations to customer-focused organizations, and back to products again. These reactions do not happen only in organizations; continuous chain reactions can also be found in complete markets. Economists speak of the pork cycle.[3] In times when there is a demand for pork meat, farmers will start breeding pigs to cater to that need. It is an attractive market; prices are high. But as all farmers do that, after a while—once the pigs have grown—the shortage quickly turns into an excess supply. As a result, prices drop and the market becomes less attractive. Farmers stop breeding pigs, and after a while the supply drops and prices go up again. The pendulum swings and it never gets solved.

The opposite reaction is to not decide anything at all. The dilemma stares you in the face and you freeze. Actually, not making decisions in time actually causes strategic dilemmas to happen. When economic times are bad, shareholders applaud decisive action. The share price increases when the CEO announces layoffs and the immediate effect on the cost structure and the profits of the organization. But it is not a brave decision at all; it is way too late. As a result, the organization suffers from a brain drain, and as a consequence the chances that the organization can benefit from the upturn are greatly diminished. It would have been much better to create a lean-and-mean organization during good times to avoid massive layoffs. As the saying goes, you need to fix the roof during summer.

Another consequence of freezing when confronted with a dilemma is that decisions are made for you. If a new business model presents itself that is conflicting with your current way of working, not embracing it and sticking to the old ways can be a danger. Think of the media industry that tried to stop distribution of music and movies via Internet channels. Although it is illegal to use peer-to-peer networks to share music, most teenagers and young professionals today do not consider this an unethical practice at all.[4] Now the media industry is catching up and fighting an uphill battle.

Displaying an anti-cyclical decision-making process helps in addressing the dilemma. Taking the time into account to breed pigs, it is best to start this process when the price of pork is low, and others are giving up on the business. The best moment to consider downsizing and making the organization more lean is in times of high profitability. There is money to do so in a controlled way, time is not of the essence so no shortcuts are needed, and the negative effects can be compensated by counterinvestments. To decide or not to decide is a clear dilemma.[i]

Another natural reaction is to seek a compromise. In you-versus-me dilemmas, through a process of negotiation each party involved gives up on a few wishes and holds onto a few other wishes. Each side makes concessions. Some requirements are nonnegotiable, others are negotiable, and some wishes are expressed only for the purpose of giving them up in the process. Particularly in politics it works that way. As a result, none of the parties involved really get what they want. The result is being stuck in the middle—hardly the way to reach a state of strategic stretch.

How to Deal with Dilemmas: Either/Or

We may have been mistaken at first and the dilemma we seem to have turns out not to be a dilemma at all. We think we have to make a choice, but this is not the case. The need for a choice is often based on the presence of a constraint. A *constraint* is a certain limit. The constraint could be time, causing the dilemma. If we wait too long making a choice, we lose momentum. And if we decide fast, we run a high risk of making the wrong call. Think of buying a house where the real estate agent gives you only 15 minutes to decide. Or think of introducing a new product quickly to have first-mover advantage. Perhaps time is not a constraint at all. The person putting us in the difficult position, pushing us to choose, may have his own agenda. We may find out there are no other buyers after all, or that there are many other comparable houses for sale. Or we come to the conclusion that there really is no first-mover advantage, and that being a fast follower in the market increases our chances of success in terms of market awareness, customer adoption, and cost of sales.

Money, like other resources such as people, facilities, and materials, could be another constraint. Given the budget we have, we cannot run all the campaigns we would want to, and we have to choose which ones. But there might be a discretionary budget that you could apply for, based on your analysis, which shows a very high probability of a positive return on investment of your marketing campaigns. Or you can barter services and piggyback on the campaigns of a partner, while offering the partner the chance to participate in one of your campaigns. Simply having

---

[i]In fact, "to decide or not to decide" is a *meta-dilemma*. It is a dilemma on how to deal with a dilemma.

a campaign strategy might make a difference. If campaigns are related, each campaign benefits from the previous one and requires less investment than a single campaign.

Constraints may also merely reside in the mind. Perhaps we feel we must choose but in reality this is not the case. The stewardess asks whether we want chicken or beef, but if we ask politely, perhaps she can give us both. Different product managers may argue over which product to position for the customer in order to get the deal, but perhaps everyone's chances improve by showing the competitive differentiation of the combination of both. Perhaps we think of either putting our money in a savings account or buying shares, but why not put part of it in the bank and speculate with the rest? Laziness or lack of effort can be another mental constraint. We say we can do only one thing today, but if we work a little harder or a little longer we can actually achieve more tasks from the overall list. Or the constraint might be a sense of complexity. The dilemma could consist of whether you should do project A first and then B, or B first and then A, when really the two projects interrelate. Why not do both projects at the same time, each with a smaller team, and simply make sure you assign a project manager who can handle the extra complexity (or give a more junior project manager the chance to rise to the occasion)?

It is important to ask yourself if you really have to choose. There may be many ways to do both if the constraints turn out not to be real.

Sometimes one of the choices can be proven wrong on objective, subjective, or ethical grounds. Upon a better understanding of the options, there simply might be a better option. There might be a lesser evil of the two, one that you can deal with in a better way. Better to overspend the budget and lose 10% of your bonus, than underachieve on your target and lose 100% of your bonus. Better to choose chicken, because that is always done the way you prefer, than to choose beef, where it may not be prepared to your liking. Better to lose an initial experimental investment in a new technology trend than to completely miss the boat on a new and promising opportunity.

Trying to keep things objective is easiest in this-versus-that dilemmas, where a clean and comparable choice has to be made. The moment the dilemma is of the now-versus-later type, psychologists will tell you, people have a natural bias for the present and a tendency to see future consequences as the lesser evil. These consequences are then rationalized: "We'll cross that bridge when we get there," "I will be in another job by then," "I am sure there will be a good solution found by then," and so on. The same is the case with you-versus-me dilemmas; people tend to choose for themselves and rationalize the consequences for others. "It really is better for him or her," or "It really is his or her own responsibility," and "Hey, it's a dog-eat-dog world out there."[ii]

An assessment of which is the better option may also be subjective in nature. It should not always be about numbers, cost, profit, or other measurable things. If two locations to put a new factory in a different country have the same tax advantages, the same cost structure, and a comparable distance to the airport, perhaps the best choice is the one where the weather conditions are better. If two people for a certain job have the same qualifications, it is perfectly normal to have a bias toward the person you feel more chemistry with. Even more, you would probably hire that person even if the other candidate has somewhat better qualifications. There is no problem in weighing in the personal commitment and enthusiasm of people for specific projects when putting together an innovation portfolio, as these can be important predictive indicators for success.

Finally, moral and ethical aspects play an important role in favoring or discarding choices in a dilemma. If any option in a dilemma is objectively realistic but compromises your personal integrity or the integrity of the organization, you should not do it. Sometimes all options have impact on integrity. Can you murder someone to save the life of others? Or more in a business sense, can you fire someone as a scapegoat to protect the interests of others in more influential positions? I remember a case very early in my own career where a consultant with a background in computer hacking was fired, because the background check by a potential customer (who was looking for a security auditor) raised questions. It was solved, or at least addressed, when the consultant indicated he was willing to quit if the employer would pay for an additional university education he was interested in pursuing. Moral or ethical dilemmas are the hardest ones of all.

How to Deal with Dilemmas: And/And

Dilemmas are a part of life. We all encounter them at some point. The question is how you approach them. Do you freeze, do you avoid them by making a quick evasive decision, do you flip a coin, or do you face them? There are different techniques you can apply to deal with them.

[ii]When you hear people use the word *really* or *actually* a lot, it is a sign of trying to rationalize something. Rationalizing is trying to convince oneself that something wrong really actually is right.

The most important thing is to embrace the dilemma. Ignoring it does not make it go away. On the contrary, embracing a dilemma is an opportunity to move forward. In the 1980s, Coca Cola had a dilemma when facing the competition with Pepsi. Pepsi was winning the "cola tests" it held in the field. Visitors in malls and other public places were asked to blind-test two colas, Pepsi and Coca Cola. As the taste of Pepsi is somewhat sweeter, it triggers the taste buds a bit faster at the first sip, which is all the testers got. Threatened by the competition, Coca Cola faced a dilemma: Respond by changing the recipe, or not? The company decided to change the flavor. After introducing New Coke in 1985, there was a large consumer outcry. People were very upset that Coke was not Coke anymore. Coca Cola was forced to reintroduce its original product, labeled Classic Coke. As painful as the whole exercise was, market share actually improved because of the reintroduction, and Coca Cola learned a very important lesson about the brand value of the product. Blind testing obviously does not address the full experience.

A dilemma forces you to think, to take a position. There is a well-known psychological phenomenon that appears when framing decisions[5] from different angles. Consider the following (famous) experiment. Let a group of people choose between two vaccination programs. Program A will surely save 200 of the 600 impacted people. Program B has a 33% chance all 600 people will be saved and a 66% chance no people survive. Most people will choose program A, avoiding the large risk of failure. Then let another group of people choose between the following options. In using program C, 400 people of the impacted 600 will die. With program D, however, there is a 33% probability no one will die, and a 66% chance 600 people will die. Most people now will choose program C; the certain death of 400 people outweighs the chance that all will die. Objectively, the two groups were offered exactly the same choice; they were just formulated differently. The way a question, problem, or dilemma is framed obviously has an impact on the bias people will have in their decision making. Changing the perspective or offering more perspectives uncovers that subjectivity and bias.

The four perspectives of the balanced scorecard and the six dilemmas derived from those four perspectives help in considering multiple perspectives. If your decision enables growth and learning, improves processes, satisfies customer needs, and contributes positively to the bottom line, you can trust the way forward. Conversely, if you ignore a vital perspective in your decision making, chances are this perspective will continue to haunt you after making the decision.

For instance, if you are a retailer and the cost of sales staff is out of control, you can fire a number of salespeople. In the short term, finances improve. At the same time, sales potential suffers and consequently the

Executive View

Publishing Corp. is in the process of consolidating its contact centers. The original business case was built on saving costs and creating efficiencies, based on an investment that needs to be earned back in two years. With the sharp decline in the economy, business (and IT) embarked on quite an aggressive cost-reduction program with head-count savings being the primary source of cost reductions. The business case for the contact center consolidation project fell apart, or in options terms, went "under water." Moving forward was not the right decision anymore, but neither was stopping the project.

Together with the project steering committee, the CIO chose to *reframe* the problem, and built a new business case based on different grounds. In addition to saving costs based on increased economies of scale, building better customer service was included. Better customer service can be translated into tangible business results, such as higher subscription retention and advertising sales, which is essential in economically difficult times. Part of the revised business case (now with a payback period of three years) also was to centralize the contact center *technology*, but not the business structures. There would still be a centralized contact center bridge, standardized call flows, central policy around agent profiles and training, as well as work-load sharing between agents. In later phases, Publishing Corp. may consolidate business functions, but that would be a different project with its own business case. This approach not only presented a better business case, but also increased business buy-in for a difficult initiative in what is essentially a decentralized company.

mid- and long-term financial results as well. It would be better to see if you can turn a number of processes into self-service. For instance, supermarkets are experimenting with self-service cash registers, and in a wide variety of industries, customers place orders via the Web. It is a scalable model that allows you to learn a lot about customer behavior, it makes business processes more efficient, it adds to a positive customer experience, and it improves the bottom line. Each of the six strategic dilemmas provides useful examples. Taking different perspectives helps to turn either/or into and/and.

The Right Mindset

People are normally unaware of their bias, as it represents their mindset and paradigm of the world. It takes a specific way of thinking to free yourself from a fixed mindset. One level up, considering complete organizations, it works the same. The organization, as a collection of people and as a living organism itself, tends to have a certain strategic bias, and needs to overcome its own paradigms as well. In his book, *Five Minds for the Future*, renowned psychologist Howard Gardner describes what it takes to have a mindset that is ready to take on dilemmas:

> *The* disciplined *mind, works steadily over time improving skill and understanding. The* synthesizing *mind takes information from disparate sources, understands and evaluates that information objectively, and puts it together. The* creating *mind breaks new ground. It puts forth new ideas, poses unfamiliar questions, conjures up fresh ways of thinking, arrives at unexpected answers. The* respectful *mind notes and welcomes differences between human individuals and between human groups. The* ethical *mind ponders the nature of one's work and the needs and desires of the society in which one lives.*[6]

All five minds are needed to successfully deal with dilemmas and to turn strategic bias, or being strategically stuck, into strategic stretch. Discipline is needed to recognize dilemmas. It is much easier to jump to conclusions and make a quick decision. Others will applaud your action orientation and there is often time pressure. It requires discipline to keep your cool when confronted with dilemmas. Dilemmas often trigger strong emotional responses such as stress, anxiety, and anger.

Only discipline takes you to the second mind, trying to find synthesis, finding a way to relate different, even opposing things. How can we make sense of all the different signals that reach us that are ambiguous, incomplete, and not well understood? We excel in this capability as children. Children in their early years do nothing but forming, testing, discarding, and fine tuning theories of how the world works,[iii] understanding the rules and exceptions in the language, and figuring out how to get attention from the people around them and manipulate them in the right way. But as we grow older, we "complete" our theory of the world (and as an

---

[iii]My eldest daughter, then at age 4 or 5, was astonished seeing a man with long blond hair and a rough beard in the street for the first time. It did not make sense to her—long blond hair fits women; a beard belongs to men. How could this be? She had to reconstruct her theory about what distinguishes men and women.

organization the theory of the business), and lose that capability. It needs to be retrained.

Based on all the information we have put together, the creative mind needs to enter the game. The insights we have created need to be turned into action. We may find ways that no one has tried before to create strategic differentiation. This requires lateral and associative thinking instead of a linear train of thought, in other words, an out-of-the-box approach. In *The Mind of the Strategist*, Japanese management guru Kenichi Ohmae argues that strategy formulation in the Western world is too analytical.[7] There are countless books and consultants preaching "12 steps to success," "7 imperatives to do tomorrow," and "the sure path to becoming rich." Ohmae makes a plea for a more creative approach, allowing more intuition and creating more intellectual flexibility, bringing in elements of Japanese culture in which vagueness, ambiguity, and tentative decisions are much more accepted and favored.

Finally, dilemmas can be solved in a sustainable way only in a *respectful* and *ethical* way. This means that we need to let go of our own preconceptions and see the good in other approaches and other people. We can respect a lazy person because he or she may come in with a very creative solution on how to eliminate work. We could respect frustration because it is a great source of innovation. We need to respect the perspective of a negative thinker, because it is better to test a plan within your organization first, than to be confronted by customers or others with its flaws after implementation. Stereotypes and preconceptions do not lead to original thinking.

Adopting these five minds does not mean you have to do all the thinking yourself. In fact, involving various people with different backgrounds, each with his or her own frame of mind, helps greatly. First, this approach is more likely to uncover multiple angles and perspectives. Further, having to formulate thoughts to share them with others often sharpens those thoughts. Finally, two (or more) know more than one.

Strategic dilemmas are mostly not unique to a single organization. In fact, the six dilemmas I derived from the balanced scorecard are almost universal in nature. They can be found in probably every organization across industries and countries. Other, comparable organizations may have come up with solutions that would work in your organization, too.[iv] Even

---

[iv]People often claim their organization is different from all others, and can be heard saying things like "That wouldn't work here" or "We've tried that already." These are signs that these organizations are in need of the five minds that Gardner described. Maybe then they will realize that their organization is not so different after all, or when they find out *it is* really different, this will inspire the creative thinking needed to make things work in their particular case.

better, a completely different industry may have already gone through a comparable cycle of thesis, antithesis, and synthesis. The specifics of the other industry then suggest a different perspective on your dilemma, while you at the same time can apply the lessons learned where there are similarities.

For instance, consider the split between the infrastructural side and the delivery business of utility companies in water, electricity, and gas that is taking place in a number of countries around the world. There are all kinds of you-versus-me and now-versus-later effects in place. Customer and process are separated, investment and exploitation are partly split up, and so on. Many formerly state-owned telecoms and railways went through that same phase of privatization and separation years ago. It is worthwhile to explore how these companies dealt with that. Or think of the struggle between integration and interoperability in IT architectures. The deeper the integration, the more specific the components become, and the more efficiently they can be built. At the same time, the higher the integration, the less these components are usable for different purposes, negatively impacting the efficiency of reusing components. This is a variation on the theme of the you-versus-me dilemma. Other industries that deal with the same dilemma are the automotive industry and the engineering industry.

On the cultural level, adopting the five minds means we learn from other approaches and other cultures. People tend to display ethnocentricity, judging other people's behavior through their own lens of what is right and wrong. They apply their cultural system to others, believing—probably even unconsciously—that their culture and view of the world is superior. We can train ourselves in dealing with other cultures by composing not only multidisciplinary teams, but also multicultural teams. This allows us to learn from each other's approaches. Perhaps, in dealing with dilemmas, we can fuse the Eastern and Western ways of thinking. Using the respectful mind, we can embrace the Eastern appreciation of ambiguity and judging facts and events not by themselves but by their context.[v] Eastern managers have more tolerance for ambiguous information, and tend to structure their decision-making process in a more collaborative and inclusive way. But in the same way, Eastern managers can also learn from the West, particularly when it comes to managing discontinuity. Easterners can

---

[v]From a Western cultural point of view, things are good or bad, or more formally: qualifications are attributes of the subject itself. In the Eastern view it depends on the effect of an event; qualifications are attributes of the context. Breaking your arm is perhaps a wonderful event, if you fall in love with the nurse in the hospital (and she falls in love with you). How many people have claimed that being fired turned out to be the best thing that ever happened in their life?

Executive View

Mr. Nirmal Hansra was chief financial officer for Fujitsu Australia Pty. Limited at a time when the Fujitsu Group was the second largest IT supplier in the world. Fujitsu, heavily competing with IBM, positioned itself as a high-quality vendor, offering mainframes with the least maintenance needed. Over the years, Fujitsu built a highly profitable business in Australia and New Zealand, based on the sales of mainframes and maintenance contracts. Then, the market changed. The mainframe hegemony was challenged by open systems, UNIX servers, and more cost-effective hardware. Fujitsu Australia was quick in recognizing these changes in the market and realizing the impact they would have. Mr. Hansra was recruited to assist the executive team to protect the company's future profitability. Fujitsu Australia identified the need to focus on new IT services such as systems integration, outsourcing, and bringing in third-party hardware and software, offering a total solution to customers. It also proposed moving the manufacturing of computers to other countries than Japan, to create a more competitive price-point. In any American company, headquarters would be the first to apply pressure to keep profitability up. In Fujitsu Australia's case, the operating company had to do it all itself, given the competitiveness of the local market.

Fujitsu Australia had to get the buy-in of headquarters, as it required a change of local strategy and business model—that is, to focus on solution selling and services, instead of hardware and maintenance. This turned out to be an incredible challenge, and led to a decision-making process of almost two years, while in the meantime Fujitsu Australia's profitability declined. In the Japanese business culture, decision making should not be hurried. There is a great loyalty to employees, which makes it hard to reorganize. Decision-making processes should be seen as a natural flow taking place within the company. This requires the buy-in of all business functions, including manufacturing, R&D, sales, and marketing, organized in a fairly complicated matrix.

For instance, as quality is a major criterion for Fujitsu, all third-party solutions that Fujitsu Australia proposed to bring in would have to undergo an extensive certification process in Japan. After two years, all stakeholders had approved and the Australian business commenced its transformation. In the meantime, Fujitsu's competitors came into the Australian market doing exactly what Fujitsu Australia

(continued)

(continued)

proposed to do. The delay in responding to the market dynamics meant that key management staff experienced frustration and lowered morale. There was also loss of staff as well as some mainframe accounts, as customers moved on with the trend toward outsourcing and switching to open systems. Entering into the outsourcing and systems-integration market became a challenge as there were by then established competitors with reference sites. The Japanese decision-making process may be very inclusive, and thorough, but it has a hard time dealing with time pressure and with expectations.

learn from the more aggressive Hegelian approach to seeking synthesis to solve dilemmas and move forward. In the Eastern approach, influenced by Taoism and Confucianism, dilemmas and ambiguity are seen as something to simply live with.

Dealing with Dilemmas Roadmap

Strategic dilemmas can be predicted and there are ways to deal with them, good and bad. In any case, they should be embraced to be solved, using Gardner's five minds. In the following chapters, I will discuss the techniques that fit with each type of dilemma that I have identified, to make sure you can attack your dilemmas with confidence.

When you encounter a dilemma, first establish whether it is a false dilemma. If it is, it is easy to identify the constraint and to lift it. There may be no time pressure at all, alternative sources of money or other resources may be available, or maybe the constraint exists only in the mind. Perhaps it is possible to disprove choices, based on objective, subjective, or ethical grounds, so that the number of choices is further limited, or only one option remains.

The next question is whether the dilemma really requires a choice. The idea of having to make a choice may exist only in the mind, or maybe you are not aware of the correct way to make a trade-off between the options. There may be cases in which no choice is needed. You can simply split the money, time, or other resources you have and do a little of both. There could be an optimal mix of all options. There is a complete field of mathematics that deals mostly with business optimization issues, called *operations research*. Other *this-or-that* dilemmas can be turned into this *and* that by decomposing the different choices. They may each look like one big decision, but in reality consist of smaller elements. Through careful analysis these smaller elements can then be recomposed into a single strategy moving forward.

You-or-me dilemmas can be tackled using three elements:

1. A successful synthesis starts with self-reflection. You cannot really understand the dilemma without understanding what it is in your mind that makes it hard to make the right decision. As in you-and-me dilemmas you are part of the dilemma itself, your position needs to be clear.
2. Further, you need to start communicating with others. A dilemma shared is a dilemma half reconciled. There are moral and philosophical considerations that need to be discussed as well.
3. The goal, making use of conflict resolution diagrams, is to find synthesis for the dilemma.

Now or later is the third special type of dilemma. There is always strategic uncertainty (we do not know if we are doing the right thing), and a bias toward the *now*. Making use of techniques such as scenario planning and real options, I will discuss how to deal with those dilemmas. Table 5.1 shows an overview of these techniques.

TABLE 5.1 Overview of Techniques on How to Deal with Dilemmas

Dealing with Dilemmas	
Chapter 7: This *and* that	■ Identify constraint. ■ Optimize portfolio on the efficiency frontier of the constraint. ■ Identify next constraint, or push or lift constraint. ■ Optimize portfolio again.
Chapter 8: You *and* me	Synthesis: ■ Self-reflect (what makes it a dilemma). ■ Communicate (explore all angles). ■ Reconcile: —What binds (not divides) all sides? —What is the higher (moral) principle?
Chapter 9: Now *and* later	Options: ■ Identify strategic uncertainty and associated risk. ■ Build scenarios. ■ Identify common options. ■ Build a contingency plan based on common options.

Table 5.1 should not be seen as a prescriptive list or a recipe for success. You will be much more successful in dealing with dilemmas if you find ways to frame the dilemma differently. In some cases, the dilemma will simply disappear. You-and-me dilemmas and now-and-later dilemmas are not mutually exclusive. In fact—and bear with me—you should see them in a meta-physical way, as a *space–time continuum*. You-and-me dilemmas take place in *space*, where space is defined as, for instance, the market space, or a network of stakeholders, or simply the people you work with. Now-and-later dilemmas take place in *time*. Bill Fitzsimmons, chief accounting officer of Cox Communications, labeled dilemmas as multidimensional problems. Taking a creative approach, reframing dilemmas, entails playing with the space and time dimensions of the dilemma.

Consider a you-and-me dilemma that cannot be reconciled between people. By introducing the time dimension, where for the time being you agree to disagree, a synthesis may appear at some point because circumstances change. Something more important may come up, one person may change his or her mind, a constraint may be lifted, rules may change, and so forth. We shifted dimension and have created the option of reconciling the dilemma later. In the interviews I conducted, several executives mentioned that the best time to make a decision is not when they *know* the right answer, but the moment they have ensured buy-in of all stakeholders.

It also works the other way around, shifting from time to space. Now-and-later dilemmas often have the element of uncertainty, as the future cannot be predicted. Making a heavy investment now, gaining first-mover advantage, also introduces serious strategic risk. By introducing the space dimension, you may involve other stakeholders first. For instance, sharing the risk by creating a joint initiative with partners to dip a toe in the water brings first-mover advantage while lowering the strategic risk to an acceptable level. In other words, we have synthesized the now-and-later dilemma.

By creatively exploring the space–time continuum, creating options and searching for synthesis become tools not only for specific dilemmas, but for strategic decision making in general.

CHAPTER 6

To Decide or Not to Decide, That Is the Question

"Fix the roof during the summer," versus "We'll cross that bridge when we get there."

As a general rule of thumb in business, the higher the reward, the higher the risk.[i] Having the first-mover advantage in a market means setting the rules of the game, gaining dominant market share, and generating higher profits as long as the competition has not caught up. But all the risk is yours as well. You will be the first one to make all the mistakes, as there are no established best practices. Conversely, waiting until you have it all figured out means others will have taken the market already. All that is left is a me-too strategy, without any brand premium or competitive differentiation. Margins are small and may even be negative if the resources left over in the market turn out to be limited. All the talented people work somewhere else, suppliers are shipping to others that did place their bets in time, and investors bring their capital elsewhere, as you appear not to be in touch with the market. If there is no risk, there is likely no reward. Over time certainty increases, but the expected performance decreases.

Figure 6.1 shows there is a trade-off between the moment to make the right decision and place your bets, and the value of that decision. If you analyze too long, the window of opportunity closes; you have suffered from *analysis paralysis*. If you jump on a new opportunity immediately–"shoot first,

---

[i]Risk and reward are obviously related. The higher the reward, most likely the higher the risk involved. However, it does not work vice versa. Taking high risks does not lead to a greater chance of a high reward. In many cases, on the contrary: The higher the risk, the lower the chance of success.

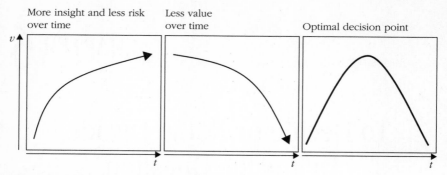

FIGURE 6.1   Risk/Reward Trade-Off Over Time

ask questions later"—your fail rate is most likely to be higher than others as well. But there is an optimum between risk and reward. Increasing your chance of success by thinking things through is worth the loss of a small amount of reward.[ii]

How can you know you are reaching an optimum? The window of opportunity is not always known. And you also do not know which vital new insights will come tomorrow. Further, while getting to the bottom of things with your analysis, chances are that instead of more clarity all you get is more ambiguity and confusion. But the point of getting more insight is not about more clarity. It is about gaining a better understanding of the problem's complexity. At the bottom of most problems a fundamental dilemma can be found. As counterintuitive as it sounds, in the case of now-and-later dilemmas this means that increasing confusion, ambiguity, and disagreement actually is a sign of progress toward the optimum decision point.

The Eye of Ambiguity

Figure 6.2 shows the dynamics of the decision-making process with a little more detail, using the idea of the S-curve.[1] S-curves describe the rise and fall of trends, the lifecycle of products, services, organizations, and markets.[iii] A trend starts hopefully; with a lot of passion, a small group of

---

[ii]For instance, a 90% chance on $90 revenue averages a return of $81. This is better than an 80% chance on $100 revenue, which averages $80.

[iii]Explanation of S-curves is loosely based on C. Handy, *The Age of Paradox*, Harvard Business School Press, 1994. The phrase "eye of ambiguity" is my own choice of words.

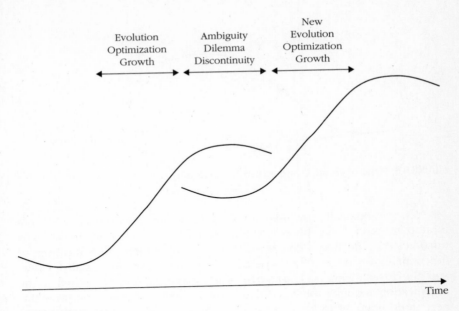

FIGURE 6.2 The S-curve

people pioneer a technology, test a new business model, or bring a new product to market. This is usually followed by a phase of disappointment. The new development turns out to be something less than a miracle. Reality kicks in. At some point, best practices emerge and a phase of evolution follows. Product functionality improves, market adoption grows, and the profitability increases. Then something else is introduced, usually by someone else. This can come from a competitor, but also from an entirely new market. Think of mobile phones replacing navigation systems, computer games challenging the market for children's books, or ready-made meals in the supermarket encroaching on fast-food restaurants and pizza delivery. This replacement then goes through the same steps.

The best place to jump to the next S-curve to secure sustained growth is obviously at the beginning of the "eye of ambiguity." While the current cash-cow business is still profitable and growing, the next wave can be adopted, preparing for future profitability. Both the now and the later are considered in an ambidextrous way. The cash-cow business can fund the new investment. The new trend has not broken through yet, so there is time to experiment in a safe way. Experimentation leads to additional insight on how to capitalize on this new trend, which decreases the risk of failure and moves you toward the optimal decision point.

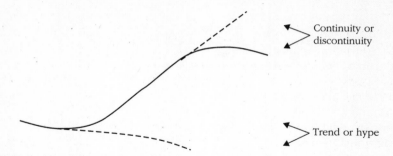

FIGURE 6.3 Hype or Trend, Continuity or Discontinuity

Yet, paradoxically, the *least likely* point to jump to the next S-curve is at that exact same point.[iv] The growth of the cash-cow business is uncontested. The new trend is certainly still underdelivering in terms of functionality or in any other type of added value. The profitability is low, and the investments will not meet the established hurdle rate that the organization requires for its current growth trajectory. And who says this new trend is going to be a success? Furthermore, the eye of ambiguity is a source of great confusion. Experts disagree on the impact of the new trend and the benefits are more of a promise than a proven reality. And in difficult times we tend to rely on what we know and what has proven to work best. As a result, most likely nothing will happen until the new trend has overtaken the old one, and it is too late.

A classic example of this is Polaroid and Kodak,[2] which missed the boat with digital photography. Another example would be the U.S. car manufacturers[3] that have missed the trend toward more economical cars and have kept building SUVs. Think of Motorola failing to see how the cellular handset business was shifting from analog to digital technology.[4] Levi's[5] did not merely misread the shift away from department stores, it also missed trend after trend, making jeans in out-of-favor colors or coming late to new looks like baggy hip-hop jeans. Plotting your particular position on the S-curves is a good start to opening your eyes for the change to come.

But as Figure 6.3 shows, how do you know that this new trend you have spotted really is the next S-curve, and not just hype that will blow over before things return to normal? And how can you know whether the curve you are on will collapse (discontinuity) or keep on growing (continuity)? When do you take a wait-and-see approach, and when should you place your bets as soon as possible?

[iv]Although Christensen does not use the S-curve metaphor, this explanation is based on C. Christensen, *The Innovators Dilemma*, Harvard Business School Press, 1997.

If you decide too soon, you could bet on the wrong trend unnecessarily. If you decide too late, it can be a missed opportunity altogether. In short, you delay decisions when the risk and cost of missing the mark is bigger than the risk and cost of a missed opportunity. You expedite decisions vice versa when the risk and cost of a missed opportunity are bigger than the risk and cost of missing the mark.[6]

Defining the optimal decision point is a *meta-dilemma*: a dilemma on how to deal with your dilemma. The meta-dilemma is solved by having the tools to create the optimal decision point yourself. Sometimes it is imperative to take action immediately, particularly in situations that may deteriorate rapidly and exponentially. Think of product recalls that have an immediate impact on the organization's reputation. Or think of any situation in which you run the risk that someone else will make the decision for you, usually not having your best interest in mind. For instance, in

Executive View

Bill Fitzsimmons, chief accounting officer of Cox Communications, identifies the jump from circuit switch to packet switch using voice-over-IP (VoIP) as a jump from one S-curve to the next. It is crucial to decide the right moment to switch. If you jump to new technologies too early, there might be issues with the maturity and scalability of the technology. If you adopt too late, the company has become a follower. A key question in determining the right moment to jump to the new S-curve is how effective the company is in meeting customer requirements. The right moment is determined by a shift in demand. Early adopters will show this shift first, and are comfortable being on the leading edge of technology. In a controlled fashion, early adopters can help iron out the wrinkles of a new technology, a new product, new business process, and related systems. Once it is anticipated that customer segments characterized as "followers" start adopting a new technology, it should be ready for primetime. This means there is a gap between offering a service, and the massive rollout. The time between those two events represents the dilemma. It can be solved by focusing on what one could call a "support capacity buffer." This constitutes the resources the company has to deal with supporting new customers. Creating different scenarios will show how the company can deal with scalability, in case early demand is bigger than predicted, and with support intensity, in case the technology is less stable than foreseen.

some industries, the major players have been given a chance to come to self-regulation before regulation is imposed on them. An example would be sustainability reporting, something most large organizations already do, although in many countries it is not a legal obligation. Or think of a code of conduct around direct-marketing activities. Another situation where it is necessary to respond immediately is in operational issues that impact the whole organization, such as a cash-flow problem. Running out of money can easily mean bankruptcy in a matter of days or weeks. Finally, all unforeseeable events might call for immediate action, such as 9/11. Reportedly, Southwest Airlines had its complete business re-planned in just four days, while other airlines were still planning the board meeting to discuss the issue.

At other times waiting is good. Let others make the first mistakes, create all the awareness, and then you hit the market with a next-generation product or technology. There is certainly an art to finding the optimal decision point. It requires reevaluation of the matter on a very regular basis, like weekly, daily, or even continuously. The law of diminishing returns is important here. When you notice that the impact of new discoveries and insights decreases when reevaluating the matter, you are nearing the optimal decision point.

At first glance, this seems to contradict the previous statement that the best moment to jump to a new curve is at the beginning of the eye of ambiguity. The more you reevaluate, the more confusion you will find, instead of more clarity. But the jump does not start with making a strategic decision, making a big choice. The jump starts by opening your eyes for it. And the increasing ambiguity can be exactly those insights that you are looking for. Remember, at the bottom of difficult problems there is a dilemma to be found. Once in the middle of the eye of ambiguity, the trick is to buy some time to increase your chances of success. You can impact the optimal decision point; it is not a given.

You need not have a strategy that aims to reap the first-mover advantage. A *fast-follower* strategy limits the risks while keeping chances of success relatively high, capitalizing on the opportunity. TomTom was not the first to offer navigation systems, but it managed to get it right. The Apple iPod was not the first mp3 player, but it has a dominant market share. The Apple Newton *was* the first PDA with handwriting recognition, but it never made it to the main stage. A variation on this theme is growth based on acquisition, something large enterprises can afford to do. Wait until a niche player becomes the successful market leader in that segment, and then—as part of a portfolio strategy—simply acquire the company. This is often the deliberate strategy of niche companies that are backed by venture capital: *to be acquired* by one of the 600-pound gorillas in the market. Other ways to dip a toe in the water would be through a partnership, a joint venture, sponsored academic research, and so forth.

Executive View

Like any manufacturing company, Novozymes needs to find the optimal production capacity. Adding capacity is not always easy, and cannot always be swiftly achieved. Having excess capacity is expensive. Novozymes uses advanced quantitative models to run multiple scenarios on how demand for capacity may change, and has a plan for each of those scenarios on how to fulfill demand, with its own capacity or with external capacity that it has an option on. This way, Novozymes delays critical-capacity decisions to decrease risk.

In another case, Novozymes decided to wait on a certain project until a partner was found.[v] Not everyone agreed with the decision, as it would create a dependency. However, when seen from the viewpoint of a performance-versus-risk dilemma, it is clear how smart this decision can be. In essence, Novozymes made the decision-making process itself a success factor. If no partner could be found, that would mean that no one else basically believed in the project's success. Or, say no partner could be found in which Novozymes had faith to bring the project to a good end. Either scenario would indicate that the initiative should not go forward, anyway. However, if finding a partner were easy, it would mean that more people believe in the project's success, and Novozymes would then be convinced that partners can add value. Either scenario would indicate that the initiative should proceed. Novozymes created a self-fulfilling or self-defeating prophecy, building the right decision into the process itself.

These are all examples of strategy as a portfolio of options. These are decisions that can be reversed when needed without too much damage. These decisions require a certain level of commitment, but not for the long term. And the different types of associated organization forms make it possible to *stage the commitment*—from a partnership to a joint venture to an acquisition. You have effectively bridged the now and the later.

---

[v]This is a very good example of a *dimension shift*, from time to space. Space here is represented by the partner environment.

A Few Examples

There are many eyes of ambiguity in today's business. Take, for instance, the whole "green" movement, or, in broader terms, the *corporate social responsibility* (CSR) wave. For every study that says there is a relationship between a company's CSR rating and its financial performance, there is another study showing there is no such relationship. And other studies show inconclusive results. *Fortune* magazine writes in 2007 that except for a few cases, such as General Electric's Ecomagination portfolio, there is no demonstrated link.[7] The *Journal for Corporate Social Responsibility and Environmental Management* states also in 2007 that the FTSE4GOOD index—the Financial Times sustainability index—does outperform the relevant benchmarks, but only due to risk differences.[8] Another study[9] shows there is no difference in risk-adjusted returns. In 2008, *The Economist*[10] quotes an exhaustive academic review of 167 studies over the past 35 years that concludes that there is in fact a positive link between companies' social and financial performance, but only a weak one. Firms are not richly rewarded for CSR, it seems, but neither does it typically destroy shareholder value. Maybe the relationship becomes stronger with time, as we have not yet figured out how to execute on CSR principles. Maybe today's effects will be visible in the longer term, and we are not yet past the incubation stage. Time will tell.

At the same time, $1 out of every $9 invested is already related to some kind of CSR-weighted fund.[11] Many pension funds weigh the management ethics and social responsibilities of corporations before making their investments. As the former chief investment officer of ABP, one of the largest pension funds in the world, says: "There is a growing body of evidence that companies which manage environmental, social, and governance risks most effectively tend to deliver better risk-adjusted financial performance than their industry peers. Moreover, all three of these sets of issues are likely to have an even greater impact on companies' competitiveness and financial performance in future."[12] Also, various CSR-driven financial indexes have emerged, such as the Dow Jones Sustainability Index, Ethibel, SERM, and FTSE4GOOD.

What should one do? There is no uncontested evidence that CSR is the right way to go, yet we cannot afford to miss such an opportunity. CSR practices are not only meant to improve the bottom line, but can also be seen as positive PR, solid risk management, or a cost saver on upcoming carbon taxes, so, it makes sense to put in some CSR options in the strategic portfolio. They have short-term merit, and benefits may materialize further over time. You can increase your stakes over time as well. Start with carbon reporting before moving to carbon planning. And look at the green aspects of a newly introduced product before applying green principles to the cash-cow business.

Another good example of the eye of ambiguity is dealing with a recession. July 2007 marked the beginning of the credit crunch. There had been many recessions before; the last one began in 2001. This present recession at first seemed to be restricted to financial services and seemed to be mainly a problem in the United States, yet—given the interconnectedness of banks worldwide and the size of the subprime mortgage problem—it was significant. The problem deteriorated, as banks lost trust in each other and were unwilling to supply short-term loans. As banks depend on the circulation of money, this soon became an issue for large banks around the world, and they needed infusions of new capital. Consumers lost trust as well and stopped spending. In many countries the real estate market ground to a halt. Banks were unwilling to provide mortgages to protect their balance sheet, while consumers were unwilling to buy a new house because of uncertain times.

From there also the real economy spiraled down, impacting the automotive industry (which turned out to be not too healthy to start with), trade and transport, travel, and so forth. Once the first signs of economic trouble appear, what should you do? One cannot be certain what is going to happen. Reacting immediately could lead to not hitting the mark. But the risk of not responding at all greatly outweighs the costs and the risk of missing the mark. Where buying time to get it right is the way to go for CSR, dealing with a recession requires immediate action. In a 2008 study, consulting firm Accenture examined why some companies manage downturns more effectively than others.[13] Their answer: The best performers watch for downturns and take action quickly. By contrast, executives in more poorly performing companies may accept that their industry is slowing down but hold their breath in the hope that things will get better before any difficult actions are necessary. Another conclusion of the study was that a strong cash position allows the winners to be flexible. This is a very good example of combining the now and the later. Cut costs quickly and decisively at the first sign of trouble, to free up cash. In fact, this is a strategy that creates options. The cash can be used in multiple ways that cannot yet be foreseen. Reacting quickly makes it possible to get through the eye of ambiguity.

One industry that seems to be in a continuous state of ambiguity is the IT industry. Paradigms succeed each other with amazing speed. Mainframe architectures were succeeded by client/server structures, leveraging the power of the then-upcoming personal computers. That paradigm lasted less than ten years before it was succeeded by Internet computing. Internet-based architectures now enable the next step: service-oriented architectures. The software paradigm has radically changed, too, with everything being 2.0, focusing on user-generated content, multimedia, interaction, personalization, and collaboration. IT organizations have greatly changed. *Sourcing* is the keyword, with derived terms such as *outsourcing, partner-sourcing, off-shoring, near-shoring, right-shoring,* and *right-sourcing.* And did I mention *cloud computing*?

Are you confused by all these buzzwords? That is exactly the point—it indicates the presence of the eye of ambiguity. The dilemma between now and later is very apparent. Having the first-mover advantage could easily lead to being on the bleeding edge where excessive initial investments may lead to underwhelming or at best unclear returns. Yet, being the first one to adopt could also lead to competitive advantage. You set the rules for the rest of the market and build deep experience. Given that technology skills can take a long time to build and that some of the skills are rare, this would be a valuable asset.

What should one do? Technology development seems to have a life of its own. It is usually not very demand driven and the actual business need can sometimes be an afterthought. And technology innovation "for the heck of it" does not seem like a good strategy. Unfortunately, there is no single answer. The best response here is situational. Some decisions are best delayed, while others need to be made upfront. An IT systems landscape can be divided in two parts: a technology infrastructure or architecture, and a set of applications. The speed of implementing applications, or modules of them, should be high. But the speed of change in the architecture tends to be very slow. If done well, radical choices are made perhaps every ten years or so. The decision for the right platform and the right architecture is crucial. Given the slower pace of development, there is time to find the optimal choice, but the decision should not be delayed. The key criterion in making the decision on how to structure your IT architecture is about what options the decision creates. The more open and flexible the architecture is, the more options it creates.[vi] If there are many options, you can delay the choice for the right application until the moment you need it. A well-defined architecture greatly speeds up the implementation time of an application, as all the basics are already arranged. Moving slowly and quickly at the same time is the hallmark of a strategically thinking CIO.

The now-and-later examples all dealt with externally inflicted dilemmas: corporate social responsibility as a trend, the economic situation, and technology development. But jumping to the next curve does not have to be a reaction—you can also drive the change yourself. In fact, this would be a preferred strategy for creating competitive advantage. The competition

---

[vi]As in so many cases, this is a dilemma in itself. Systems that are flexible may at the same time be more complex, or score lower on performance and efficiency. This is the price of having many options.

is facing the eye of ambiguity—whether you will be successful or not—while you have the advantage of following your plan and knowing your intentions. Creating a portfolio of options is a more active task than waiting to see which options actually pan out. This would lead to uncoordinated diversification—a financial portfolio of activities mostly based on maximizing return on investment. In a more active approach, the portfolio of options is used to create new and unique combinations that lead to innovation and competitive advantage.

For example, in the early 1970s, starting in France, *bancassurance* became popular.[14] Bancassurance means an integrated product, marketing, and sales approach to both banking services and insurances. This leads to cross-sell opportunities, products that combine elements from both businesses—such as life insurance as part of your home mortgage—and it is also good for customers if it leads to better prices. These combinations started out as partnerships and the creation of internal subsidiaries, but in the 1980s and 1990s, bancassurance triggered large acquisitions, creating huge financial services institutions. The bancassurance concept also spreads the risks. In economic good times people may be more interested in investment projects, whereas in uncertain times people focus more on being well insured. Although both types of business are about financial services, the business model, the value drivers, and the customer relationship strategies are very different. For instance, insurance companies do not interact with their customers very often, while banks try to have a continuous line of communication with their customers. In light of the recession of 2008/2009, the pendulum swings again. Bancassurance combinations have become "too big to fail," and are now seen as a liability to society. Some financial institutions behave proactively, and again split up.

Unfortunately, sometimes unique combinations do not work out the way they are envisioned. In 2002, online marketplace (auction web site) eBay[15] acquired online banking system PayPal for $1.5 billion, followed by the acquisition of Internet phone company Skype in 2005 for $2.6 billion. The idea was not only to combine the flow of goods (the online market) with the flow of money (the payments), but also to include a flow of communication (Skype). The combination did not materialize at all; no synergies emerged. In 2009, Skype was sold again to Silverlake (an investment firm), at a considerable loss. In the end there is always strategic uncertainty.

CHAPTER 7

This and That

In the Batman movie, The Dark Knight, *District Attorney Harvey Dent flips a coin three times. "Heads it's me, tails it's you," he tells Rachel Dawes, deciding who will be lead counsel at a trial. The coin comes up heads. "Would you really leave something like that up to luck?," she asks him. "I make my own luck," he replies.*

You could be lucky, and the dilemma you are facing is simply a complex optimization problem.[i] Most managers are not mathematical experts, and there is no need to be one. However, it is important to know when someone with those specific skills is needed to do some serious number crunching. The good news is that there is a substantial body of techniques that can help find an optimum choice between various alternatives. Complex organizations generate complex decision problems. A rigorous, even scientific, method of investigating and analyzing these problems is necessary. During World War II, requiring better decision making in both economic as well as military issues, the discipline of *operations research* (also known as *management science* or *quantitative decision making*) was born.[1] Operations research (OR) includes techniques such as simulation, decision trees, linear programming (maximizing results while working with limited resources), and dynamic programming (e.g., to find the shortest route for deliveries). Unfortunately, operations research is not widely used. The Dealing with Dilemmas survey showed that 60% of respondents have never heard of it, or are not using it. OR is a standard in only 5% of companies.

It may not be necessary to master all these techniques, but it is important to recognize that a certain complex problem could in fact be tackled

---

[i]You could also argue the opposite, that finding out you are dealing with a false dilemma should be disappointing, as dealing with a true dilemma represents a chance to come to synthesis, and fundamentally solve a problem.

with one of these techniques. Here we concentrate on recognizing how to optimize between various alternatives that could be seen as a dilemma if we were not aware of these techniques.

Some cases represent what I call a *many-of-these* versus *many-of-those* problem. Should we buy lots of handguns (cheaper, so we can afford more) or rifles (offering more firepower) to maximize the effectiveness of our platoon? What mix of vegetables of 200 grams per person provides the most vitamins and variety within a single portion of food? What is the best marketing mix to reach as many people as we can? Another type of problem involves merely a *one big this* versus *one big that*. It is either this strategy or that one, to save costs. Either focus on cost savings or on investing in growth. Either buy a motorbike or go on vacation.

Many of These versus Many of Those

Putting together a mix of marketing communications is a question of optimization. The goal is to maximize the number of responses, or *leads*. These can then be qualified as to how serious they are and passed on to the sales department, whose job it is to convert those leads into actual sales. Let us consider how to optimize the mix.[ii] GloAsia (fictitious name) is a global trading firm that tries to reach customers worldwide. For a particular campaign the question is raised whether it should be done by traditional direct marketing (DM) or via Google ads. Logically, there can be three outcomes of the analysis. In its simplest form, one choice always turns out to be better than the other. Alternatively, both choices could be equal; it does not matter what you choose. Finally, there could be a true optimum, a mix of DM and Google ads that yields the best return.

For instance, assume the budget is $1,000. One Google ad costs $40 and you get 10 responses. A direct-marketing letter may cost $1 and you get a response in only 10% of cases. If you stick all your money in Google ads you will get *250* responses from 25 ads. And if you spend the complete budget on direct marketing, you will get *100* responses from 1,000 letters. With this example, putting all your money in Google ads is the best choice and cannot be bettered with any other combination (see Figure 7.1).

This is not always the case. Make a small tweak to the assumptions and we can generate an example with numerous "optimal solutions." Assume

---

[ii]I would like to express my thanks to Dr. Ziggy MacDonald for helping with these examples. I am "quantitatively challenged," but Dr. MacDonald has the gift of bringing complex matters back to an understandable set of steps that even I understand.

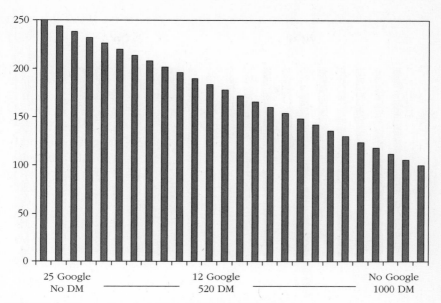

FIGURE 7.1 Choose Google Ads for the Highest Return

the budget is still $1,000. A Google ad now costs $50, and you will still get 10 responses. Assume a direct-marketing letter still costs $1, but, by using improved messaging and more targeted delivery, you now get a 20% response rate (i.e., 1 in 5 letters gets a response). If you focus completely on Google ads you will get *200* responses from 20 ads, and if you decide to use only direct marketing, you will get *200* responses from 1,000 letters. In this example, it is impossible to pick which is the best option, as in addition to these two equally good choices, there are a further 18 choices that will also give you the maximum return of 200 responses (i.e., 19 ads and 50 letters, or 18 ads and 100 letters, or 17 ads and 150 letters, and so on). Each uses up the entire budget and each combination gets you 200 responses (see Figure 7.2).

Again, there is no dilemma. Every choice is perfect. You could argue that this is a dilemma in itself: which one to pick if it does not matter. This can be a surprisingly difficult choice. The key to picking one is to identify other objectives in addition to creating a maximum return of responses. For instance, Google ads might be a new communication medium for you and you would like to test how it is working for you, although you and your customers are used to direct marketing. Allocating a small part of the budget to Google ads would be a logical result. Perhaps using two channels creates a bit more complexity in reporting the results; different

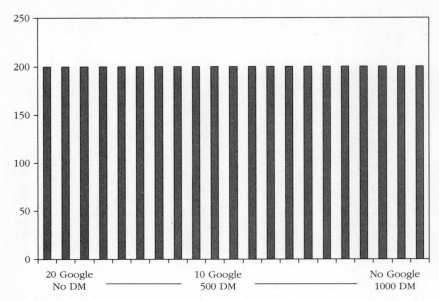

FIGURE 7.2 All Combinations Provide the Same Return

systems have to be used to get to the right numbers. In that case, choosing one or the other makes more sense. Or, you are equally experienced in both ways of customer communications and you would like to compare them on an even basis. Spending half the budget on one and the other half on the other may make sense.

In most cases, reality is a bit more complex. Usually more constraints apply. Let us go back to the original problem and assume that the budget is $1,000 again, a Google ad costs $40, and you get 10 responses, whereas a direct-marketing letter costs $1 and you get a 10% response rate (i.e., 1 in 10 letters gets a response). Say that there is a budget for Google ads for all campaigns, and this budget allows you to purchase only a maximum of 16 ads in a given period. Also, assume there is a minimum print run for letters of 500.[iii]

[iii]Mathematically, if you let R be the total number of responses, G be the number of Google ads, and DM be the number of letters, then the problem is written as:

Max $R = 10G + 0.1DM$

Subject to

$40G + 1DM \leq 1000$

$G \leq 160$

$DM \geq 500$

$G, DM \geq 0$ and integer

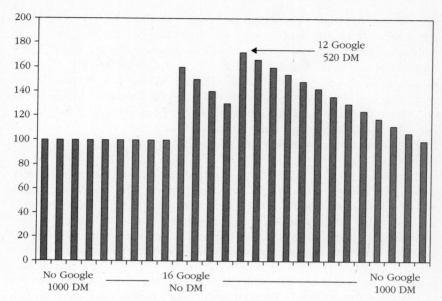

FIGURE 7.3 Optimal Solution with a Mix of Google Ads and Direct Marketing

If you spend as much as you can on Google ads, your maximum response would be 160 from 16 ads (the limit), costing $640, but you cannot get any letters from your remaining $380, as the minimum print run is 500. If you spend your entire budget on letters, then you will get 100 responses from 1,000 letters. Can we do better than this? Yes: By spending $480 on 12 Google ads and $520 on 520 letters, you will get 172 responses. This is the optimal solution to this "constrained optimization" problem, which cannot be bettered. Again, there is no dilemma, but a single solution (see Figure 7.3).

Finding the optimal solution for this problem requires going through all combinations of Google ads and direct marketing, in other words, creating a linear program. *Linear programming*, as part of operations research, is a key technique for optimization.

Lifting the Constraints

There is more to business than mathematics. In fact, lifting constraints is the basis of most innovation. *TRIZ*, a Russian methodology for problem solving, is based on a classification of different constraints (or contradictions)

that can be the cause of a certain problem.[2] For instance, everyone wants the battery life of their mobile phone to be better, but not many would be willing to accept a heavier or bigger mobile phone to hold a more powerful battery. Battery size and weight are at odds with battery life. The TRIZ classification identifies a total of 39 different constraints, including cost, weight, speed, strength, shape, temperature, complexity, stability, and so on. Although TRIZ was originally developed for engineering, it can also be used for business management. Business management is also constrained by factors such as cost, time, sustainable growth rate, available skills, and resources.

Once we understand the impact of the constraints, we can find ways to lift the constraints and get more responses. The GloAsia example showed three constraints: the budget, the amount of Google ads, and the minimum number of letters. One way of finding additional budget would be to team up with a partner and make it a joint campaign. Or you can combine campaigns within the company that each target the same audience. You could find alternative online or direct-marketing channels that are lower priced, say by 20%, but with a response rate that is less than 20% lower. Direct marketing was possible only as of 500 letters. Perhaps working with a different vendor or technology lowers that number. The maximum number of Google ads perhaps was based on a concern not to depend on one channel too much and to spread the budget over multiple channels, reaching more individual "eyeballs." Is this assumption true? Perhaps this logic can be challenged and turned around. It could very well be that the power of repetition creates leverage for future campaigns. In this way, every campaign creates a certain percentage additional response in the next campaign. This spillover effect can also be used within the mix of a campaign. Clicking on the Google ad may lead you to a web page where you can register for a direct-marketing newsletter, improving DM response. And the direct-marketing piece could refer to the web site that the Google ad refers to, to further increase web responses. Obviously, the mathematics of calculating the expected response become more complex, but the results improve.

Efficient Frontiers

In order to maximize the return on investment, organizations need to operate on the productivity frontier. In other words, resources such as capital and labor must be deployed in such a way that they deliver the highest productivity and returns. Get the most out of what you have. The optimization exercises that compared Google ads and direct marketing provided a good example. *Modern portfolio theory* further builds on the idea of optimizing results, specifically addressing risk versus reward.[iv] Modern portfolio theory is based on the premise that investments (like stocks, or bonds, or real estate, or just about anything you can buy in the hope of making money) have three important properties:

1. The return generated by the investment
2. The risk of the investment (the uncertainty that we will get the return)
3. The correlation of investment returns

For example, we could look at investments like government bonds of a stable country and forecast that, based on performance of these bonds over the past 10 years, the returns are low (perhaps 3% per year), the risk is also low (over the 100-year history, the government has never defaulted on its bonds), and its tendency to behave like other investments is relatively low. Other investors, perhaps with a higher risk appetite, would consider investing in a venture capital firm that supports startup companies in biochemistry. The return could be considerable (perhaps 1,000% over time), but the risk is extremely high (80% of all investments may not provide a return at all).

Harry Markowitz (who later won Nobel recognition for his work on modern portfolio theory) looked at a collection of possible investments by generating a chart with risk increasing to the right on the horizontal axis, and return increasing upward on the vertical axis. In its simplest version in Figure 7.4, the small dots are possible investments, and three of those possible investments (A, B, and C) are highlighted.

In Figure 7.4, first note that as the risk of investments increases, it is possible to get greater returns. This illustrates the rule, "no risk, no return." Now, look at three possible investments, A, B, and C, each representing stocks in a well-known company. Given a choice between A or C, which would make the best investment? The correct answer would be A, because it provides the same return at a much lower level of risk. An investor would be foolish to invest in C, taking unnecessary risk. Now consider between investing in B and C. B would be the superior investment, because you are receiving a much higher expected return, within the same risk profile.

So Markowitz concluded that investments up toward the efficient frontier curve would generate the highest return for whatever level of risk the investor could tolerate. So both A and B would represent more "efficient" investments, with both providing maximum returns at their respective risk levels. A conservative investor would prefer A and take smaller returns in

---

[iv] I would like to thank Steve Hoye and Jim Franklin for contributing their description of modern portfolio theory.

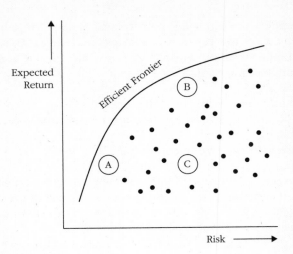

FIGURE 7.4 Efficient Frontier

exchange for lower risk, whereas a more aggressive investor would prefer B—being willing to take more risk for higher returns.

That leaves the third property of investments, the tendency of an investment's returns to behave in a similar way to the returns of other available investments. In other words, investments correlate. *Correlation* is very important, because when investors buy multiple investments (a portfolio) that include stocks whose returns are weakly correlated (i.e., their returns do not behave in exactly the same way), then something very beneficial happens: Their portfolio becomes diversified. This means that if one of the investments held in a portfolio suffers a loss, perhaps other investments will dampen the loss the investor would have suffered if she had held only the one investment. Diversification of a portfolio makes it possible to achieve higher returns for a given level of risk than most individual investments that are available.[v]

One Big This versus One Big That

The idea of portfolio management can also be applied in a broader sense, to deal with one-big-this versus one-big-that dilemmas. Classical strategic thinking

---

[v]This is another example of a dimension shift between space and time. You can wait for a stock to perform well over a period of several years, smoothing the ups and downs over time, or you can look for a portfolio of stocks (the space dimension here), smoothing ups and downs immediately.

stresses the important of making big choices: either cost leadership or differentiation. Or in a more subtle version: You need to be sufficiently successful in all value disciplines, such as operational excellence, customer intimacy, and product innovation, but excel in one of them. It is strategic thinking like this that creates strategic dilemmas, either one strategy or the other. However, there is also a good body of evidence that pure strategies are not necessarily the best ones. A combination of differentiation and cost leadership could also lead to superior business performance.[3]

There is a way to break the one-big-this-versus-one-big-that strategic dilemma, and create an effective hybrid strategy. First, we decompose the strategies into smaller elements, the strategic goals into smaller goals, the choices on the table into smaller choices. Then we start to recompose those goals into a single picture, or into a new strategy, thus avoiding an either/or choice.

Cost Cutting

Particularly in a downturn economy, cost cutting is important. How to cut costs poses a common dilemma. It is easiest to cut a complete business activity, such as a product, geography, or a business unit. The disadvantage is that you will be cutting revenue streams as well. The alternative is shaving costs across the board, where each unit will have to cut, for instance, 5 or 10%. However, this means that every business function suffers and handicaps its execution. Essentially, it is a sucker's choice again. Who says these are the only two options, and you have to choose? Perhaps it can be a combination of the two: selling off a small activity representing just a part of the needed cost savings, so that other units need to cut less. Perhaps cost cutting is not even necessary, but scrutinizing working capital management would be enough

In case these are indeed the two choices, how can you cut costs without harming revenue streams, and without harming execution of the total business? This can be done if we can identify the costs that do not influence revenues, directly or indirectly. These costs can be identified if we understand what the "value drivers" in the company processes are, for instance, through an activity-based management initiative. Value drivers could be the reliability of a production process, or the reputation of the company, or, indirectly, a certain information system, the speed of externally reporting business results, or the rigor of working capital management. Once we understand those value drivers, all costs not associated with this can be cut without greatly impacting the health of the company.

The actual problem here is hidden under the surface: thinking about efficiency when it is too late. Not making the right decisions early on has led to your range of options all having negative side effects. The dilemma is self-inflicted. In fact, it would be better to display anti-cyclical behavior and make sure to create an optimal cost structure during better times. Getting to a deep level of insight into value drivers and restructuring accordingly takes time.

Improvement of Return

Consider Direct Bank,[vi] which offers simple loans and savings accounts via only two customer contact channels, the Web and the call center. Direct Bank has operations in multiple countries. The Web infrastructure is centralized, and there is a call center in every country, as consumer confidence is partly based on physical local presence. As part of its growing ambitions, corporate increases its targets for the return on capital employed (ROCE). The management team brainstorms and comes up with a few options. Trying to increase the operational excellence by centralizing call centers in multiple countries will certainly cut costs and increase margins. Another option is to reinvest the assets under management in a more aggressive way. The marketing director offers to start a large campaign to increase market awareness. Finally, a junior manager brings in the idea to create a product for "Islamic banking," unlocking the large ethnic communities in various countries where the bank is active. The management team summarizes the options as shown in Table 7.1.

TABLE 7.1 Direct Bank Options to Improve Return

	Advantage	Disadvantage
Close call centers	Easy cost saving calculation	Negative impact on consumer trust
Change reinvestment policy	Higher return, no change in operations needed	Higher risk
Market awareness	Top-line improvement	Process for handling large numbers of new customers not scalable enough
Islamic banking	Blue ocean growth	No direct return

[vi]Example is based on F.A. Buytendijk, *Performance Leadership*, McGraw-Hill, 2008.

This is a true dilemma: Each choice has unacceptable disadvantages. But why look for just one alternative to reach the new objective, when a *portfolio* of improvement activities might do the trick? (See Figure 7.5.)

Each option is represented with a line, from "low" to "high." Low here means only moderate changes are made; high means drastic redesigns are carried out. The line provides a visual explanation of how much impact the performance can have. The line can be horizontal, which means the performance improvement activity can be scaled up without additional risk. The line can go up, as it will do in many cases, to show how the risk will increase proportionally or disproportionately when the performance improvement initiative is implemented more aggressively. And there are cases where the risk actually goes down at the same time as the initiative has more impact. This last case is preferable because the initiative reconciles the natural dilemma between risk and performance.

None of the options provides a perfect answer, as long as they are viewed separately. However, the picture changes once you consider multiple options, each contributing at an acceptable risk level. Instead of the point solution to performance improvement in the traditional way of thinking, a *performance improvement portfolio* emerges.

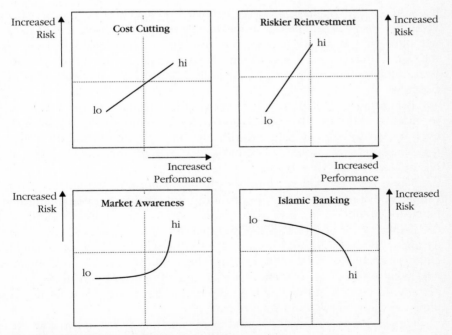

FIGURE 7.5 Performance/Risk Map per Option

Changing the risk profile of the reinvestments should be dismissed by the management. It would increase the risk significantly while the returns would be marginal. Cost cutting in call centers is still possible, not by closing call centers but by investing in an infrastructure that integrates call centers so that local employees who speak multiple languages can also help customers in another country. By itself, that might not save enough costs, so it helps to also increase market awareness, yet not so aggressively that the current processes and systems cannot cope with the follow-up. The joint performance improvement more than makes the goal. The idea of Islamic banking remains. With the strongly improved contribution, a part of the returns can be invested in setting up an Islamic banking pilot in a single country and serving a single ethnic group. It allows the bank to follow-up on the results and build up the necessary competency. The bank is investing in its next round of performance improvement.

One Big This or One Big That: Round Two

There are always cases where the choices you are confronted with include no elegant way out by creating a portfolio of small solutions that together tackle the one big, hairy problem. Those are dilemmas in the classical sense: You have to make a binary choice. And no matter what you choose, values you hold dear will be compromised. People are going to get hurt. In our personal lives, we may have experienced this going through a divorce, and sometimes in the newspaper we read how parents turn in their criminal children to the police. We can also recognize this in business.

For instance, you have to lay off a significant part of the workforce in order to make sure the shareholder value does not totally collapse, or even to prevent the company from folding. Or you need to sell off a strategic business unit in order to refund a new strategic initiative project that has massively gone over budget.

These are cases where all options have significant disadvantages. You can also be confronted with the sort of dilemma that forces you to choose between multiple priorities, while there really is no chance to mobilize the resources for all priorities. As the minister of social affairs, you need to invest in a project either for homeless people or for disadvantaged children while the budget allows only the minimal possible investment. And what if there are only enough skills and resources available to comply with just a part of the new regulations, and the clock is ticking? If you were the CEO, what would you choose?

Perhaps there is no way out, and there is no choice but to live with the consequences of whatever decision you make. Preventing it from happening was the only thing you could have done, by having made the right choices and decisions *beforehand*. But that is history; now it is too late. Hopefully, as a professional, you learn from this, and you find a way to prevent something like this from happening again.

Still, the question remains as to how you will communicate those choices, and which moral appeals you have to make. This is also an integral part of dealing with you-and-me dilemmas.

CHAPTER 8

You and Me

I think intellect is a good thing unless it paralyzes your ability to make decisions because you see too much complexity. Presidents need to have what I would call a synthesizing intelligence.

Bill Clinton

People have different requirements. We sometimes forget that; we simply presume there is "us." We do not even acknowledge the diversity of what people expect from an organization in the way we define the term *organization* itself. Most people define an organization as a group of people sharing the same objectives. Seldom is this the case. Employees are looking for career opportunities, a stable income, and a chance to develop their skills. Shareholders look for a financial return. Customers look for a good deal, while suppliers see your organization as a source of profit themselves. Not only do people have different requirements—often they are flat-out conflicting ones.

Organizational theorists will be quick to point out that having different requirements actually is the whole point of paying out a salary to employees, instead of seeing them as individual entrepreneurs. A salary can be defined as the compensation for giving up your time and personal objectives and contributing to the organization's objectives. However true this may have been in the industrial age, and for the larger part of the twentieth century, a salary is not what motivates employees today. Today's generation is motivated by meaning and purpose, and creating a healthy work/life balance,[1] a true you-and-me dilemma to start with.

You-and-me dilemmas can be found everywhere, in multiple shapes and forms. They can exist between stakeholders of the organization, such as shareholders having a different goal than the unions, or the regulators, or society at large. In fact, an organization is better defined as a unique collaboration of stakeholders that through the organization each reach goals and objectives that none of them could have reached by themselves. For that, they need to reconcile their differences.

You-and-me dilemmas can be found within organizations, where the back office and the front office have conflicting requirements. The back office may look for standard processes and smooth operations, while the front office is served better with all the flexibility to match customer demand exactly. And the two responsible managers need to strike a balance and overcome their differences. You might be one of those two managers, or you might be part of the senior management team, having to deal with managers who have conflicting views: "You versus you, and me," in a sense.

The most common you-and-me dilemma that can be found in almost every organization is between "me" and the rest of the company: local versus global—the choice between local optimization and corporate alignment. For instance, one business unit may introduce a product or service with high-growth potential that competes with a cash-cow product from another business unit. Think of the hardware vendor that sees the growth of the personal computer at the expense of large corporate mainframes. Or think of a savings account offered by the direct-banking division offering more interest than the standard full bank savings account that is connected to retail checking accounts. You may argue that it is better to cannibalize yourself than allowing the competition to do so, but your fellow manager in the other division is still not going to like it. Your success will cost him his bonus. Or think of corporate marketing banning one business unit's marketing campaign, as the target audience has been bombarded and exhausted already by other parts of the business. And what about the needs of a small and growing corporate startup unit, while the overall business has to deal with a hiring freeze? Come to think of it, the budgeting process is nothing other than battling a big dilemma: how to distribute the resources for the coming period across the various departments and business functions. Or consider serving a customer in one country while there are legal issues about that in other countries (such as the tobacco industry, weapons industry, or companies under investigation). Or the opposite: choosing to *not* serve a class of customers, although there is no legal basis to refuse such customers, such as legitimate businesses in the sex industry.

These are all examples of *social dilemmas*. A social dilemma can be defined as "a situation in which a group of persons must choose between maximizing selfish interests and maximizing collective interests." It is generally more profitable for each person to maximize selfish interests, but if all choose to maximize selfish interests, all are worse off than if all choose to maximize collective interests.[2] How do we make the right call?

Morality and Ethics

It is impossible to look at you-and-me dilemmas without taking the ethical side of decision making into account. *Morals* (or *ethics*; the terms are often used interchangeably) form a code of conduct to refer to in judging what is right and what is wrong. Ethics revolve around three central concepts: *self*, *good*, and *other*.[3] You display ethical behavior when you do not merely consider what is good for yourself but also take into account what is good for others. This does not mean that you should be completely altruistic and always do good to others without considering your own needs. That is not sustainable. Moral dilemmas arise when the division between what is ethically right and wrong gets blurred.

Executive View

General (ret.) D.L. Berlijn, former commander of the Dutch Armed Forces,[i] has faced many dilemmas during his career in the army. At the end of 1999, the commander of the Air Force suggested Gen. Berlijn to be his successor. Although this would mean an attractive promotion and a huge honor, there were many risks involved. At that point there were serious cost control issues, and severe criticism from auditors about financial management. Further cost savings and cuts were to be expected, which is not the most pleasant of responsibilities. After careful deliberation, Gen. Berlijn accepted the assignment. In another case, Gen. Berlijn was invited, as the formal representative of the combined Dutch forces, to attend an important soccer match, including the complete VIP treatment. Although this could be seen as a representative task, Berlijn chose to politely decline the invitation. In the words of Gen. Berlijn: "If you are faced with a difficult choice, and one of the options compromises your integrity, don't make that choice. If you hesitate to make a certain choice, because you are afraid you lack the courage, go for it anyway. It is a good opportunity to step up to the plate." Although the dilemmas that Gen. Berlijn describes are more personal in nature, they point out a vital component: morality.

---

[i] Quotes taken from an interview with Mr. Dick Berlijn, combined with D.L. Berlijn, *No Guts, No Glory*, NRC Focus, Netherlands, March 2009.

Global Survey

The Global Dealing with Dilemmas Survey asked for respondents to describe dilemmas they dealt with, without qualifying what type of dilemma. Most of the described dilemmas were moral in nature:

- "As managing partner of a law firm, I was faced with allegations of sexual misconduct against a senior partner who was a true 'rainmaker,' bringing in the majority of firm revenue. Firing him would mean losing that revenue and the associated jobs. I fired him."
- "I have resigned from my job as a senior general manager of an insurance company. I was not satisfied with the owner's/chairman's business ethics. This was a very important decision for me. I had financial freedom, but no personal and ethical freedom in my position. Seconds after my resignation, I had total personal freedom but no job and thus no financial freedom. Now after two years I can say it was the best decision ever, but not without financial consequences. I kept my integrity. Never an easy decision!"
- "As an IT consultant, I had access to the clients' contracting data. My supervisor asked for their proprietary information, which would aid our company in bidding future contracts. With a family to support, I was concerned that he would sack me if I didn't give him the information. It was a tough decision, but I had to inform my supervisor that his request was unethical. In the end it was a win-win. I retained my job and my self-respect."
- "I was in charge of development for an acquired product that simply did not work. It was damaging customer careers, hurting their compensation, and getting them fired. The issues could be resolved, but it would be expensive and time consuming. The company did not want to admit there were issues. I quit—despite tremendous efforts and offers on the part of the company to keep me. That is a real ethical issue."

The philosophers agree to disagree on what is morally right or wrong.[ii] There can be two moral approaches to dealing with dilemmas.[4] The first school of thought defines morals as universally applicable (this is called

---

[ii] In fact, the philosophers have found their own synthesis in this discussion, and address this as *meta-ethics*, understanding that there are multiple ways of deciding what is ethical behavior in the first place.

the *universalist* approach, or *ethical absolutism*). Things simply are right or wrong. It is wrong to kill, it is wrong to lie, it is wrong to steal. In this way of thinking the consequences of doing the right thing are simply not relevant. It is *always* wrong to lie; abortion is *always* wrong; *under no circumstances* should you kill—even if there is a "greater good," such as saving many lives, or protecting many jobs. For people subscribing to this school of thought, dealing with a dilemma means finding out what is the right thing to do, and following through, no matter what—making the tough calls that come with the job. Some associate this style of thinking with Western culture; others have called it the "male way."

The other school of thought does not consider an act to be morally good or bad as such, but weighs the consequences in making that determination (called the *consequentialist* approach, or *ethical relativism*). In more formal terms, good and bad are not attributes of the subject at hand, but rather its context. Robin Hood stole from the rich, but did it to help the poor. A few years ago, a Roman Catholic bishop in my country stated in the press that it was not necessarily all bad for a poor person to steal bread if he were hungry. And sometimes it is necessary to sacrifice the needs of a few for the benefit of the many. Good things can come from bad decisions.

Subscribers to this school of thought will weigh their options when facing a dilemma in a different way. What makes a problem a dilemma is that all options have negative consequences. Choosing between them is not a preferred solution. There must be ways to satisfy everyone's needs and avoid negative consequences. Take care of the baker's trash and sweep the courtyard, and then ask for bread. Breaking your arm is not necessarily a bad thing, if you fall in love with the nurse in the hospital (and it is even better if she falls in love with you, too). The consequentialists might develop a more creative way of dealing with dilemmas, being more comfortable with ambiguity in decision making. After all, the consequences are known only after the decision has played out. This type of thinking is more associated with Asian cultures, and sometimes is called the "female approach." See Table 8.1, which compares these two approaches.

A dominant paradigm in philosophy today is *postmodernism*. It is accepted that there are different ways to define *truth*, and different ways to display moral behavior. Even if you are a universalist and believe in universally applicable morals, as a rational decision maker you should be able to accept that there may be others who hold different, conflicting views to be equally universally applicable. At least, you would recognize their equally persistent behavior. As not everyone will agree on what is right or wrong, there can be significant *moral dissensus*. For instance, some point out that the social responsibility of a

TABLE 8.1 Universalism versus Consequentialism

Universalist Approach	Consequentialist Approach
■ Actions are inherently good or bad, regardless of the consequences. There is a right and a wrong way of doing things.	■ Whether an action is morally good or bad depends on the consequences. The ends sometimes justify the means.
■ Associated with European culture, and a "male way of thinking."	■ Associated with Eastern cultures, and a "female way of thinking."
■ Also known as or related to the *deontological* view.	■ Also known as or related to the *teleological* view.

company is to maximize its profits and that other use of resources factually is stealing from the shareholders. It should be up to the shareholders to decide what to do with the returns. Others reject that reasoning and point out the need for organizations to give something back to society. Morals change over time. The whole discussion around corporate social responsibility was not very prominent in the 1980s—it simply was not expected of large corporations. And perhaps, 10 years from now, the discussion will have completely died down again, and corporate social responsibility will have become an accepted standard set of behaviors.

It is universalist moral dissensus that creates most of the you-and-me dilemmas. All involved parties insist on their view being the correct one. Their solution is good, and the other solution is bad. Because moral dissensus is a reality, it does not help much to purely analyze the you-and-me dilemma on the table. Universalists will not discover a different view of the world, as analysis will drive them to the conclusion that is dictated by their paradigm. And the analysis of the consequentialists will focus on what consequences they feel are acceptable, and most likely will also not look for an answer outside the options on the table. A different approach is needed.

Three Elements to Resolve You-and-Me Dilemmas

Different people have different ways of dealing with dilemmas, and there are some cultural differences, too. According to the Dealing with Dilemmas survey, there is a correlation between the decision style respondents have, and the biases they display in the six business dilemmas I

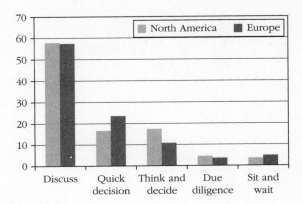

FIGURE 8.1 Decision Styles

described in Chapters 3 and 4. In addition to all the questions on how organizations deal with dilemmas, the survey also asked people about how they tackle dilemmas personally—their decision style. People who have a "sit-and-wait" attitude have a bias for the short term. Sometimes waiting for something to blow over is good, but not always. Knowing when to act and when not to act is key to stretching the strategy elastic in the long- and short-term dilemma. I discussed choosing the optimal decision moment in Chapter 6. Others see discussing the dilemmas with others purely as going through "due diligence." They tend to have a bias for leading instead of listening to customers. They also have a bias for inside-out thinking. This makes complete sense. Usually, they have the answer in mind already, and the rest is implementation. Finally, leaders who think long and hard before they make a decision—without consultation with many others—have a higher chance of bias toward a top-down approach, and have a long-term view.

Figure 8.1 shows that respondents from Europe tend to favor making a quick decision, and this percentage is much lower in North America (there were not enough responses from Asia to make a meaningful determination). The percentage of respondents who think long and hard,[iii] and then decide, is much higher in North America. However, most respondents across the regions favor discussing the issue with others, to collect multiple opinions. This approach is central to successfully dealing with you-and-me dilemmas.

[iii]Or, as one respondent called it, "Go for a ride on my bike."

I have found three elements to be important in resolving you-and-me dilemmas.[iv] These are *elements*, not steps, because all three of them may take place at the same time, and in the process of resolving the dilemma, you may revisit them multiple times. You need to (1) examine your motives, (2) communicate, and (3) try to reconcile the opposites.

Examine Your Motives

The first element, whether you are a universalist or a consequentialist, is to realize that analyzing the options on the table may not always help you. The whole point of a dilemma is that it is pretty clear from the outset that each of the options has negative consequences, or that constraints keep you from doing everything that you need to do. A first analysis should point out whether you might be facing a false dilemma that in truth is an optimization problem, as I describe in Chapter 7. But once it is confirmed that you are dealing with a true dilemma, and particularly a you-and-me dilemma, additional analysis is merely going to confirm this more and more.

Instead of examining the options, dilemmas require a close examination of your own motives. Assume that you have to fire someone from the team, which is a difficult decision for most managers (and it should be). For many, this may form a dilemma, based on the implicit desire that most people have, which is to be seen as sympathetic, friendly, nice. You may have loyalty both to your firm and to the person on your team. Once you understand your desire to be thought nice, as a universalist you may, for instance, decide that this should not play a role in the decision you have to make, and the dilemma disappears. You have found the right choice for you. As a consequentialist, you may want to define what it means to be thought nice. Is it nice to not fire a person, but simply sidetrack him or her, and never provide the feedback that this person has no future in this company? That is the consequence of not firing this person. Or is it perhaps nicer to the rest of your team to fire this person, as the team is suffering from a lack of performance and productivity because of the whole situation? You may still not like firing this person, but your desire to be thought nice actually tells you what is the right thing to do as well.

[iv]I do realize that this is a rather universalist remark. I am prescribing three universal keys here that lead to the right answer. But I would like to point out there is a greater good here, a higher motive, which is getting my point across without getting it blurred by too much subtle discourse. Of course, it depends on many things, but the three keys certainly help. This footnote reconciles my dilemma, unfortunately, by compromise: making a strong point (main text) while at the same time trying to provide a subtler view here in the footnote.

In many cases, the solution to a problem comes to mind immediately. You need to buy a bigger car (if only you had the money), you need to invest in a certain technology (you are lagging behind the competition already), or you need to start discounting (as the economy is turning bad and demand is collapsing). Examining your own motives and thinking process may uncover the fact that you jumped to conclusions, that it is time to take a step back and look for alternatives, and that it does not have to be an either/or choice. Maybe a bigger car is not needed, as—once you think about it—you would need the extra capacity only a few times per year, and renting a car for those occasions might be much cheaper. And perhaps it is smart to wait a little longer and invest in the next generation of technology, leapfrogging the competition. And is discounting really the best option to keep demand up? Perhaps you can unbundle the product and sell a basic product at a lower price while adding services to upsell.

Dilemmas are full of emotion. We feel we are put on the spot, and that the situation is not under control. Anger, frustration, fear, and anxiety may all be part of the mix when you are confronted with a you-and-me dilemma. Why is there always someone who does not agree with you? Why can't people simply do what you want *for once*? Why is it always he or she who is such a negative influence? And in the heat of the fight we can confront others (or be confronted) with a sucker's dilemma: "My way or the highway." Did you really mean to say that? Would you not rather find a common denominator than escalate? The old advice to count to ten before responding might not be a bad idea. All too often we regret words spoken to air our emotions, instead of asking ourselves what it is we are trying to achieve—take a firmly entrenched position, or build a bridge? Examining your motives is the start of successfully dealing with a you-and-me dilemma, as the dilemma might say more about you than about the actual tough choice to be made.

This goes for organizations as much as it goes for people. An organization faces dilemmas all the time, being confronted with conflicting stakeholder requirements.[v] Dealing with stakeholder dilemmas starts with self-reflection, too. What is it your organization is trying to achieve? How can profit and value be reconciled? What is it that stakeholders expect from us, and what contributions do we expect from them? How can we align these contributions and requirements? If we spend more time discussing how to spin a strategy to the market than actually rolling it out, we are setting ourselves up for many dilemmas of the ugly kind. Without self-reflection, open communication, and reconciliation, there is no hope of improving our strategy elastic.

---

[v] I describe *stakeholder dilemmas* in greater detail in Chapter 10.

Communicate

The second element is to make sure that the parties involved communicate. In most cases, when people state their position regarding a certain problem, they will state their solution to their side of the problem. In Chapter 1, I described Western management culture with a few statements, such as "If you are not part of the solution, you are part of the problem." However, this attitude *creates* dilemmas instead of preventing or solving them. When dealing with dilemmas, it is important to discuss the problem first. In other words, if you are not part of the problem, you are also not part of the solution. The solution comes from seeing things from multiple perspectives. By being part of the solution from the start, the only angle you will see is your own.

We all know many examples of this. "This sales assistant has to go, because he or she is just not performing," or "We need stricter laws in place to make sure this type of accident will never happen again," or "We need to change the price of the product, as our competition is beating us." Immediate solution orientation *creates* the dilemma. Different solutions are compared, and the underlying problem is forgotten. Even worse, the moment another party has a different, opposite opinion, emotions flare up again. People may reject the idea of being part of a dilemma at first; they will probably tell you that as far as they are concerned, there is no other choice but to see their side—an ultimatum.[vi] How can someone not see the problem, particularly when the solution is so obvious? It takes professionalism to also listen to the other side: "The sales assistant should not go—he or she has other very important qualities," "There is a country-wide initiative in place to actually decrease the number of laws," or "We cannot lower the price of the product; otherwise it is not profitable anymore." Acknowledging there are multiple sides to the story, even if you do not agree, is the key to reconciliation. The key to these conflicting positions, which are posing a dilemma, is to figure out the actual problem underlying the presented solution. Perhaps the problem with the sales assistant not performing is that he does not communicate very well with customers, but he never makes a mistake with complex offers and revenue recognition. A position in sales operations would be better. And regarding the accident, in the end we do not want more rules; we just do not want accidents to happen again. Are there other ways of prevention? And, there are many ways to compete; how is the competition beating us?

[vi]An ultimatum poses a dilemma in itself, regardless of any other side to the dilemma. If you give in to an ultimatum, you decide based on pressure instead of trying to solve the problem. And if you do not give in to an ultimatum, the threat might be carried out.

By asking questions, we uncover not the proposed solution to the single-sided problem, but the actual problem. Comparing proposed solutions leads to a you-or-me dilemma; a common understanding of the problem is halfway to a you-and-me solution.

A powerful way to reconcile a dilemma is to find a way to switch roles. This works in cases where people know they need to find a way to work together; the dilemma is that they have seemingly irreconcilable differences on how to do that. For instance, think of a newly formed management team of two merged companies, each based in very different corporate cultures. They have to find a way to make it work. Or think of a coalition of two political parties that need to collaborate to form a majority government. Despite different opposing views, and the election battle that has been going on, they need to find a way to come to a program, and a fair division of ministerial posts. Switching roles requires creating an environment of trust in which you ask the people involved not to talk about their own convictions, but to talk about the convictions of the other side—in other words, to defend their opponent's point of view. This not only helps in understanding the position of others, but also triggers examination of your own preconceptions.

If this is not possible, at least make sure all involved parties openly discuss their opposing views, and more important, what they are based on. Are they based on past experiences (but times have changed), religious beliefs (that may not belong in the workplace), or personal goals (which could be reconciled with the goals of the other parties involved)?

In fact, communication is also the key to solving the prisoner's dilemma that I referred to in Chapter 1. Recall the situation: Two suspects are being charged for a crime and offered a deal, independently of each other. If both remain silent, they will be charged with a lesser crime and will each receive a short sentence, one year in prison. If they both confess, they will each receive a longer sentence, five years in prison. If one confesses and the other remains silent, the one who confesses will be released, and the other will be sentenced to ten years in jail. They cannot talk with each other. Although the best solution for both would be to remain silent, the fact that they are not able to talk it over means that most likely both will talk, each hoping that the other does not. The result is five years in prison, instead of only one year. Communication during the arrest is indeed not possible, but it is possible beforehand. In fact, criminal organizations such as gangs and mafia invest quite a bit of time building strong relationships based on motivation and communication. Belonging to the organization is like being part of a family, with a very strong sense of loyalty. The rules of engagement are very clearly communicated, in word and in deed. For members of the organization, it is clear that talking may lead to a shorter jail sentence, but will have negative consequences for the suspect after the jail sentence, and perhaps immediate consequences for family and friendships. At the same time, not talking to the police is rewarded handsomely. The organization takes care of the suspect's loved ones during jail time.

Most organizations have a very well-developed hierarchy, with objectives, clear responsibilities, and a high degree of accountability. Managers all report up into the organization to their managers, until the consolidated results reach the executive team. This structure is the cause of many strategic dilemmas. The back office has different objectives than the front office, but has—through the management structure—no insight into what the front office really does. It is a different set of responsibilities. Vertical management structures with mutually exclusive domains and responsibilities do not invite managers to openly discuss their problems, other than in the executive team. Even if managers wanted to discuss problems, exploring multiple angles, there would not be a logical structure to do so—except, of course, when it is too late and a "multidisciplinary taskforce" is instituted to fix what has gone wrong.[vii] Alignment does not have to be vertical. Alignment can also be horizontal, where managers are required to optimize the work across the whole value chain, instead of just within their own unit. In addition to business domains, organizations need to define their business interfaces.[viii] A *business interface* is where work gets handed off between one system and the next, between one activity and another, between one process and the next, between one department and another. Business interfaces need to be managed as conscientiously as do business domains.

Reconcile the Dilemma

Together with self-reflection and communication, *reconciliation* forms the third element. Can you find a way to bring the opposite sides together? Figure out how to achieve both goals at the same time? Realize that you want the same thing, just in a different way?

The Western way of thinking does not make it easy to answer these questions, as we tend to see the different sides of a dilemma as mutually

---

[vii]The sad thing is that instituting taskforces like this is being seen as decisive action, whereas in essence it is an example of "too little, too late." Too late, because the damage is done; too little, because the structure that actually caused the problem most likely will not be changed. Any reorganization coming out of exercises like this is bound to be equally vertically structured. The pendulum swings and the organization sets itself up for yet another set of dilemmas.

[viii]There is more on business interfaces in F.A. Buytendijk, *Performance Leadership*, McGraw-Hill, 2008.

Western View

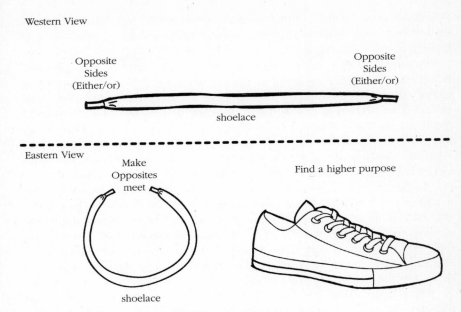

Opposite
Sides
(Either/or)

Opposite
Sides
(Either/or)

shoelace

Eastern View

Make
Opposites
meet

Find a higher purpose

shoelace

FIGURE 8.2 Western and Eastern Views on Opposites

excluding opposites—either/or thinking (see Figure 8.2). Figure 8.2 also visualizes a more Eastern point of view, where opposites are alike. For instance, love and hate are very similar emotions.[ix] From a business perspective, different people may have different solutions for a certain problem or strategic direction, but after examining their motives and discussing them, they come to the conclusion that they want the same thing: to be successful. If one executive is looking to acquire a certain company, to get access to a particular market or technology, while another executive is opposed to the acquisition because of the risks involved, these two opposites could be bridged by starting a joint venture or another type of partnership between the two companies.

Or consider the different schools of strategy, as discussed in Chapter 2. One group of people claims that structure follows strategy. The strategy comes first, and the organization should adapt to that strategy. A new strategy therefore often requires reorganization. Another group of people would claim the opposite: Strategy follows structure. Strategies are put together by existing structures and it is unlikely that thinking from such a structure can be seen as independent from that structure. But are these really opposites? Both points of view can be easily combined. Strategy and structure are

---

[ix]So the opposite of love and hate would be indifference.

interdependent. Strategies are formed by a structure, and based on strategic feedback that structure may be changed, leading to an adapted strategy, leading to . . . , and so on.

Another example comes from the field of intercultural management.[5] For global organizations there is always a dilemma between creating a global corporate culture and creating space for local national cultures. The effects of this dilemma can be found in something as simple as the use of the word *yes*. According to one local culture, it can be very impolite to say *no*, whereas in another country's culture, it is equally impolite to say *yes* without following up on it. Still, reconciling such cultural dilemmas can be as fundamental as aiming to create a culture that celebrates diversity.

As an alternative to connecting both opposites, you can try to find a higher objective. You could discuss among fellow board members the necessity of firing a high-performing CEO because you fundamentally disagree with his views on life and the political statements that he aired in a high-profile business magazine. But freedom of speech may be an even higher goal, as in the Voltaire paradox: "I despise what you say, but I will defend to the death your right to say it."

On a larger scale, consider one of the core dilemmas in the tobacco industry. As smoking poses a health risk, should this industry simply stop its business? Is it morally defensible for a responsible company to sell products that are unhealthful and addictive? And even under all current regulations and restrictions, could you call producing and selling tobacco a *responsible* business? But what is the alternative? People have been smoking various things since the beginning of time, and simply not producing and selling cigarettes anymore is not going to take away the demand. Is the alternative to leave the business in the hands of less responsible companies, effectively letting the market go underground? It seems the tobacco industry is complying with all regulations in trying to protect its business. Fundamentally, the dilemma is not addressed, at least not visibly to the general public. The higher objective is to answer the key question of what happens *next*. What comes after cigarettes? Would that be nicotine sticks or nicotine chewing gum? Would it be nicotine- and tar-free cigarettes, or something else? As long as the tobacco industry is looking to reinvent itself—Tobacco 2.0—the industry is on its way to reconciling its dilemma, to creating a synthesis. Yes, its business is unhealthful, yet the players show their sense of responsibility by actively trying to change their product.

In Chapter 1, I discussed thesis, antithesis, and synthesis. The thesis represented a certain situation that suffers from a dominant disadvantage, that is being addressed by a reaction, the antithesis. However, the antithesis probably displays the opposite dominant disadvantage. The synthesis then combines the best of two worlds. As one of those little ironies of life, the synthesis becomes the new thesis. The "best of both worlds" seems to have some disadvantages as well, and these will be addressed by an antithesis, and ultimately a new synthesis—a potentially endless cycle. Take, for instance, the example of the joint venture as the synthesis between acquiring or not acquiring a certain company. The joint venture combined getting access to a certain market or technology while at the same time not significantly increasing strategic or financial risk. But the disadvantage of this joint venture might be in not having the same market power as both its parents have, or in having less access to corporate resources. A reaction will occur eventually. Or consider the tobacco industry that shows its responsibility by investing its profits in a new generation of products that do not have such adverse health effects. How can it do that in a responsible way if there is no certainty of the demand for such new products? The tobacco company also needs to be responsible toward its employees, and other stakeholders such as its investors. Reconciling one dilemma usually reveals yet another. Dealing with you-and-me dilemmas is a continuous process of synthesis.

A Structured Approach

In *The Mind of the Strategist*, Japanese strategist Kenichi Ohmae writes:

> *Phenomena and events in the real world do not always fit a linear model. Hence the most reliable means of dissecting a situation into its constituent parts and reassembling them in the desired pattern is not a step-by-step methodology such as systems analysis. Rather, it is that ultimate nonlinear thinking tool, the human brain. True strategic thinking thus contrasts sharply with the conventional mechanical systems approach based on linear thinking. But it also contrasts with the approach that stakes everything on intuition, reaching conclusions without any real breakdown or analysis.[6]*

One of the most important characteristics of a successful strategy is that it distinguishes the company from its competitors. Clearly, this calls for lateral thinking and a creative approach. But as Ohmae remarks, strategic decision making is more than a seat-of-the-pants approach based on experience and intuition, or an advanced form of art. The same is the case in dealing with dilemmas. Although perhaps not linear, there is logic to it. And although creative in nature, there is a process.

Manufacturing is known for its focus on continuous improvement. Lean and Six Sigma are perhaps the two best-known approaches.

According to the DwD survey, around 50% of organizations use them in some form. However, there is another methodology that I think is even more fundamental, called *theory of constraints* (TOC).[7] Unfortunately, TOC is not very well known. The DwD survey shows around 2% of organizations have it in their standard toolkit. A third of respondents have never heard of it, and an additional 40% claims to have heard of it but are not using it. In addition to ways of creating continuous improvement, it introduces a way of arriving at performance breakthroughs. The original author, Eliyahu Goldratt, dramatically refers to it as "evaporating clouds"[8] others prefer a more business-oriented term: *conflict resolution diagrams*.[9] Define a problem precisely and you are halfway to a solution, is the promise of a conflict resolution diagram.

As in every continuous improvement methodology, conflict resolution diagrams work their way backward, with the end in mind. The goal must be identified first. This helps us to create a synthesis or reconciliation between the advantages of both strategies. Other than trying to optimize for one side of the dilemma, followed by the pendulum swinging to optimizing the other side, conflict resolution diagrams help questioning the requirements and prerequisites to see if the problem itself can be eliminated. Perhaps we have chosen the wrong goal. First, we decompose the choices on the table into smaller choices. Then we start to recompose those choices, into a single picture or into a new strategy, thus avoiding an either/or choice.

Although originally implemented in manufacturing environments for improving throughput, decreasing operating expenses, and lowering inventory, conflict resolution diagrams can also be used for dealing with dilemmas. In Chapter 3, I identified three fundamental intraorganizational you-and-me dilemmas. Value and profit, outside in and inside out, and top down and bottom up. Let us discuss a number of these dilemmas using the conflict resolution diagrams.

Top Down and Bottom Up

On one hand, organizations should be managed top down. Strategic objectives have to be set, and the organization has to adjust. On the other hand, organizations require a bottom-up approach, where we look for ways to get the most out of the resources we currently have. As a result, organizations go through a continuous cycle of centralization and decentralization. For instance, once in a while, organizations have to fix their cost structure, because growth has led to cost control issues. The logical solution is to centralize functions in the organization, a top-down approach.

Control is increased, economies of scale are reached, and as a result costs go down. The organization is now more efficient. A centralized environment also has some disadvantages. The decision power is unnecessarily far removed from operations and concrete market opportunities, inhibiting growth. This means middle management should be empowered to make their own decisions and find their own solutions to deal with opportunities and problems. This leads to a more decentralized environment, a bottom-up approach. After a while, however, this leads to cost inefficiencies, and the pendulum swings again. The thesis of centralization leads to the antithesis of decentralization, and vice versa.

In a conflict resolution diagram, the dilemma would look like Figure 8.3.

Let us decompose both the centralization and decentralization strategies (see Table 8.2).

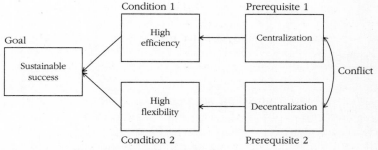

FIGURE 8.3 Centralization and Decentralization

TABLE 8.2 Dilemma Decomposition

Centralization	Decentralization
+	+
■ Control	■ Flexibility
■ Economies of scale, lower cost	■ Market focus, growth scenario
■ Uniformity	■ Empowering people
−	−
■ Less flexible	■ Less control
■ Less focus on specific markets and growth	■ Higher cost
■ Less empowerment	■ Fragmentation and no learning

Source: Adapted from B. Johnson, *Polarity Management: Identifying and Managing Unsolvable Problems*, HRD Press, 1992.

Centralization and decentralization seem to be mutually exclusive. The advantages of one are the disadvantages of the other. How can we be in control and flexible at the same time? How can we focus on economies of scale and keep a focus on the needs of specific markets? How can we empower people to make their own decisions, and maintain uniformity?

This last question gives the first clue as to how to reconcile. How to maintain uniformity, while empowering people. That is what a *standard* does. A standard is a uniform approach for people to apply in different situation. Standards also offer economies of scale, as everyone is working in the same way. Best practices can be developed and shared across the various functions of the organization. Standards do not take away focus from specific markets; they are simply applied differently. Once you have strong standards in place, it does not matter anymore whether you are centralized or decentralized. We have created a higher level of understanding— we have achieved synthesis.

Executive View

Cox Communications has been very successful in redesigning its financial processes. In transitioning the historically decentralized environment that Cox operated in, a "touch-it-once" philosophy was initiated in the accounts payable process, where all invoices need to be collected, checked, approved, and paid. The pre-existing way of working had proven to be too costly. Furthermore, it is better to optimize working capital across the group, instead of (sub)optimizing it on the local level.

However, the magnitude of swapping out the heart and soul of how Cox remits transactions across the organization is not without risk. There was the fear that a centralized organization would not have the same level of accuracy and reliability, and would not have the same sense of ownership. Furthermore, centralized environments often are not that flexible. In a project called CornerStone, under the leadership of Chief Accounting Officer Bill Fitzsimmons, Cox Communications chose to go another route. Instead of falling into the trap of the centralization/decentralization pendulum, it went for *standardization*.

First, within the existing processes and systems, Cox standardized its chart of accounts across all lines of business. Between February 2004 and August 2005, it created what is often called the "single version of the truth." The time was right for taking this step. As difficult as most organizations find it to go through a politically complex initiative like this, the problem was reframed by an external factor: the need for Sarbanes-Oxley (SOx) compliance. For many organizations, SOx compliance had made things possible that otherwise would have been more difficult to achieve.

Then, as a next step, Cox implemented a new financial system. It chose to redesign the financial processes based on the standards in the software, instead of tailoring the system to the specific requirements of the users. Although this approach is a best practice, usually there is some resistance. Should IT follow the business, instead of the other way around? And what is in it for the business? Again, Mr. Fitzsimmons found a way to reframe the problem, and avoid the central/local dilemma. He assembled a team of 45 people consisting of the broadest range of backgrounds from a variety of locations. They helped gain support, provide perspective, and spread the word, and found a way to get people vested in the project. The "what is in it for them" became a personal objective. Helping to redesign financial accounting became a career tool and a result for all to be proud of.

In November 2008, Cox Communications took the final step and centralized the accounting process. This turned out to be the most straightforward step of all because of the standardized nature of the accounting process. The final step of centralization was not a dilemma, anymore, but simply a linear step forward, based on increased cost effectiveness. All that happened was moving doing the accounting transactions from the business units to Corporate Accounting. Trust was an important factor in making this final step, which is always crucial in solving critical business dilemmas. Mr. Fitzsimmons had shown over the various steps in the project that he communicated openly, and was transparent to the business. Successes were openly celebrated, but also the activities that did not go as planned were equally openly shared. Another key success factor was the fact that Mr. Fitzsimmons had worked in the business for many years, both in field positions as well as on the corporate level, giving him a strong recognition.

Standardization represents the synthesis, combining the thesis and antithesis of centralization and decentralization. Once the standardization is in place, it represents the new situation, in other words, the new thesis. The challenge in a standardized environment is how to handle exceptions, and how to deal with the innovation that so often comes from diversity.

Once this becomes problematic, this will lead to an antithesis, solving the exceptions problem, but compromising the standardization. Another synthesis will be needed.

Value and Profit

If you treat business as a zero-sum game, in which your profit automatically means someone else's loss, there will always be a dilemma. The key is to define value for the customer that is profitable for yourself and all others in the value chain. Perhaps one of the best examples comes from the Apple iPod mp3 player. The product itself may have had a stunning design over the various generations, but the device itself is not the key innovation.[x] It was not the first mp3 player on the market, most of the materials are freely available on the market, and with the exception of the user interface, most functionality is not unique. The key innovation is in the business model,[10] reconciling an important dilemma.

Before the music store that is part of the Apple iTunes software, mp3 files were very much associated with illegal downloads. However, downloading music as mp3 files ("rip, mix, and burn" as Apple called it) is the way forward, the future. Despite various legal procedures by musicians and music companies (remember Napster?), the popularity of downloading mp3 files could not be denied. The music industry was in danger. The profitability of the industry was in the declining model of selling CDs, physical products with a fixed number of tracks in a fixed order. This is a clear strategic dilemma: embracing a future that consists of an unprofitable business model (how to compete with "free"?) versus unprofitable prospects of the current business model. The conflict resolution diagram could look like Figure 8.4.

This is the classic you-and-me dilemma. The customer value conflicts with the music industry's profitability. Let us explore this further by decomposing the options (see Table 8.3).

Table 8.3 shows that the disadvantages of embracing the trend and sticking to the old model at least outnumber the advantages. It is hard to cannibalize your own business model if you do not know whether the

---

[x]It should be said that Apple goes out of its way to cannibalize itself with new designs, new functionality, and new convergence areas, such as the iPhone, to keep a product lead. The new iPad is another example. The functionality of the product is not special, in fact, it is criticized for lacking certain functionality. The innovation is in offering a platform for mobile applications, unlocking new creative ideas for working and leisure that don't even exist today.

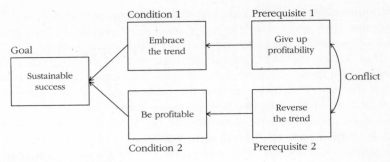

FIGURE 8.4 Value and Profit

TABLE 8.3 Dilemma Decomposition, Value and Profit

Embrace the Trend	Be Profitable
+	+
■ Create customer value.	■ Profitability.
■ Set new standards, gain first-mover advantage if you get it right.	■ Keep control over the complete end product.
	■ Well-understood business model.
—	—
■ No profit; how to compete with free?	■ Less perceived customer value.
■ No control over the product; users may not download a complete album, just a few tracks.	■ Risk of becoming a market laggard, following the rest.
■ Strategic risk of not getting it right.	

new business model is going to be successful. This is a very clear case of being in the eye of ambiguity between two S-curves, as described in Chapter 6. And the choices seem to be completely mutually exclusive. The advantages of one are the exact disadvantages of the other.

But let us question the assumptions. Do we really have to reverse the trend to keep up profitability? Is there no way to compete with downloading music for free, and make that profitable? Apple understood that the "free" model was not without disadvantages as well. The quality of the downloaded mp3 files was far from guaranteed, and it was quite a hassle to convert those mp3 files to an mp3 player, using different types of software that often felt like an afterthought. Apple, with a strong reputation for alignment of hardware and software, solved that problem: perfect integration of downloading and managing music with its iTunes software from a demand chain point of view, and a high availability of music through distribution contracts from a supply chain point of view. Distribution and integration: This was enough to justify asking users for the modest price of less than one dollar per track. Value and profit go hand in hand.

That leaves the issue of the strategic risk of not getting it right. Obviously, strategic risk cannot be avoided completely. There is always a chance that the chosen direction or the product solution will not pan out the way it was intended. But here is where the win-win approach of the you-and-me dilemma starts to work. The Apple iPod is not only Apple's success. Myriad partners offering accessories are part of the success and share in the success, and the same goes for the music companies. This risk is distributed, but with so many parties involved, the chances of success have been maximized.

In the meantime, the entire music industry has changed, and is building a new S-curve. Artists have had to reexamine their sources of income. Concerts, not CDs, are now in many cases the main source of income. As a result, fans get to see the artists more. The balance of power is changing. In October 2007, Madonna signed a new deal not with a major record company, but with LiveNation, a concert promoter.[11] Hip-hop legend Jay-Z and rock band U2 did the same in 2008.[12] Prince gave away his new CD in the Sunday edition of the UK newspaper *Mail* to promote his series of concerts in the London O2 stadium.[13]

Even the traditional business of selling CDs has changed. There are hardly any CD stores left in shopping malls and on the streets—sales have moved online. Current stores focus more on DVDs and games. But it stands to reason that the same thing that happened with CDs will happen to all forms of information not stored in an openly accessible way. What happened to Napster enabling downloading mp3 files has now also happened to web sites such as The Pirate Bay enabling sharing of complete movies. Newspapers struggle with a declining subscription base, and authors putting their books online for free sometimes actually see an uptick in traditional sales. Games are moving online as well, and advertising is becoming a more important source of income for game studios. Value and profit are realigning.

CHAPTER 9

Now and Later

Luck favors the prepared mind.

Louis Pasteur

In managing the short term versus the long term, it would help to know where things are going, to be able to leverage short-term investments for the long term. Knowing where things are going would help in knowing how to place the right bets in terms of innovation, leading your customers. And insight into the future would certainly help in putting the business case together to justify innovation over optimization. However, there is always strategic uncertainty. There is no telling what the future will bring. There are simply too many factors that influence our environment and internal operations.

And even if we would have all the information we can think of, there is still no telling if we would make the right decision. One of the core principles in decision-making theory is that we human beings suffer from something called *bounded rationality*. The capacity of the human mind for formulating and solving complex problems is very small compared with the size of the problems whose solution is required for objectively rational behavior in the real world.[1] It is hard enough to think through the consequences of a decision in the short term, let alone the longer-term choices.

The Global DwD Survey showed that managing the long term and the short term at the same time, and managing innovation as well as optimization, are indeed seen as the most difficult dilemmas in business. Most organizations could benefit from improvement there. The core recipe for dealing with now-and-later dilemmas, shown again in Figure 9.1, is not trying to predict the future, but being ready for it.

The traditional way of making decisions around an uncertain future, dealing with now-and-later dilemmas, is to use metrics such as *net present value* and *discounted cash flow*. This way of translating future results

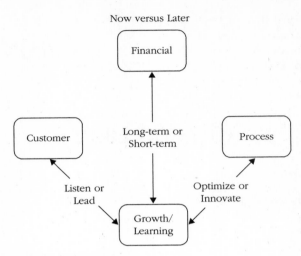

FIGURE 9.1 Three Now-and-Later Dilemmas

back to today's circumstances is widely adopted, but has a major flaw; it assumes the future will be no different from today. Concerning investment decisions impacting the future—and which investment decisions do not?—you just cannot know whether you picked the "right" strategy, and whether you are executing it in the "right" way. Unfortunately, there is always strategic uncertainty.

However, if you define strategy as a process of creating options, as discussed in Chapter 2, you might be more ready for the unpredictable future. The idea of *real options* is very helpful in this regard. The idea dates back to 1977.[2] Unfortunately, it is not very well known.[i] According to the DwD survey, 55% of all respondents have never even heard of it, and it is a standard practice in only 2.5% of companies.

The term *options* is used in the sense of financial options, acquired with the express purpose of being exercised at will. *Real options* are like

---

[i]Part of the reason why real options theory is still relatively obscure is that the financial analysts and academics took control of it. This means an enormous focus on the quantitative side. In the average paper on real options, the first "Black-Scholes" formulas start to appear on page 3, and by page 17 they transcend the complexity of Einstein's special theory of relativity. Practitioners have rightfully shied away from the complexity of highly complex option valuation exercises. However, the strategic background of real options is crucial for modern strategy management.

financial options, but in the "real world." The concept of real options is a strategic decision-making paradigm that allows for making flexible or staged decisions under uncertainty. It captures the value of managerial flexibility to adapt and revise decisions at a future time under the right conditions with the benefit of better information.[3] It should be seen less as a valuation tool (how much your options are worth) and more as a management process. If you look at your portfolio of subjects that require a strategic decision at a given moment, it would be helpful to have the flexibility to be able to expand on a certain initiative when needed, delay certain investments or projects without losing the benefits so far, have the agility to switch halfway through, and use the investments so far for another opportunity, or once in a while, when having to abandon the investment, enjoying the tactical benefits of the investment up to that point.

Executive View

Thinking in terms of strategic options is part of Vopak's DNA. Its complete strategy is based on a portfolio partly because risk diversification comes naturally to the business. First, there is a natural geographic spread. There is a global need for the consumption of bulk liquids, while at the same time the different oil and chemical products are produced all over the world. There is no complete dependency on one line of products, or one part of the world. Also, bulk liquids are being used for many different purposes, ranging from providing fuel for transportation (cars, airplanes, boats) to the creation of plastics, to human consumption of vegetable oils. As a result, the demand is diversified. Vopak's business and financial model is also diversified. Forty percent of contracts have a term longer than three years, 35% have a contract term between one and three years, and 25% are short-term contracts for shorter than 1 year. One could say that diversification is all over the company's balanced scorecard: It runs a portfolio from a financial perspective (contracts), from a customer perspective (demand for different products, which drives Vopak's business), from a process perspective (terminals all over the world), and from growth and learning perspective (servicing new bulk liquids in addition to oil).

The company's strategic decision making is deeply rooted in portfolio and real options thinking. Take, for instance, an investment proposal. Like every company, Vopak has "hurdle rates," the minimum return that investments must provide. In many companies this means

(continued)

(continued)

each investment must reach this hurdle by itself; otherwise, it is not approved. Vopak's philosophy is more subtle and sophisticated; a return can also come from a new option that a new investment generates. The return may then be allocated somewhere else, but was generated by an initial investment. Take, for instance, the company's early investments in China. The business case for other investment proposals for terminal expansion in established areas would show much higher returns. Yet, Vopak chose to approve some investment proposals that had a calculated return lower than the hurdle rate. For instance, there are long-term advantages to being an early adopter in new geographic markets. Think of being the first to build local relationships, and of the opportunity to build terminals with an infrastructure that is optimal for the company's processes. Once, through Vopak's brand, other terminal services and new customers are attracted, the return on investment rises to levels that do outpace the other "traditional" opportunities.

Of course there is a risk. If those synergies do not materialize, the company is stuck with a long-term investment that, while cash flow positive, does not cover the cost of capital. This is where the rest of the portfolio, the company's existing 79 terminals, comes in. The risk being taken can be seen as a calculated one.

Thinking in terms of real options helps in determining the optimal decision-moment as discussed in Chapter 6. For instance, if you believe the time is right for making a certain decision, and waiting any longer only decreases the chance of success, or the return on investment, you must exercise that option immediately, and perhaps invest even more to increase the return even more. If you believe that there is no chance of success, and the longer you wait, the more sunk cost you will incur, there is no choice but to abandon the initiative immediately and discard the initiative as an option. But there is also a middle ground. Perhaps you feel the option is currently "under water" (meaning, if you were to decide now to start an initiative, it would not succeed or it would not generate the return you expect), but circumstances might improve. For instance, the market will grow, the oil price will change, the cost of technology needed to implement the initiative will go down, the political climate will improve, or scarcity will increase. In those cases, you decide not to make a decision yet, and wait on exercising the option. Of course, you can always shape the business case, and switch the investment to serve another goal.

In essence, according to real options theory, you construct decision-making processes and you craft decisions in such a way that they leave the option to change open. You are not sticking to a single plan, but keeping your eyes open for change under way.

As with financial options, where you need to purchase them, there is a cost to real options as well. Consider outsourcing. It frees up internal capacity, such as managers and employees, and their time and skills can now be invested in other options. Although usually a cost benefit is expected by achieving economies of scale by using a large outsourcing company for your shared financial services center, or a large catering firm, or a large systems integrator, your partner needs to be profitable as well. Furthermore, there is often a larger cost for long-term change. You could argue that given the increased cost of change, outsourcing activities actually reduces your future ability to adapt. Utilities companies and telecoms invest in peak capacity, introducing overcapacity. Or think of production plans that actually allow for slack, to be able to innovate processes while the core business is running on full speed.

In fact, mass customization—being able to tailor every individual transaction that goes through a production process or administrative process—has become the norm in many industries. Already since the beginning of the 1990s, Hewlett-Packard has experimented with real options.[4] In the 1980s, HP was manufacturing printers in a centralized manner. All types and customizations were produced in the central plants, and then shipped to the warehouses worldwide. This was the most efficient solution from a manufacturing point of view as the product was only "touched" once. However, forecasts are not always right, and the company would end up with customized products that were not sold. The company found out it was smarter to ship partially assembled printers to the warehouses, and then customize them there, based on local orders and specifications. This approach certainly was more expensive, but the company saved $3 million per month by better matching supply and demand. Increasing the cost of production was the price HP paid to create more options for customization.

It should also be said that the comparison between strategy and financial options is not entirely accurate.[5] For instance, financial options are a monetary instrument—you can sell them to anyone. Real options are very much connected to your strategy, and your resources. It is likely that investments, once done, cannot be sold to others. Furthermore, in the case of financial options, the market, based on supply and demand, sets the price. In the case of real options, the valuation—if any—is based on subjective assessment. Finally, as assessments are subjective in nature, so is decision making as to which initiatives to expand or delay, where to switch, and how to abandon. Compared to financial options, it is harder to make the right calls.

Real options are a powerful way of thinking, but how do we create a decision-making process that reconciles an uncertain future with the tangible needs of today? There are five things you can do:[6]

1. Bet on the most probable future, based on your assessment.
2. Bet on the future that best fits the goals of the firm (which is basically the same as hoping your predetermined strategy works out).
3. Hedge your investments and initiatives so that you get satisfactory results no matter what future becomes reality.
4. Preserve your flexibility, so that you can apply growing insight, and adapt to changing circumstances.
5. Exert your influence to make the most desired future a reality.

The first two options represent traditional thinking of having to make definitive choices, and are rather dangerous. The only thing we really know about the future is that it is most likely different from today, and if we add some humility, most likely also different from what we can imagine. Betting might not be the best idea. Exerting your influence is always a good idea, and as of a certain size or innovative position in the market, this is certainly a viable strategy.[ii] Preserving flexibility and hedging your investments and initiatives creates a more conscientious decision-making process (but has the disadvantage that this process is harder to communicate than those all-or-nothing, bet-the-farm strategic decisions).

Using the now-and-later dilemmas, I will discuss what such decision-making processes look like, and elaborate on one of the most important methodologies for creating options for the future: scenario planning.

Long Term and Short Term

Strategic decision-making is not a single-step process. Long gone are the times of the detailed three-to-five-year plans. In a turbulent environment, it is of no use to stick to the plan—you need to stick to reality. And reality changes. Strategic decision-making more likely is a sequence of decisions,

---

[ii]Indeed, you could reason that when you have a certain market dominance, because of size or innovative impact, you do not have to bet anymore. Once you have determined what the most desirable future is, you simply create it. As valid as this may seem, it closes your eyes to change, and easily leads to arrogance. Smaller competitors that are more focused on customers' needs will take advantage.

each following the other. Some actions are taken immediately, while others are deliberately deferred so that managers can optimize as circumstances evolve. The strategy sets the framework within which future decisions will be made, but at the same time it leaves room for learning from ongoing developments and for discretion to act based on what is learned.[7]

Most organizations struggle with the long-term versus short-term dilemma. How can you meet Wall Street's expectation for maximizing shareholder value in the short term while at the same time investing in long-term results? And given the fierce competition, it is sometimes necessary to keep the intended results of these investments under wraps.

Executive View

Reconciling long term and short term is also very present in marketing. By definition, marketing is a long-term investment. As part of the marketing cycle, building awareness does not necessarily lead to generating short-term leads. For Polycom, the answer is in building relationships with the channel. Heidi Melin, the company's chief marketing officer, preaches a high-touch marketing strategy. Having built those relationships over the longer term, it becomes possible to use those relationships to satisfy both short-term and long-term needs. Sometimes it is necessary to call channel partners and ask for favors, to contribute to a short-term campaign. This can be done only if, at other moments, Polycom takes the long-term approach and advises the channel to wait with certain promotions. For instance, a price decrease may be in the pipeline, or a new version of the product. A high-touch marketing strategy is essential in creating a strategic stretch, covering both long- and short-term success.

Each decision is based on the best information available at that time. By staging a decision-making process, you can successfully push out the optimal decision-making moment, as discussed in Chapter 6. To service the short term, each decision in the sequence needs to have an immediate positive impact as well. For instance, for a business, a phased approach to implementing a new system in three-month increments might be more expensive than a big-bang approach that takes a year. But the chance of success, getting user buy-in, being able to detect any issues early, or reaping cost benefits from current use by a small user group, combined are worth the extra cost.

Executive View

Commercial organizations can learn from public service.[iii] Dr. Edmund Stoiber, the former prime minister of Bavaria, Germany, points out that decision-making processes in the public sector are structured differently than in commercial enterprise. Where executives in companies are agents representing the shareholder's interests, which is reflected in their decision making, government officials are required to take the needs of all stakeholders into account, such as the various groups in society. Therefore, the decision-making process is more consultative, collaborative, and transparent than in commercial enterprise.

What strategic decision making in the public sector and in commercial enterprise have in common is that there is never enough time to think through the consequences and immediately make the right decision. There is a conflict between conscientious decision making and the time that is needed to do this.

This is why in the public sector decisions are explicitly made in various steps. Social groups and their representatives can lobby for certain proposals. Proposals are being discussed in parliament, and through a process of revision, fine tuning, and various signoff steps, ultimately become a final decision, for instance, in the form of a law. This means decisions start on the preliminary level, stating a general direction ("There should be less bureaucracy"). The process then moves to intermediate steps, applying the general direction to specific areas ("These are the areas where less bureaucracy has the most positive impact"). The process ends with concrete initiatives ("What we will achieve over the coming two years"). This system of checks and balances makes sure that the consequences for all stakeholders are considered, and growing insight can be taken into account (reducing the strategic uncertainty), while at the same time not delaying fundamental decision making until it is too late.

In that sense, public sector decision making resembles an options-based strategy. Each step in the process has value, but leaves room

---

[iii]I am not suggesting that commercial organizations adopt the same process, as a competitive environment simply presents a different dynamic. However, it helps to compare decision-making processes that perhaps are more implicit in commercial life with the structured and transparent way the governmental process is structured. It should also be acknowledged that the governmental process is also not perfect.

for circumstantial changes and new insights. At each stage, as many options as possible are kept open until there is more certainty.

Both Publishing Corp.'s CIO and Heidi Melin (CMO of Polycom) made the same remark: Do not make a decision until you understand the consequences for all stakeholders. And according to the Global Dealing with Dilemmas Survey, broad consultation to collect as many angles as possible is also the preferred decision-making style.

Listen and Lead, Optimize and Innovate

The listen-and-lead, and optimize-and-innovate dilemmas are very alike. Listen and lead concentrates on the dilemma between what customers are asking for today, and what is needed to cater to their requirements tomorrow. Optimize and innovate represents the same tension, between the organization's processes of today and the ones that are needed to do well in the future. All the more interesting is that in the Global DwD Survey, respondents report they do relatively well in listen and lead, while at the same time they indicate that innovation versus optimization is one of the hardest dilemmas they encounter. Perhaps some of the lessons learned in the front office should be applied to the back office as well. Respondents indicate that they can combine customer intimacy with product innovation, by listening to customers better than anyone else (leading in listening). In creating better business processes, are finance people, business analysts, and IT professionals listening equally well to their colleagues that run these business processes? And while putting the business processes together, are they also monitoring how they use the business processes continuously?

Executive View

Innovate and Optimize

It is hard to both innovate and optimize current processes at the same time. The more you optimize toward maximizing output, the more you hardwire the process. And the more you hardwire the process, the harder it becomes to innovate that process. The only way out is to design and implement an entirely new process, and a new cycle of optimization starts. Novozymes is able to optimize its production and

(continued)

(continued)

gain efficiencies of about 7 to 8% each year, while not compromising the flexibility of the process. This is because the efficiencies do not come from a better process, but from better ways of transforming the raw materials into products. It is the technology itself that becomes more efficient. In biotech, technology is an important constraint. It defines what Porter called the "productivity frontier," on which every company should operate. By investing in new technology, pushing the frontier out, Novozymes is able to both innovate and optimize at the same time.

Listen and Lead

Like many technology companies, Polycom has a strong engineering culture. Innovation is often driven by technological advancements. New products or new versions of products are characterized by, for instance, image resolution, speed, bandwidth efficiency, compression techniques, and other advancements. Within the culture of Polycom, it is then the task of marketing to find out how to position the product, come up with useful real-life applications, and target buyer segments. In the listen-or-lead dilemma, Polycom displays a strong strategic bias toward leading the customer.

Sometimes this bias goes too far, and leads to a counterintuitive user experience. Polycom's chief marketing officer, Heidi Melin, describes her own experiences with videoconferencing. Every time she used the remote control to move the camera from her desk to a meeting table in her office, it would go left when she wanted it to go right, and vice versa. The "left" and "right" buttons on the remote were defined from the camera's point of view, not the user's point of view.

The opposite approach to innovation would be to work market driven. Marketing would listen to customers, see how they collaborate over a long distance, gather product requirements, and work with development to shape these into new products and features. Given Polycom's business model, which sells exclusively through partner channels, this is not easy. Between the company and the end-consumer, sometimes there are two or three steps.

The marketing dilemma here is how far to push in changing the way of working. Push too hard, and Polycom loses its innovative edge. Accept the current way of working, and Polycom runs unnecessary risk in not being able to earn back development investments, in case there is less than expected demand for new products and features.

Consider one of the new Polycom products, called People-on-Content. As with the meteorologist on TV, it projects the presenter on top of his or her presentation material, whether this is a PowerPoint presentation, or, for instance, an X-Ray. Through the videoconferencing system, People-on-Content creates a seamless presentation experience. Marketing saw itself confronted with the difficult task of successfully positioning this new technology innovation, as the possibilities are almost endless. One way to fuse both approaches, to come to listen *and* lead, is to use the customer base to generate ideas for applications. For instance, the development department could create a so-called mashup application on the web site. Customers could upload their own visuals and their presentations, and simulate their own People-on-Content application. This could be shaped as a contest, where the best applications will actually be built or promoted. The interesting aspect of this approach is that the engineering talent in the company in this way actually drives the listen approach, by using modern technology to gather customer information.

The DwD survey reports a bias toward optimization at the cost of innovation. Indeed, most studies show that while companies can manage short-term bursts of high performance, only a few sustain it over the longer run. Companies that can both execute and adapt are very rare indeed. There are three main reasons for that:[8]

1. **People**. There is a price to pay for the experience that people build over time; they become used to a certain way of working and cannot see alternative ways anymore. What helped companies execute in the past constrains their ability to adapt in the future.
2. **Structure**. The more interdependencies exist within organizations, the more potential for conflict that constrains the range of solutions. In general, larger organizations find it harder to adapt than smaller organizations, as more and more specialized functions become involved.[iv]
3. **Resources**. By executing on a plan, management determines a company's configuration of resources. Hiring people and investing in assets define future opportunities. Structure determines strategy just as much as the other way around.

[iv]This is a dilemma in itself, as allowing large organizations to act in a fragmented way may also not turn out to be very successful. See Chapter 8 on you-and-me dilemmas for a discussion on centralization versus decentralization.

What helps most in stretching both innovation and optimization, both listening and leading, is *diversity*. People see only the thing they are used to seeing. Different people have different frames of mind, and tend to focus on different things. Bringing diversity to a management team or a project team helps the team notice things that otherwise would have gone unnoticed. It allows a team to listen better to customers, or to come up with ideas for innovation that people who are stuck in the process they have been working with would never be able to see. The late C.K. Prahalad, who was one of the world's foremost management gurus, refers to the need of "genetic variation" within organizations.[9] There might be a genetic variation of skills within a team. For instance, a sociologist as a project manager will see different things than someone with a background in business administration. An econometrist may come to the conclusion that a certain problem he has in building a predictive model is solved already by physicists, dealing with their particular problems. There might be generic variation coming from mixing industries. Financial services may be able to learn about mass customization processes from automotive experts. Utility companies can learn from telecoms when coping with deregulation. And of course there is the need for cultural diversity. An American manager will tackle innovation in a different way than his or her Japanese counterpart. One methodology that can aid in sharing and learning from each other's views on the future is called *scenario planning*.

Scenario Planning: Seeing What Others Do Not See

Scenario planning[v,vi] is a way to depict possible future states. Some have tried to do this in a mathematical, quantitative way, but mostly it is a qualitative exercise—creating parallel narratives that describe how the future might unfold under different circumstances. In more formal terms, "scenario planning is a tool for ordering one's perception about alternative future environments in which one's decisions might be played."[10] The least important goal of scenario planning is to be *right* about the future. If we

---

[v]Most of the text on scenario planning is based on P. Schwartz, *The Art of the Long View*, Currency Doubleday, 1996; and K. van der Heyden, *Scenarios: The Art of Strategic Conversation*, John Wiley & Sons, 1996. Scenario-based strategy maps are based on F. Buytendijk, T. Hatch, and P. Micheli, *Scenario-Based Strategy Maps*, Academy of Management, Chicago, 2009.

[vi]Different authors have used various terms such as *scenario analysis*, *scenario planning*, and *scenario development*, yet the difference between these terms is loosely defined at best. Here I am using the term *scenario planning* synonymously with the other terms.

imagine 100 possible futures, number 101 will be the reality. It helps to think of future performance not as a single plan to stick to, but as a number of options. Once the future plays out, they need to be recognized. If we opened our eyes to change, which is the most important goal of scenario planning, we would recognize these different directions—whatever they may be—a bit better. Seeing only what we are used to seeing is deeply rooted in human behavior. Training yourself to think in terms of scenarios and options broadens your horizon, and creates a prepared mind. People experienced in thinking in terms of scenarios will be less likely to stick to an established strategy even if reality is moving in a different direction. Scenario planning by itself, regardless of the outcome, may very well have a positive effect on the decision-making process.

The key to a scenario planning exercise is to formulate the assumptions in the business, and challenge them—to think the unthinkable, both internal and external. External assumptions can be economical in nature, such as the growth of the economy, the cost of capital, and the cost of labor. There are also social assumptions, for instance, around fashion trends, attractive product design, effective messaging, or demographics. There may also be political or legal assumptions, around tax pressure, subsidies, compliance, or accepted business practices. Many assumptions are based on technology restrictions; what is possible today is being extrapolated into the future. Internal assumptions may be based on the company's typical business processes, for instance, from order to cash, or decision-making processes around, for instance, financing projects. What if the price of oil triples almost overnight, or goes to near zero? What if the greenhouse-effect does not exist? What if mobile phone signals indeed turn out to have negative health effects? What if the economy completely breaks down if the financial system does not work anymore?[vii] What if the government decides to store everyone's DNA pattern? What if we could close the financial books instantaneously? What if we could measure the impact of marketing to the dollar specific? None of these things are necessarily good or bad; they may be situations or opportunities to simply deal with.

The most-often-recited, best-known example of the enormous business impact of scenario planning comes from Shell. When the 1970s oil crisis hit, although it did not plan for it, Shell had the scenario ready. As a lot of the thinking had been done, it was easier for Shell to drastically change strategy while still being in control. Shell came out as a strong market leader. Scenario planning is experiencing a revival. Nearly 60% of respondents in the DwD survey indicate they use it themselves, it is used

---

[vii]No, wait, that unthinkable thing happened already—was anyone ready to respond?

elsewhere in the organization, or it is a standard practice (in 10% of cases). Still, 10% of respondents have never heard of it.

Scenario planning differs from forecasting and other planning methods in a number of ways. Where budgeting, planning, and forecasting focus on a single future—and in advanced cases even assign a probability—scenarios keep the element of uncertainty. Different scenarios stand side by side as equals. Scenarios are much richer than a plan; through storytelling they describe a complete possible world of tomorrow. As a result, scenarios go beyond objective analyses to include subjective interpretations. Finally, forecasting is an inside-out activity, based on the existing situation, where scenario planning is an outside-in activity, opening up new areas of thinking.

Scenario planning is a relevant method to deal with the eye of ambiguity for two principal reasons. First, it is fundamental for organizations to think creatively about the future in order to avoid the risk of being surprised and unprepared, once there is a discontinuity. We cannot predict which discontinuity will happen, other than certainly there *will* be discontinuities. The list of discontinuities in the past has been endless in its variety. Think of the various recessions, 9/11, the SARS or H1N1 epidemic, the volcanic activity in Iceland, and so on. Therefore, and this is the second reason, since the future is inherently uncertain, organizations need to prepare for multiple plausible futures, not only the one they expect to happen.

A scenario could be defined as "a view of what the future might turn out to be—not a forecast, but one possible future outcome."[11] Usually, two to four scenarios are created, as shown in Figure 9.2. If it is only one scenario, it is simply a prediction. Practice shows that with more than four, the number of scenarios becomes unmanageable and loses its impact.

I think different situations each specifically ask for one of the three variations. You use the two-scenario approach when you are at a crossroads and have to make a strategic choice. The scenarios describe the future of

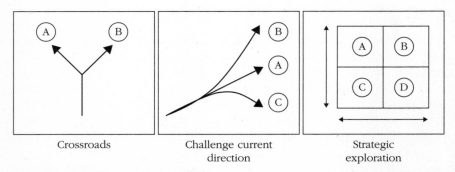

Crossroads   Challenge current direction   Strategic exploration

FIGURE 9.2 Two, Three, or Four Scenarios

the company in both these choices. The three-scenario approach is better if "steady-as-she-goes" is a valid option. One scenario can be an extrapolation of the present. A second one describes a bright future in which, for example, you deal well with a discontinuity, because the organization was prepared. The third scenario could describe a more gloomy perspective (for instance, a discontinuity that could not be dealt with successfully, because the organization was not ready). The aim of the exercise is to challenge the current direction as the default way forward. The four-scenario variation you use as a strategic exploration in situations where there is most uncertainty, and where there is a need for out-of-the-box thinking. You take a number of the key assumptions in the business and reason what happens if all of a sudden the opposite would happen. These two opposites then form dimensions, typically ranging from "low" to "high."

Take the example of a software vendor.[viii] At a certain point the firm starts a strategic exploration, wishing to find out where the market could go, and how it would be ready for those possible futures in term of a development roadmap, competitive position, and market messaging. Figure 9.3 shows the four scenarios.

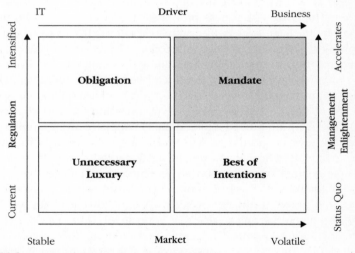

FIGURE 9.3 Scenario Planning in a Software Firm

[viii]Scenario planning, like strategy in general, requires a process, a context, and content (domain expertise). Going through the process alone does not lead to a good set of scenarios. That is why I am using the example of a business software firm, as those are my strategic roots. Thanks to Howard Dresner, with whom I created this scenario.

The scenario planning describes the four dimensions that have the greatest impact on the development of business software:

1. The regulatory environment may stay as it currently is, or it may intensify even more, providing stricter laws and more rules. I did not consider a regulatory environment that becomes looser.
2. The markets in which the customers operate may become more stable, finding a new equilibrium, or may continue to be volatile. This impacts the amount of change they need to deal with.
3. The business software discipline may be driven by the IT department and technological developments, or may be driven by business trends and governed by business executives.
4. The attitude of managers toward business software may stay tactical, looking at a single business case at a time, or management might be "enlightened," using business software to create new business models and adopting the principles more enterprise-wide.

These four dimensions lead to four scenarios. In a tough economic future, where regulations do not intensify, the management attitude does not change, and IT is driving implementations, strategic use of business software is a luxury. The costs of business processes need to be minimized and not many people are interested in the subject. The mood is dispassionate. The software vendor should focus on integration and lowering the cost of running the software (TCO). If regulations intensify and the attitude toward business software becomes more strategic, the discipline becomes obligatory. There is no choice but to invest. The focus will be on risk mitigation and compliance. The sentiment will be highly conservative, searching for and copying best practices. The software firm should add many templates and examples.

In a future of economic growth and a stronger business focus, however, in an equal tactical environment, under today's regulatory environment, implementing business software becomes a discipline that is full of the best of intentions. There is money to invest, people are looking for quick ways to grow, and many projects appear; however, they are largely disconnected given the quick pace that is believed to be needed. The sentiment is *getting things done*. The software firm should allow customers to start with deploying a single application for a single purpose. When, however, a more strategic thinking develops. Compliance alone is not enough to be competitive—a more aggressive approach is needed. Running perfect business processes becomes a mandate for survival and thriving. The sentiment toward business software is purposeful and passionate. New business models appear that leverage the investments in compliance into higher levels of transparency. The software firm should offer an integrated, scalable system, but consisting of different modules for various lines of business.

Scenario-Based Strategy Maps

Continuously considering different courses of action asks for an agile strategy implementation process. And that is where it starts to go wrong in strategy management. So far I have been discussing the now and the later from a strategy formulation perspective, but what about managing uncertainty in strategy implementation and evaluation? Peter Drucker stated that the root of most strategic problems is that the assumptions on which the organization has been built and is being run no longer fit reality.[12] The theory of the business has to be tested constantly. The theory is a hypothesis about things that are in constant flux. Your assumptions underlying your strategy may be right, or may turn out to be wrong. In Chapter 2, I argued that the three phases of strategy—formulation, implementation, and evaluation—become a single process. It is a continuous pretzel-shaped cycle, where changes are picked up in daily operations through a process of escalation evaluated on their strategic impact, and course corrections are immediately implemented.

Unfortunately, today's reality is often different. We have gone over all the strategic options and picked the best one, based on the information at hand and with an understanding of the assumptions. And then we stick to a single strategy, the one thing to focus and concentrate on. To the outside world, in our guidance, we still work within a certain range, for instance, with a low-end and high-end prediction of the earnings per share, but internally we live within a single budget.[ix] Strong leadership often means making sure everyone sticks to the plan. But, the longer you stick to a plan, the higher the chance you get disconnected from reality. After all, it is only a plan. It is better to stick to reality. In order to be successful, it is, of course, important to stick to your goals, but while you are on your way to reaching them you should continuously ask yourself if there are better, faster, or cheaper ways of making it to your goals. The budget should never keep you from doing the right thing. How can we be goal-oriented and also keep our eyes open for change?

In Chapter 3, I discussed the balanced scorecard, and the concept of strategy maps as a way to visualize the cause-and-effect relationships between an organization's strategic objectives. They were developed to provide "the missing link between strategy formulation and

---

[ix]That number is by definition not "right," as you can never know for certain what is going to happen throughout the year. Strongly put, everyone who is exactly "hitting their numbers" has been playing with them. What are the odds you would exactly reach an abstract number?

strategy execution,"[13] so they should prove useful in making strategy a continuous process. Let us use the idea of the strategy map, but to support an options-based strategy.

Strategy maps aim to be predictive, as they aspire to show how decisions made in the present could impact future results. This is done through linking leading and lagging indicators. A leading indicator predicts future performance; a lagging indicator reports past performance. For instance, for a postal service, the percentage of mail delivered within 24 hours is a leading indicator for customer satisfaction. For a movie studio, the initial reaction of the test audience is a leading indicator of the financial success of a movie. Empirical data and statistical techniques are used to discover and test these relationships. However, relying on the causal model represented in the strategy map is not sufficient to reflect the evolution of strategy over time.[14] You can use statistical techniques only if you have enough data. Data, by definition, describes results from the past. Given that all we can truly predict about the future is that most likely it will be different from today, you can question the predictive value of correlations found in data describing the past. Putting it in stronger words, you could even argue that validating a strategy map based on correlating past data, by definition, *invalidates* it.

The best practice developed in strategy measurement (traditionally following strategy formulation and implementation) is to create a circular approach. Implement a strategy map describing the current strategy, use leading metrics to analyze (weak) signals that indicate strategic change, modify the strategy, and let a new strategy map reflect that change. However, from a strategy formulation perspective, the question is which strategy leads to meeting the organization's goals and objectives in the first place. Here, the use of scenario planning could expand the effectiveness of strategy maps. The joint use of the two methods, by creating something I call a *scenario-based strategy map*, is a substantial step forward.[x]

---

[x]As with every technique or methodology, there are limitations. Although scenario-based strategy maps address several weaknesses of "standard" strategy maps, this remains a qualitative method. As such, its inputs and outputs will be hard to quantify. Moreover, the process of development of the maps will be likely to reflect only the views of the stakeholders involved. Although this issue could be mitigated by involving a wide range of stakeholders, dominant personalities, groupthink, and power relationships will affect the results. Another limitation is related to the trade-off between number of scenarios and possibility of keeping the exercise practical. Of course, the more scenarios included, the more future-proof the strategy map becomes (and the more the analysis starts to lend itself to quantitative analysis). However, as the literature suggests, two to four scenarios seems to be the most practical approach.

Given the popularity of balanced scorecards and strategy maps, I will assume that the organization already has a strategy map:

1. Consider your organization's existing strategy map and identify the strategic objectives that describe the assumptions for the business model—for instance, "cost leadership" for a budget airline, or "ultimate safety" for a car manufacturer, or "superior service" in a hotel chain.
2. Create different scenarios, for example, using PESTEL analysis. (*PESTEL* is an analysis of six external factors: political, economical, social, technological, environmental, and legal). Identify the new (or unchanged) critical success factors in each of those scenarios.
3. Create a strategy map with objectives for each of those scenarios, based on the specifics of that scenario.
4. Establish the commonality of objectives across the various scenarios. The more an objective is present across scenarios, the more future-proof such an objective will be, and the higher the probability that these goals could be reached in a changing environment. In order for this commonality analysis to work, objectives will have to be specific; this implies that predominantly high-level objectives such as "maintain profitability" and "seek growth" do not provide practical guidance and will most likely change only in the gravest of discontinuities.

Case Study: Tier 1 Talent

Let us see how this works in practice. Tier 1 Talent (a hypothetical firm) is a large recruitment firm for people with technology skills, such as software developers, support specialists, and database administrators. In a market full of job mobility, and many people building IT skills, there is an ample supply of talent. Tier 1 Talent's (T1T) competitive differentiators are its superior matching process, and customer relationships. It has developed global contracts with its large multinational customers, yet retains local management for personalized service. Account managers know their customers inside and out and know what skills to look for; instead of asking customers to fill in forms, T1T offers "live services," creating job profiles based on interviews and mutual understanding. In other words, T1T focuses on the "customer intimacy" value discipline.[15] T1T created a strategy map (see Figure 9.4) to articulate how they intend to meet their goals for the next few years.

T1T is known for its advanced matching system, consisting of very specific technology that provides better results than off-the-shelf packages. This translates well into its customer value proposition, as T1T can offer better candidates in a shorter period of time—an important driver of revenue growth. T1T is also working on expanding the footprint of the technology.

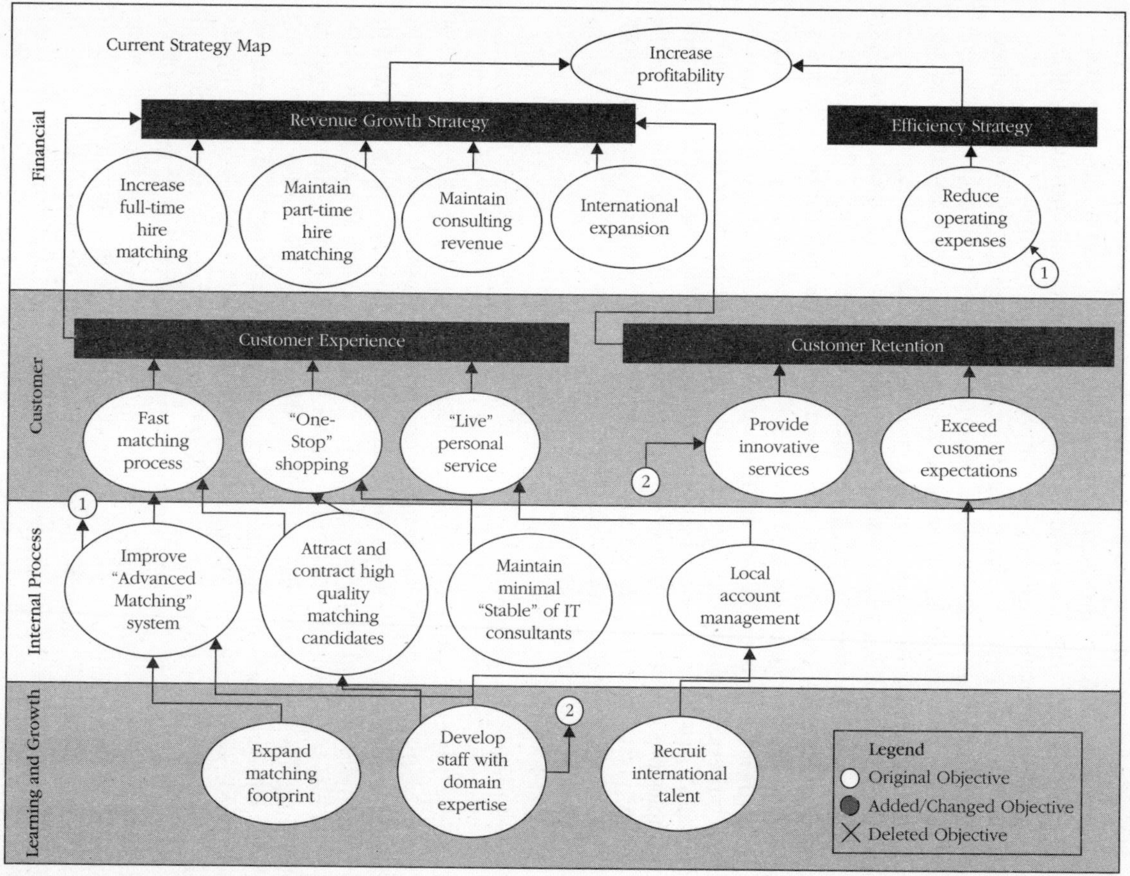

FIGURE 9.4 Current Strategy Map

160

This means adding candidates and adding matching criteria to further improve the system, and opening up the system for candidates and customers to search themselves, providing an innovative service. T1T's focus is to increase the number of full-time placements and maintain its part-time placements in order to meet its revenue growth objectives. Customer intimacy implies not only knowing the customer very well and having local account management (increasingly internationally), but also having staff that understands IT. This adds to qualifying candidates effectively, a positive customer experience, customer retention, and ultimately revenue growth.

To further differentiate from the competition, T1T employs a small unit of IT consultants who take on projects, mainly focusing on project management. This is an hourly-rate consulting business, aimed at creating a "T1T" way of doing IT, adding to the customer experience. This service is particularly aimed at smaller customers who do not have their own professional IT department.

In order to test the validity of the strategic objectives and make the strategy map "future-proof," T1T has prepared three scenarios:

1. **Steady-as-she-goes**. The economic market stays the same and the company continues to grow organically.
2. **It's a networked world**. The labor economy starts to boom and T1T needs to focus on hypergrowth.
3. **Cost-cost-cost**. The economy takes a severe downturn, IT strategies change, and T1T needs to change the business model to survive.

Scenario 1 can be completed using the same strategy map. T1T simply ramps up efforts to hire and retain employees, and find and contract new candidates for matching. The current objectives in the "learning and growth" perspective would be sufficient.

Scenario 2, "It's a networked world," sketches a different situation.[xi] With "Generation Y" entering the workforce, the independent professional is on the rise. Where lifelong employment had already moved to job-hopping, now professionals hop from project to project. Governments support entrepreneurship by offering various tax rebates, thus lowering the risk for people who become self-employed. Open-source working styles dominate the IT world. The 2.0 wave rules the business, and commerce shifts even more from traditional channels to social web sites. "Green" is the key, causing many professionals to work at home serving multiple customers. New projects are found using Internet markets.

[xi]I used the six factors of PESTEL analysis to create this sample scenario: *political/ legal influence:* tax rebates; *economic/social factors:* Generation Y self-employed professionals who use Internet markets to find work; *technological:* rise of the 2.0 world; *ecological:* focus on green.

This scenario has a clear impact on T1T's strategic objectives (see Figure 9.5). The dynamics of the market will change, too. Currently, being a recruitment firm, T1T may have to shift focus to become more of a temp agency, matching customers and candidates on a project-by-project basis. Given the huge growth of the market, T1T may have to acquire a temp agency in order to keep up with the competition and the market growth. Another opportunity would be to acquire a training firm, to educate new graduates and to provide them with a few months of basic experience. With a huge demand for flexible employment, T1T's customer intimacy would have to shift focus to the supply side, understanding the networks of self-employed professionals and building close relationships with colleges and universities. In this scenario, it is no longer necessary to have staff with in-depth domain expertise about IT. T1T's "live services" would not scale, and matching would have to become a self-service process between customers and candidates. This then becomes the innovative service of choice. In addition, T1T would have to take a hard look at their lines of business to ensure it is maximizing revenue. For this reason, T1T would no longer have the luxury of maintaining its own staff providing hourly consulting for smaller clients.

In this scenario, T1T's customer intimacy strategy turns out not to be very future-proof. Yet, given the enormous market growth, the matching system and the planned expansion still hold.

This scenario depicts only one of several potential realities. Scenario 3—"Cost-cost-cost"—draws a different picture. In this scenario, the economy declines and the cost of living increases. People are looking for secure jobs. Companies are not willing to invest in IT innovation, but instead outsource IT activities to other countries that offer economies of scale. IT professionals focus on managing sourcing relationships, instead of developing or maintaining systems themselves. Consequently, IT becomes a utility; government regulations intensify, and more IT budget is spent on compliance. Being green is not a consideration.[xii]

Also in scenario 3, T1T's strategy is heavily impacted (see Figure 9.6). New sources of business are needed. The traditional recruiting business will take a hit. T1T will have to differentiate even more. It will need to emphasize its live services and needs to prove even more the superior capabilities of the matching system. The IT people customers hire will be of a more senior level, and IT managers will manage the outsourcing relationships instead of IT development and operations. T1T will need to position the matching system as a mechanism between the customer and

---

[xii]The PESTEL analysis related to this scenario is as follows: *political/legal influence:* increased compliance regulations; *economic/social factors:* job security in a declining economy; *technological:* Internet largely used to globalize and source operations, as IT becomes a utility.

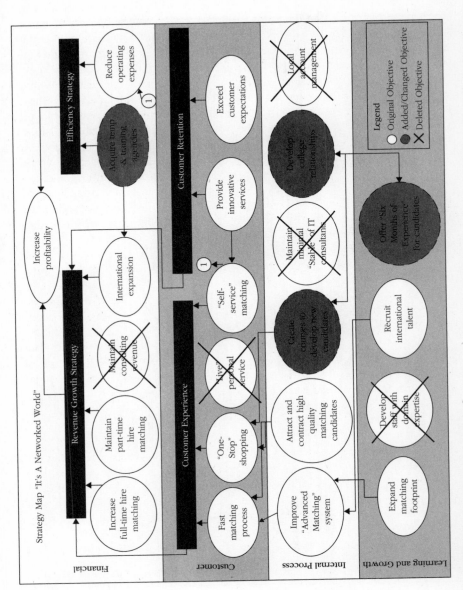

FIGURE 9.5 Strategy Map, Scenario 2

163

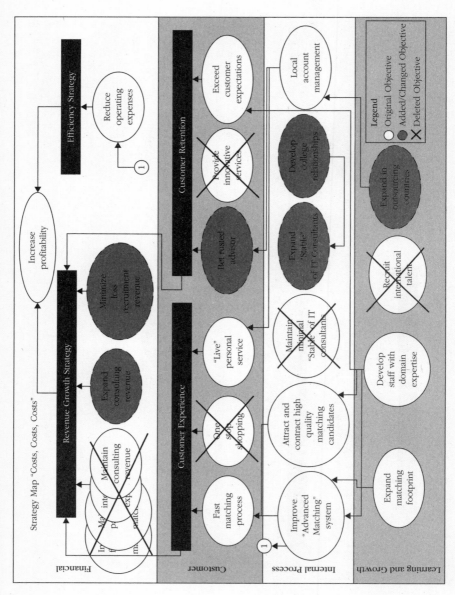

FIGURE 9.6 Strategy Map, Scenario 3

the outsourcing party and show how resources can be matched between those parties. T1T then will mediate between outsourcers and customers, based on an annual contract. Given the additional complexity of this work, T1T will need to ramp up its consulting business, advising large customers on outsourcing strategies, and manage outsourcing relationships for smaller customers as a trusted advisor. T1T will need to hire more IT professionals. Instead of expanding in North America and Europe, the company would need to invest in India and other countries where outsourcers run their operations. Like in scenario 2, the company needs to intensify relationships with the supply side. There are more than enough candidates, but it needs to find the right ones with a multitude of skills. Customer intimacy is now more important than ever; however, the company now needs to specialize and therefore no longer has the luxury of offering one-stop shopping.

Key objectives in this scenario are expanding the matching footprint, and expanding the consulting business. In every scenario, setting up college relationships emerges as important.

Considering all scenarios, a new, synthesized strategy map can be created. This is T1T's new, more future-proof strategy map, based on the common strategic objectives throughout the various scenarios, and other objectives that were evaluated and considered important to T1T's future. The objectives are categorized into two types: strategic imperatives and strategic options.

- The **strategic imperatives (SI)** include all objectives that remained stable throughout all scenarios. Strategic imperatives also include the objectives that appear in all the new scenarios (other than "steady as she goes") that do not harm the original scenario and fit the new strategic direction. The objectives that were formulated on a level that is too abstract (too high) did not change, but are likely not useful. These should be examined to see if they can be made more relevant, or be removed.
- **Strategic options (SO)** include all objectives that did not appear in all scenarios but do fit the strategic direction moving forward.
- The objectives in scenarios that are **neither imperative nor a strategic option (Not Chosen)** are removed from the strategy map.

The assumption is that it is safe to make long-term investments in strategic imperatives. It is less safe to invest heavily in strategic options unless the investment can be made in such a way that it is possible to reconsider or alter the investment if required by a future reality.

Table 9.1 compares the objectives for the three scenarios being considered. The evaluation column describes whether the objective was considered a strategic imperative, or a strategic option (in some cases modified based

TABLE 9.1 Finding Commonality Across All Scenarios

Strategic Objective	Current and "Steady-as-She-Goes"	Networked World	Costs, Costs, Costs	Evaluation
Financial				
Increase profitability	✓	✓	✓	SI
Increase full-time hire matching	✓	✓	✗	SO Modified
Maintain part-time hire matching	✓	✓	✗	SO Modified
Maintain/expand hourly consulting	✓	✗	✓	SO
International revenue expansion	✓	✓	✗	SO Modified
Minimize loss recruitment revenue	✗	✗	✓	Not Chosen
Reduce operating expenses	✓	✓	✓	SI
Acquire temp & training agency	✗	✓	✗	Not Chosen
Customer				
Fast matching process	✓	✓	✓	SI Modified
One-stop shopping	✓	✓	✗	SO
Live personal service	✓	✗	✓	SO
Self-service matching	✗	✓	✗	SO
Provide innovative services	✓	✗	✗	Not Chosen
Exceed customer expectations	✓	✓	✓	SI
Be trusted advisor	✗	✗	✓	Not Chosen
Internal Process				
Improve matching system	✓	✓	✓	SI
Attract and contract high-quality matching candidates	✓	✓	✓	SI

TABLE 9.1 *(continued)*

Strategic Objective	Current and "Steady-as-She-Goes"	Networked World	Costs, Costs, Costs	Evaluation
Create courses to develop new candidates	✗	✓	✗	Not Chosen
Maintain/expand stable of IT consultants	✓	✗	✓	SO
Local account management	✓	✗	✓	SO
Develop college relationships	✗	✓	✓	SI
Learning & Growth				
Expand matching footprint	✓	✓	✓	SI
Develop staff with domain expertise	✓	✗	✓	SO
Recruit international talent	✓	✓	✗	SO Modified
Expand in outsourcing countries	✗	✗	✓	SO Modified
Offer six months of experience for candidates	✗	✗	✓	Not Chosen

on the insights gained by the scenario planning process), or not considered at all for the synthesized map.

As shown in Table 9.1, a few strategic objectives of T1T remain solid throughout all scenarios and can therefore be labeled imperatives. T1T's key competitive differentiator, the matching system, is fortunately future-proof. Expanding its technology footprint works in all explored scenarios and using it in various ways remains an important part of the customer value proposition. Monitoring operating expenses and reducing them where possible is also important as is the main strategic objective, increasing profitability. It is also logical that attracting candidates remains a strategic imperative throughout all scenarios as it is T1T's core business.

Scenarios 2 and 3 both suggest it is wise to invest in college relationships, and, since this objective does not negatively affect the "steady-as-she-goes" scenario, it can be considered a strategic imperative as well. Exceeding customer expectations endures throughout the three scenarios, therefore it is also present on the new strategy map. This objective is meaningful in all scenarios; however, it is not clear whether this is truly a strategic imperative or that it did not change from scenario to scenario because it has been defined at too high a level to be of significance.

Based on the scenario planning, T1T chooses to change its strategy. As T1T already has a reasonable share of the market, the strategic choices it makes not only will affect them, but will have an impact on the market as well. T1T decides to move away from a high-touch business model for all customers. Consequently, it will supply local account management and live personal service for key accounts only. For other customer segments, the company will move to a self-service model where customers and candidates get access to the matching system themselves. For non-key customers, T1T will still offer a wide range of services for all areas of the business, thus retaining its business model of "one-stop shopping" for IT recruitment.

As long as the consulting activities are profitable and there are no drastic changes in volume, this objective should remain on the map. The revenue stream from maintaining a group of consultants should be retained. Given the lower service costs of the self-service model, it makes sense to continue providing and even expanding full-time and part-time contracts. Currently, T1T does not need to actively pursue acquiring a temp agency, another recruitment agency, or a training company. However, it is prudent to continue to monitor the mergers and acquisitions market in case good opportunities arise and the market conditions change again.

In the learning and growth area, T1T will continue to invest in developing IT domain expertise in its own staff. This expertise is needed to carry on improving the intelligence of the self-service matching system, from which customers and candidates will benefit. On a more strategic level, international investments will be rerouted to countries that may hold large outsourcing businesses. Attracting staff in these local communities will not only help grow business and revenue in the emerging economies, but also add to the intelligence of the self-service system.

The objective to provide six months of experience was not inserted in the synthesized strategy map as currently it is not needed and the program can always be started later. Although it makes sense in a number of scenarios (scenario 3 and, with hindsight, in scenario 1) to focus on being a trusted advisor, this path of thinking is not followed. Indeed, it does not fit the self-service model and local account management should already have that role in key accounts. Providing innovative services is also not on the strategy map anymore, because the self-service model has become the innovative model of choice.

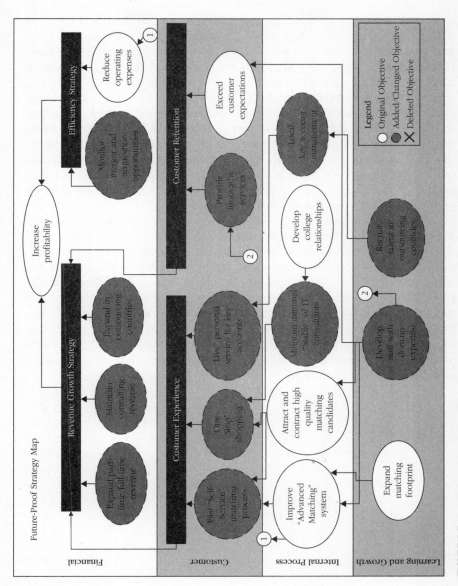

FIGURE 9.7 Synthesized Strategy Map

Figure 9.7 shows the effects of the new approach on the development of the strategy map. If we compare this new strategy map with the initial one (see Figure 9.4), a number of differences are evident. Based on the scenario-based strategy mapping exercise, T1T has effectively decided to change its strategy. Strategic uncertainty will always be present, and T1T's new strategy, although more future-proof, may not necessarily be *right*. However, the new strategy map has informed T1T's decisions on which strategic areas the company could invest in safely for the long term, and which options should be kept open.

Although intuitively our reaction would be to find ways to minimize that risk or uncertainty, risk is not necessarily a bad thing. In fact, uncertainty is the ultimate source of all value in business.[16] If there were no risk in business, how would an organization be able to outperform, say, putting the money in a savings account in the bank? Risk should not necessarily be minimized. The scenario-based strategy map shows how an options-based strategy can actually reconcile risk and performance.

Through the case of T1T, a large recruitment firm for people with technology skills, I have exemplified the development of a scenario-based strategy map. In this instance, it is clear how T1T could, and should, consider a suite of factors that may have a significant impact on the way the organization and its market operate. By considering three scenarios, T1T could modify its current strategy and prepare itself for possible future conditions. Differentiating among strategic imperatives, strategic options, and marginally relevant objectives (particularly in the light of future states), the organization could design a more future-proof strategy map. This could enable it to face strategic uncertainty in a more effective way and make it more sustainable in the longer term.

CHAPTER 10

Increasing the Stakes

*Like all organisms, the living company exists primarily for its own sur-
vival and improvement: to fulfill its potential and to become as great as
it can be.*

Arie de Geus, author of *The Living Company*

The goal of every organization is to sustain itself. And management
gurus all over the world have been looking for the elixir. Jim Collins
introduced the BHAGs (Big Hairy Audacious Goals) and Level 5 leadership.[1] Peters and Waterman introduced eight attributes, among which are a
bias for action, being close to the customer, and sticking to one's knitting.[2]
Another study[3] adds quality of management and employees, as well as a
long-term orientation and a focus on continuous improvement. One of my
own studies,[4] in 2005, showed that many disciplines were searching for
the high-performance organization, each from its own angle. Management
gurus would focus on leadership, customer relationship management evan-
gelists would focus on the customer, and HR specialists would emphasize
teamwork.

I have come to the conclusion that the key to sustainable success is the
ability to deal with dilemmas. Thinking about it, it is only logical. The two
corner pillars for dealing with dilemmas that I described in the book are
creating synthesis and *creating options*. Synthesis is the tool of innovation.
Most innovation comes from solving a contradiction.[5] Making something
light enough to be powerful *and* portable; making something safe *and* fast;
making something functional *and* easy to use—these are all examples of
synthesis. Innovation is a prerequisite (although not a guarantee) for a sustainable business. Creating options makes it possible for a company to adjust
when reality changes. It creates organizational agility. And according to
Darwin, the ones that adapt are the ones to survive.

Furthermore, the notion that dealing with dilemmas is key to sustainable success is supported by the most important themes of what is considered sustainability today: environmental concern and corporate social responsibility. The Brundtland Commission, also known as the World Commission on Environment and Development (WCED), defines *sustainability* this way: "Sustainable development is development that meets the needs of the present without compromising the ability of future generations to meet their own needs."[6]

The most common definitions of *corporate social responsibility* (CSR) come from the International Standards Organization (ISO) and from the European Union (EU). ISO defines CSR as "a balanced approach for organizations to address economic, social, and environmental issues in a way that aims to benefit people, community and society."[7] The European Union defines CSR as "a concept whereby firms integrate social and environmental concerns in business operations and in the interaction with their stakeholders on a voluntary basis."[8]

The ISO definition highlights the triumvirate of economic, social, and environmental issues, but focuses on benefiting not the organization itself, but people, community, and society. The EU explicitly mentions business operations, but fails to mention that CSR needs to be beneficial. My own definition of CSR is a combination of these two definitions:

> *Corporate social responsibility is a balanced approach for organizations to integrate social and environmental concerns in business operations in a way that aims to benefit the organization and its internal and external stakeholders.*

Although CSR is only one side of sustainability, and sustainability—as we will see—is much more than environmental protection, these definitions reveal something interesting. Meeting today's needs while protecting the needs of tomorrow is almost a literal translation of the now-or-later dilemma. And the definition of CSR highlights that it must benefit the organization as well as its stakeholders. That is a classic you-or-me dilemma.

Sustainability, therefore, is being able to deal with you and me, as well as now and later. As the goal of an organization is to sustain itself, the management needs to successfully deal with dilemmas.

The current focus of organizations on social and environmental issues as their interpretation of sustainability has its pluses and minuses. On the positive side, it shows that focusing on shareholder value only while ignoring other stakeholders leads to problems, and that a different approach is needed. On the flipside, as always in situations that are in the middle of the eye of ambiguity, opinions on what to think about it and how to tackle it vary widely,[i] clouding the bigger picture. Nobel Prize–winning economist Milton Friedman is quite clear in his opinion that the social responsibility of corporations is to maximize profits.[9] It is up to the shareholders to decide what to do with those returns. Then there are the proponents of corporate social responsibility as a goal in itself. In their view, organizations have a moral obligation to society. Environmentalists take this approach even further. Corporations need to invest in saving planet Earth, regardless of cost or loss of profit.

There are, it seems, two opposing schools of thought: those who feel CSR should not be part of a management agenda, and those who feel CSR is by default part of management's concern. However, those two sides can be synthesized. Peter Drucker starts out by stating that an organization is not entitled to put itself in the place of government or to use its economic power to impose its values on the community. But he also introduces an exception, which is when contributing to easing a social problem creates an opportunity for performance and results.[10] But Michael Porter takes the synthesis a lot further. Porter sharply analyzes the shortcomings of these opposite schools of thought because they focus on the tension between business and society rather than on their interdependence. Running a business does not preclude being a good citizen. In fact, these two objectives should be aligned. Being a leader in CSR, in Porter's view, is an opportunity to differentiate from the competition.[11] In our terms, CSR, which is about *you and me*, leads to a better competitive position, and a more favorable *now and then*.

However, given the current ways in which organizations, their hierarchy, and their strategic focus are structured, the odds are against an enlightened view. In the usual contrarian words of Henry Mintzberg, as early as 1983:

> *The economic goals plugged in at the top filter down through a rationally designed hierarchy of ends and means . . . [the] workers are impelled to put aside their personal goals and to do as they are told in return for remuneration. The system is overlaid with a hierarchy of authority supported by an extensive network of formal controls. . . . Now, what happens when the concept of social responsibility is introduced into all this? . . . Not much. The system is too tight.[12]*

---

[i]Discussion is based on F.A. Buytendijk, *Performance Leadership*, McGraw-Hill, 2008.

As I argued in Chapter 8, traditional management structures *create* strategic dilemmas.

So far, I have discussed dilemmas within the organization (intraorganizational). But based on the definition of sustainability, we need to expand our focus. We also need to manage stakeholders (of which social responsibility is one angle) and their conflicting requirements, in other words *interorganizational dilemmas*.

Interorganizational Dilemmas

Most studies define the high-performance organization as an organization that outperformed its industry peers for a number of years. This is very much in line with traditional organizational theory, with its focus on shareholder value. In the classical sense, an organization is defined as a group of people sharing the same goal. Here we look at sustainability from an ecosystem point of view. Organisms have a reciprocal relationship with their environment (they give and they receive) and this relationship is circular in nature (the more you receive, the more you can give, which leads to receiving more). This view requires a focus on stakeholder value.[13] From a stakeholder value perspective, an organization is defined as a unique collaboration of stakeholders who realize that they can reach their own goals only by working together. Stakeholder theory defines the role of management as balancing the fiduciary responsibility of looking after shareholders' interests with the competing interests of other stakeholders for the long-term survival of the corporation.[14]

Redefining the concept of the organization has become a necessity. Globalization and technology have had an extreme impact on the transaction costs organizations have in interacting with others. Today, in many cases it is much better, cheaper, and faster to outsource activities, compared to the quality, cost, and speed of internally coordinating those activities. Outsourcing comprises support functions such as facilitary services, finance, and IT, but also logistics, manufacturing, and increasingly even R&D. In fact, over the past 20 years, there are indications that the average size of organizations has been shrinking.[15] Business is not a hierarchy anymore, based on command and control, with a CEO at the top of the food chain deciding which direction to take. Business should be seen as a network of organizations that communicate, negotiate, and collaborate when discussing strategic direction. Organizations are part of an overall "performance network." A performance network recognizes all stakeholders in a value chain, and aligns their objectives in order to optimize the performance of the overall network, instead of the performance of each individual stakeholder.[16]

The majority of business decisions impacting your bottom line are actually made outside the walls of the organization itself, in the wider performance network. You need to take stakeholders into account as part of strategy management. This starts with asking the question, "What do my stakeholders contribute to my success?" This question leads to a much higher leverage; as we aim to reach our strategic goals, we are not alone anymore. This question can be asked only if the opposite question is asked as well: "And what do I contribute to the success of my stakeholders?" These questions are the key to the performance network.

A huge contribution in how to manage the performance network comes from a methodology called the *Performance Prism*.[17] One of the key messages of the Performance Prism is that stakeholders have requirements, and they offer contributions. The methodology describes in great detail, among other things, what stakeholders could (and perhaps should) expect from each other. With this in mind, it triggers the right strategic and planned discussion. The requirements of different stakeholders or the requirements between a single stakeholder and the organization may not align, may provide tension, and may even be conflicting. Without realizing this, we may act on wrong assumptions, or worse, be ignorant of these needs. By understanding these objectives, we can find a solution to reconcile these differences; this probably will lead to much smarter solutions than optimizing a single set of objectives. Figure 10.1 and Table 10.1 provide an overview of an organization's stakeholders and their needs, according to the Performance Prism.

Figure 10.1 clearly shows how customer/supplier relationships are the basis of all value creation in the performance network. The suppliers of the organization view the organization as a client, while the organization again has its own clients. Organizations are looking for profit, growth, opinion, and trust downstream the value chain, and for fast, cheap, and easy products and services upstream the value chain. Other stakeholders, such as employees, the community, regulators, and investors, supply the means to propel value creation, making it possible. Regulators ensure fair competition, the community provides a platform to work in, such as infrastructure, investors supply the necessary capital to operate, and employees provide the needed labor. With this view in mind, none of the stakeholders can be ignored as each represents a vital component in making the value chain flow smoothly.

Each stakeholder has different requirements, and sometimes they can be conflicting. Employees are looking to be treated with care, and view the organization as their main source of income. The organization is in need of dynamic capabilities and may be looking for ways to quickly shrink and expand the organization, based on the state of the economy. As described before, between customers and the organization there is the

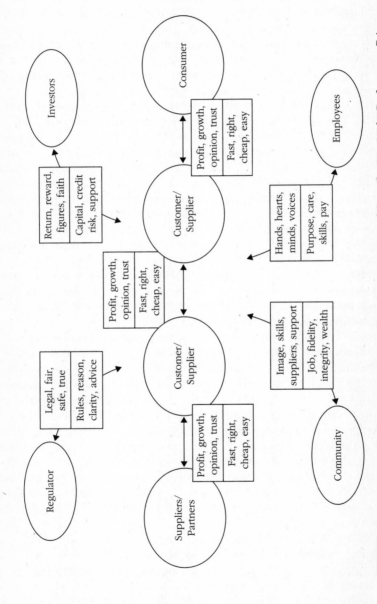

FIGURE 10.1 Graphical Representation of Stakeholder Requirements and Contributions in the Performance Prism

TABLE 10.1 Stakeholder Contributions and Requirements According to the Performance Prism

Organization Needs	Stakeholder Needs
. . . from investors	**Investors** need from the organization:
■ *Capital*, to operate and invest	■ *Return*, capital appreciation
■ *Credit*, facilities from banks	■ *Reward*, dividend
■ *Risk*, to be taken by investors	■ *Figures*, justification
■ *Support*, loyalty and advice	■ *Faith*, confidence in management team
. . . from customers	**Customers** need from the organization:
■ *Profit*, to sustain the business	■ *Fast*, rapid delivery
■ *Growth*, increase of sales	■ *Right*, high-quality products and services
■ *Opinion*, feedback on performance	
■ *Trust*, for repeat business	■ *Cheap*, reasonably priced
	■ *Easy*, no barriers to buy
. . . from employees	**Employees** need from the organization:
■ *Hands*, headcount, productivity	■ *Purpose*, support, direction
■ *Hearts*, loyalty, commitment	■ *Care*, respect, fair treatment
■ *Minds*, qualifications, teams	■ *Skills*, training, knowledge
■ *Voices*, suggestions, diversity	■ *Pay*, compensation package
. . . from suppliers	**Suppliers** need from the organization:
■ *Fast*, rapid delivery	■ *Profit*, to sustain their business
■ *Right*, high-quality products and services	■ *Growth*, increase of sales
	■ *Opinion*, feedback on performance
■ *Cheap*, reasonably priced	■ *Trust*, for repeat business
■ *Easy*, no barriers to buy	
. . . from regulators	**Regulators** want from the organization:
■ *Rules*, for fair competition	■ *Legal*, compliance to laws
■ *Reason*, sound purpose and reasonable to implement	■ *Fair*, no monopolistic or anticompetitive behaviors
■ *Clarity*, not ambiguity	■ *Safe*, no endangering society
■ *Advice*, on implementing rules	■ *True*, be open and honest
. . . from the community	**Communities** want from the organization:
■ *Image*, be viewed in a positive way	■ *Jobs*, regional employment
■ *Skills*, availability of workers	■ *Fidelity*, sustain and grow employment
■ *Suppliers*, local vendors for particular needs	■ *Integrity*, open, honest, responsible
■ *Support*, supportive of aims	■ *Wealth*, making the community healthy and prosperous

value-versus-profit dilemma, and the same is the case between suppliers and your organization (as you are the customer). Many sales-driven organizations wrestle with the trade-off between the direct and indirect channel, figuring how much to do themselves and how much to leave to partners. Further, in regulated industries, the regulators and the competitors in the market can live at odds with each other. Businesses are trying to compete and are looking to surprise their competitors, whereas the regulators value predictability the most.

There is an interesting dynamic between shareholders, the organization, and its other stakeholders. We may think there is no dilemma—after all, it is a common view that the goal of the organization is to maximize shareholder value. But shareholders, whether they are acting in the short or long term, are looking to maximize *their* returns, which is not necessarily the same as optimizing the performance of the organization. Further, in terms of the Performance Prism, shareholders, supplying capital, are only one necessary type of stakeholder. And if you follow the visualization in Figure 10.1, shareholders are not the central stakeholders in the performance network. In fact, optimization toward shareholder value *creates* stakeholder dilemmas, as their requirements are disregarded. Investors may press for short-term layoffs, whereas you know a brain-drain will cause issues in the longer term. Investors may focus on immediate improvement of working capital, leading to upsetting customers when collecting invoices is done in an overly aggressive manner. Investors may see corporate social responsibility as frivolous, whereas society sees it as mandatory. It is best if such dilemmas are solved. In order to have a sustainable business, one of the most important tasks of senior management is to reconcile the dilemmas between all relevant stakeholders—the interorganizational dilemmas.[ii]

How is this done? No differently than with the other you-and-me dilemmas we have discussed. First, the organization needs to examine its motives. What is it trying to achieve with a specific stakeholder relationship? Different relationships have different intensities. Some relationships are not very strategic, and there are low switching costs. Outsourcing certain forms of logistics, the cleaning service, or the cafeteria is a very transactional decision. Boiled down to its essence, it is "not being bothered too much" that drives the success of the relationship. One notch up, what we might expect from other business relationships is added value. We would

---

[ii]This does not mean that dealing with intraorganizational dilemmas is less important. If the internal organization keeps requiring all of management's attention, there is no time to focus on stakeholder management. And on a more strategic level, if your own organization is not healthy and transparent, how can you expect the same of your stakeholders?

like to establish an integrated supply chain with our preferred suppliers. We would like to get close to our customers. We would like to invest in employee education together with the unions. In these cases, switching costs are high. Finally, there are relationships based on co-innovation. Both parties go to market with a joint product or service. Our motives are to grow a business together. Problems and dilemmas arise when the parties do not have the same understanding of the relationship. Opening up to the unions to improve relationships can be a true dilemma if we expect to be treated transactionally in return. Suppliers may not be willing to invest in value chain integration if they believe it will only lead to more dependency and less of a negotiating position. Open and honest communication about both stakeholder contributions and requirements is needed. Then find ways to reconcile any differences that are found. Some retailers have insight into the margins of their suppliers, making sure the relationship stays profitable for both. Some car manufacturers have business improvement teams that suppliers can use to lower their costs. Both suppliers and manufacturer benefit. Some oil companies have established activist group boards in which they actively seek the opinion and advice of pressure groups.

Executive View

The biggest dilemma Global Soft Commodities Singapore (GSCS) has been facing is how to grow the company over the long term while keeping the shareholders happy in the short term. There are multiple ways of growing. It is possible to seek additional market share for the products the company is active in within existing markets, for instance, seeking volume expansion in a soft commodity such as coffee. Another growth option is in moving into new product categories or into new markets, and the company has done so as well. The company's growth is plotted with care. It does not shy away for more risky investments, but always starts small. When an investment turns out to be successful, the company is geared toward scaling it fast.

The dilemma is not in new products and in new markets; rather it has been in deciding to expand its footprint in the supply chain. This means growing from being merely a trade company focused on logistics, to becoming a company that is also growing and harvesting soft commodities, processing them, and even marketing the products. How will customers that have traditionally been in the business of

(continued)

(continued)

adding value to the soft commodities take that? Will they start seeing GSCS as a competitor, if GSCS starts adding value by processing the products itself? And what about large suppliers that grow the soft commodities? At what point will they start to see GSCS as a competitor? Would GSCS have the size and the power in the value chain to create this space for itself?

The keys to finding the solution to this you-and-me dilemma are communication, and not jeopardizing the customer relationship. For instance, GSCS has been offering these added services only to private labels, avoiding direct competition with the company's current customers. Perhaps the most important element in this communication, and in the way the expansion is executed, is addressing the "What's in it for them?" question—reframing the company's growth plans into customers' and suppliers' benefits.

For instance, there are benefits to building experience with processing and other value-added services, and also for GSCS's customers. It teaches GSCS about the challenges its customers have first hand. With this experience, the company can improve its traditional logistical services to large customers, offering better integration with its customers' operations. This should be more than just marketing; changes and improvements in the business should actively reflect these lessons learned, and there should be a clear cost, quality, and/or speed advantage for customers. The intention to build an even better customer relationship needs to be authentic—it has to be real. It is particularly strengthening the customer value proposition that reconciles the competitor/customer relationship dilemma. Anything else will pose a long-term threat to the business's health.

Building a supplier proposition might sound odd at first. After all, they are the suppliers, and they should build an attractive proposition. However, this works only in transactional relationships, not in the case of GSCS, which takes responsibility of the complete supply chain. The experience built with growing and harvesting soft commodities can be used to help suppliers improve their operations as well. This in turn benefits GSCS.

Growing the footprint in the integrated supply chain does not necessarily mean displacing other stakeholders. In fact, it could (and should) strengthen existing relationships. GSCS implements a philosophy in which everyone wins.

The Performance Prism helps us define those reciprocal relationships, and even guides us in telling how to manage those relationships. However, one thing is missing: It does not help us solve stakeholder dilemmas. The Performance Prism merely states the themes that need to be managed. To successfully reconcile conflicting requirements between the organization and its stakeholders, and among stakeholders surrounding the organization, we need to align the different value propositions.

Stakeholder Alignment Map

Strategy is the glue that aims to build and deliver a consistent and distinctive value proposition to your target market.[18] A value proposition is "what we promise to do for you." Stakeholder alignment could be defined as the common understanding of a value proposition. The moment there is no common understanding of that purpose, the stakeholder relationships and consequently the long-term success of the organization are in danger. It is the task of each organization to manage its stakeholder relationships and the alignment of the value proposition.

Kim and Mauborgne argue for the alignment of three value propositions.[19] They state that "a strategy's success hinges on the development and alignment of three propositions: (1) a value proposition that attracts buyers; (2) a profit proposition that enables the company to make money out of the value proposition; and (3) a people proposition that motivates those working for or with the company to execute the strategy." Why not extend the concept of the value proposition to all stakeholders? The promise of what to achieve for investors is commonly known as the *investor value proposition* (which is different from a *profit proposition*, as this serves the organization itself). A less commonly accepted term would be a *supplier value proposition*, stating what the organization promises to achieve for its suppliers. This may seem strange at first. They are suppliers; what they require is being paid on time. What else is there to it? However, there is logic in this concept. If an organization requires the contribution of its suppliers in order to live up to the customer value proposition, it needs to reciprocate. Unless the switching cost to another supplier is negligible, firms need to mind the requirements of the supplier for sustainable success.

The value propositions to all stakeholders need to align. In a transparent world, promising customers to be reliable while at the same time treating suppliers badly impacts the firm's image and authenticity.[20] Promising the shareholders high returns while the margin on the core business does not support that leads to dysfunctional organizational behavior. Many of the corporate scandals in the early 2000s and business failures in the economic crisis of the late 2000s were caused by putting more emphasis on using the company as an instrument of the stock market and making money there, instead of minding the core business. Think of the super-market chain that treated its operating companies as cash cows to finance even more acquisitions, or the car manufacturer that made more money trading shares of a competitor in pursuit of acquiring that company than the profit from actual car sales.

To see how a stakeholder alignment map could look and how it is built, let us consider an example of a food processing firm. Let us assume its value proposition is very customer-centric, to avoid commodization. Many food processing firms employ food technologists to work with customers to ensure the best use of the products. At the same time, utmost attention is paid to the consistent quality of products. In other words, its customer value proposition is being a safe bet for its customers. See Figure 10.2.

However, organizations should realize their value is broader than their customer value proposition. Companies for instance also have a *supplier* value proposition, what its promise is to its customers. In the example of the food processing company, it should pay a fair price to its suppliers, and it should pay in time, but more is possible. Some firms in the agri-cultural/foods markets are known to help their suppliers (farmers) when there are crop issues due to unforeseen weather circumstances. This can be financial aid or to provide other services, helping farmers improve productivity and efficiency[iii]. This supplier value proposition can be sum-marized as being a safe bet. See Figure 10.3.

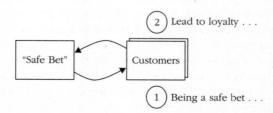

FIGURE 10.2 Stakeholder Alignment Map, Customer Value Proposition

---

[iii]In Germany, some agricultural and community banks are known to even organize farmer's markets to support local communities and the local economy. There is no clear difference between customer and supplier value proposition, the bank offers community value.

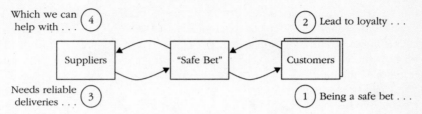

FIGURE 10.3 Stakeholder Alignment Map, Supplier Value Proposition

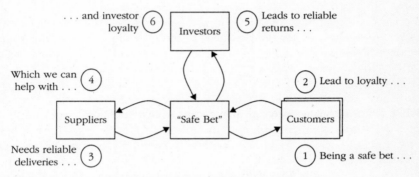

FIGURE 10.4 Stakeholder Alignment Map, Investor Value Proposition

The investor value proposition usually is very straightforward, to provide a competitive shareholder return. The returns of the food processing company may not be as high as in other industries, but instead they may be relatively stable. In other words, they could be a safe bet in the portfolio of investors. See Figure 10.4.

Companies are part of society as well. They need to show they are responsible citizens. By for instance investing in green technology, encouraging suppliers to do the same, and through products making customers greener, companies can create a high level of societal approval. This creates more stability, which is appreciated by investors and customers. See Figure 10.5.

Also, regulators should be considered. As our food processing company is in control of its value chain, does not have a lot of volatility coming from investors and shareholders, and treats its environment with care, it will not easily get the regulators on its back. This leads to a consistent press and image, which is appreciated by customers, suppliers, investors, and society. See Figure 10.6.

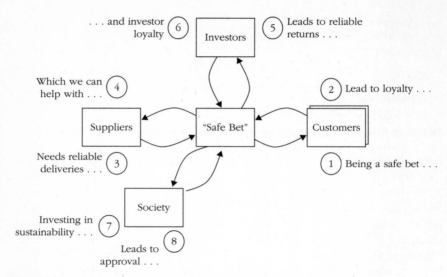

FIGURE 10.5 Stakeholder Alignment Map, Society Value Proposition

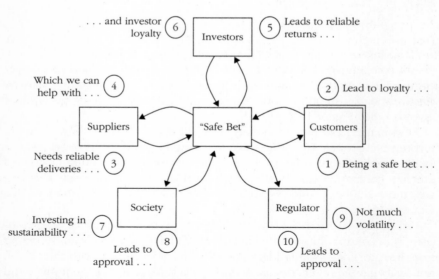

FIGURE 10.6 Stakeholder Alignment Map, Regulator Value Proposition

Conclusion

It seems a tall order, not only stretching intraorganizational dilemmas, but also managing all stakeholder contributions and requirements. You probably have your hands full managing your own organization as it is. How can all this be managed at the same time? The reality is that there is no such thing as a perfect world. I do not believe in guaranteed sustainability, or being a high-performance organization as a final stage in an organization's maturity. Again, organizations are like living organisms. They strive for survival, but it is a constant struggle. The moment you focus on investors, there is the risk of taking your eyes off the customers. Investments in process improvement may shift your attention away from innovation. Managing company performance means working in a constantly changing dynamic. You need to keep your options open, as the environment changes. By keeping your options open, change becomes a natural flow. Change is not a process that costs energy and disrupts operations. In fact, it is the other way around: Change is a process that brings energy into the company, because of positive stakeholder interactions and constant reconfirmation. And it is disruption of processes that actually brings change.

By seeking stakeholder alignment, you create synthesis. Our example shows that improvements start to have multiple effects. For instance, improving supplier relationships also improves customer relationships, investor relationships, and all other stakeholder relationships. Synthesis is the process of taking two or more ideas and morphing them into one. That means not only one thing less to manage, but creating a flywheel, a fundamental step forward in improving business performance.

As promised in the Preface, *creating options* and *seeking synthesis* are the two keys to dealing with dilemmas. And I believe that dealing with dilemmas is the key to driving an organization's sustainable performance.

CHAPTER 11

Closing Thoughts

You can't have your cake and eat it, too.

I have never understood this expression. Why can't I have my cake and it eat, too? Isn't that the whole point of cake, to be able to eat it? In this book I have described multiple ways of having your cake and eating it, too. I have shown that dilemmas are nothing to be afraid of. They are there, whether you deal with them or not. Given that reality, it is better to confront them.

How do we do this? Unfortunately, management theory can be truly confusing. Management is not like physics, where a single theory describes reality until it is proven wrong and substituted with a better theory. Management is part of the social sciences, where multiple conflicting and even contradicting theories can perfectly well coexist. For every study that says that innovation should be kept separate from the day-to-day business, there is another one that proposes combining the two. Leading academics claim that pure strategies are the best, yet other research suggests hybrid strategies perform much better. The reason is that we cannot control the circumstances, like we do in physics. There is no such thing as a true management laboratory in the real world.

You could actually call this the *theory dilemma*. If you believe a theory, and you know there are competing theories, you could pick the wrong one and fail. If you do not subscribe to a certain way of thinking and do a little of everything, you may not be able to focus and could fail as well. However, the theory dilemma actually is good news. It does not invalidate strategy management. In fact, it is the ultimate validation: It forces you to think. The more you are confronted with competing theories and conflicting advice, the more you can be convinced you have found a dilemma. You are in the eye of ambiguity. This makes you understand the true fundamental management problem: strategic uncertainty. You cannot predict the future and you cannot fully control your environment; the only thing you can do is be ready. And if you are really good, you can shape the future and your environment—a bit. In order to do this, you need to remove two important constraints. One is using the traditional vertical management structure for decision making as well. It actually creates dilemmas as it drives people to take a position based on the solution they see for their side of the problem. Strategic decision making should be a *multidimensional* exercise, exploring all intra- and extra-organizational angles. The second is the classical understanding of what strategy actually is. Thinking of strategy as making those big choices leads to dilemmas, too. Strategy should be seen as a *continuous process* to create and exercise options.

Meta-Synthesis

I started this book by arguing that we analyze too much. You could see *analysis* as the thesis that is currently reigning in the world of management. Am I opposing analysis? Absolutely not; not all problems are dilemmas, and proper analysis solves problems before they become dilemmas. This book itself is full of analysis—all the survey analysis, the concept of scenario planning, the conflict resolution diagrams, and so forth.

But there is more than analysis. The opposite of analysis, *synthesis*, perhaps acts as the antithesis to analysis. Synthesis helps us to think outside the box in as structured a manner as analysis does. Synthetic thinking provides a chance of reconciling the opposites of a dilemma, and a great way to truly advance instead of letting the pendulum swing back and forth.

So, if analysis is the *thesis*, and synthesis is the *antithesis*, there must be a *meta-synthesis*[i] that brings analysis and synthesis together. You cannot successfully create synthesis without analysis. In many cases, synthesis comes through deconstructing the opposing sides of a dilemma and reconstructing a new reality. This is what the conflict resolution diagrams do. Deconstruction is analysis.

There is a time for everything. In discussing S-curves, I focused on the eye of ambiguity. But a large part of the S-curve obviously consists of growth within the curve. Sometimes that growth can even be exponential. Being on top of what is happening, creating insight that is deeper than that of the competition, and the ability to act on that are crucial for an organization's

---

[i] Don't worry, read the sentence twice. When I came up with the concept of meta-synthesis I knew it was time to stop writing, before I would completely detach myself from planet Earth.

survival. Analysis is the main toolkit. And there is a time when it is necessary to reconfigure, and move to another S-curve, another strategy, another way of working. In those cases, synthesis is the way to go. This is how I see it: Strategy is like a Chinese puzzle, a *tangram* that consists of seven pieces that can form many different puzzles. Sometimes the puzzle stays as it is for a while, and sometimes it is necessary to put together a new puzzle.

Relationships, Human Behavior, and Culture

Although the book is full of strategy and management methodology, in the end I think I have written a book about relationships, about human behavior, and about culture. Consider being a soldier in the army. By military law, you are required to follow orders. But you cannot hide behind just following orders if that means breaking the law. How does one deal with such a fundamental dilemma? Soldiers need to invest time in getting to know their commander. If you truly know your supervising officer and he is behaving in an unusual manner, this is a warning sign to double check orders, or to involve others. Likewise, the commanding officer needs to invest time in his troops, so that they can truly trust him. The officer should be open, should be known and understood by his people. In well-functioning relationships, you can distinguish between following the right order and following the wrong order.

Independently of each other, Heidi Melin (CMO Polycom), Publishing Corp.'s CIO, and Bill Fitzsimmons (CAO Cox Communications) stress the need to build relationships and trust, something that requires time to do. Without trust, it is not possible to reconcile dilemmas. It is not a coincidence that this insight comes from these executives. Finance, IT, and marketing are each supporting functions that need to work with the conflicting requirements of different stakeholders within the company on a daily basis.

Executive View

In order to be successful, organizations need to be profitable and have an appropriate market share. The "profit and market share" of a political party can be translated into being reelected. This means listening very carefully to what the voters have to say. At the same time, the fundamental goal of decision making in politics is to improve conditions in society in general. This does not always entail

(continued)

(continued)

making popular decisions, or producing results in the short term that will be beneficial in the next elections. There are many decisions, for instance, involving special taxes, or public health, or anything else that is considered restrictive, that serve the greater good. This perhaps is the most important political dilemma.

The way to deal with it is to see the party not as a goal in itself (to build the biggest party), but as a means to govern the country in a better way. A political party is not a static construct, but a dynamic organism consisting of many politically engaged people. The political party connects the government to the grassroots of society, the individual voters. An effective political decision-making process mobilizes the political party to create a basis for the decisions to be made. Top down and bottom up do not have to be contradictory forces. General directions and preliminary decisions can be set from the top, but to create voter buy-in, the next step, translating the guidelines into concrete measures, can be tasked to the communities. These can be lower levels of government as well as the various segments of the party. Successfully engaging people requires strong leadership. And as with all leadership matters, results come from building relationships and building trust over time.

How you deal with dilemmas has a lot to do with behavior as well. Dilemmas are very self-confrontational. It often makes more sense to examine your own intentions and assumptions than to try to analyze the options on the table. It is a deep human emotion to want to be perceived as nice, making it hard to fire a nonfunctioning person. But is it truly nice not to give honest feedback, and not to allow the person to move on? And is it nice to all other colleagues, whose productivity and success is held back by this one dysfunctional person? "Being nice" sometimes needs to be redefined to align with doing the right thing. Understanding your environment starts with a strong understanding of yourself.

This is also a book about culture. I have tried to pay tribute to fusing Eastern and Western thinking. In the West, we should try to better understand the Eastern sense of ambiguity, instead of jumping to the easiest and fastest solution. Taoism and Confucianism embrace ambiguity and define what is good or bad based not on the facts that occur but on their context, which may change. The Eastern style of thinking could learn from the Western style, which is based on the more aggressive Hegelian approach—to seek synthesis and move forward instead of trying to preserve the ways of the past.

All of these management techniques and logical thinking aside, dealing with dilemmas requires creativity. The best example I know actually comes from *Star Trek*, in a story about the Kobayashi Maru. The Kobayashi Maru is a spaceship that features in a computer simulation for young cadets at the academy. Cadets taking the test are confronted with a distress signal from another ship. It is in trouble and is asking for help. The problem is that the ship is marooned amid enemy territory. Will you save the ship and risk an interplanetary war, or will you simply let the crew of the ship die? This is a true dilemma; the simulation represents a no-win situation—there is no way out. Its purpose is merely to test how cadets treat the dilemma. James T. Kirk, a young cadet, achieves the impossible after failing the test a few times, and finds a way out. Kirk hacks the computer program and alters the simulation. His defense: I cheated the simulation because the simulation cheated me.

Kirk showed true out-of-the-box thinking, looking beyond the obvious and immediate solutions. We need more of that. In Chapter 1, I criticized the popular management yell, "If you are not part of the solution, then you are part of the problem." Well, if I really must choose between the two,[ii] I would choose to be part of the problem every day of the week.

[ii]Then again, why should one choose? That is a sucker's dilemma. The way out is simple: Truly understanding the problem you are dealing with means you are halfway toward finding a solution. This book has shown you how.

APPENDIX

Company Profiles

This appendix contains a short description of each company that appears in the executive overviews of the book, as well as short introductions of the interviewed executives.

Achmea (Europe)

Achmea is part of Eureko, a leading European conglomerate in financial services. Eureko is the holding company for a group of strong insurance brands in 11 countries: Belgium, Bulgaria, Cyprus, France, Greece, Ireland, the Netherlands, Romania, Slovakia, Turkey, and, since 2008, Russia. Eureko is a cooperative organization. As a result, the company's mindset is a balanced stakeholder approach, rather than a focus primarily on shareholders. Eureko's goal is to create value for all its equally important stakeholders: customers, distribution partners, shareholders, and employees. Eureko's core business is insurance—life, non-life, and health—and services relating to pensions and health. Eureko has over 10 billion euro revenue, and has close to 24,000 employees.

Jeroen van Breda Vriesman, member of the board of Achmea, held various positions in financial services before being appointed chairman of Division Occupational Health in 2004. He became chairman of Division Achmea Health in 2006. As of October 2008, he became a member of the Executive Board of Eureko. His core responsibilities include Health, Life & Pensions and Group Information Management & Technology.

Cox Communications (United States)

With more than 6 million customers and nearly 21,000 employees, Cox Communications is the third-largest cable entertainment and broadband services provider in the United States. It is part of Cox Enterprises, founded in 1898 by James M. Cox, who served three terms as governor of Ohio and eventually ran in the 1920 U.S. presidential election as the Democratic Party nominee. In that same year, Gov. Cox purchased his first newspaper, the Dayton (OH) *Evening News*—the first step in creating the company that is Cox Enterprises today—a company with extensive interests in newspapers, television, radio, and automobile auctions and broadband residential and commercial services. The company proudly emphasizes its focus on customer care, which has led to industry accolades in customer satisfaction. Cox Communications is the only communications company to win top satisfaction honors in video, Internet, phone, and business categories.

William (Bill) J. Fitzsimmons is chief accounting officer of Cox Communications Inc. Fitzsimmons is responsible for overseeing all aspects of accounting and financial planning, including accounts payable, property, financial systems, general ledger, tax, budgeting and forecasting, internal reporting and analysis, program cost accounting, and payroll tax reporting. Since joining Cox in 1993, Mr. Fitzsimmons has built extensive experience with the company, both in the field and on the corporate level.

Global Soft Commodities Singapore (Anonymized, Singapore)

Global Soft Commodities Singapore (GSCS) has been in business since 1989. With more than 8,000 employees worldwide, the company operates an integrated supply chain for 20 products in over 60 countries worldwide, delivering these products to over 4,500 customers in over 60 destination markets. The soft commodities in which the company trades include wood, rice, cotton, coffee, cashew, and others. The integrated supply chain is managed from origination to processing, logistics, marketing, and distribution. This allows GSCS to achieve operational efficiencies, add value, and manage the various risks along the entire supply chain, enabling the company to appropriate the margins that exist in each part of the supply chain.

The COO is responsible for finance, the products portfolio, and a number of the regions in which the company is active.

Publishing Corp. (Anonymized, English-Speaking Country)

Publishing Corp. is the largest publishing group in one of the English-speaking countries. The group has interests in newspapers, magazines, Internet businesses, book publishing, printing plants, and distribution companies. Millions of its magazines are sold on a monthly basis. Publishing Corp.'s Internet business reaches more than half of the country's online population. Publishing Corp. currently publishes more than 60 magazine titles, and has licensing agreements with international titles. The company's roots go back to the early twentieth century.

The company's CIO started out as a practicing engineer before he moved into the world of IT. He has kept his academic involvement alive as a part-time lecturer.

National Central Bank (Anonymized, Europe)

Central banks are responsible for safeguarding financial stability. This central bank in one of the European countries (which I refer to as *NCB*, for *National Central Bank*, to distinguish it from the European Central Bank) has a broad set of responsibilities. First, its monetary policy is aimed at creating price stability. In cooperation with all other central banks, and the European Central Bank, inflation is controlled through the interest rates. NCB also exercises oversight of all payment systems in the country, and is responsible for the circulation of cash. NCB is also responsible for the prudential supervision of the country's banks. Finally, NCB acts as an advisor to the national government on monetary policy and on other social and economic matters.

After a career in academia, the official I interviewed has had multiple roles in NCB for the past ten years. Currently, he is responsible for macroprudential analysis, evaluating the health, soundness, and vulnerabilities of the country's financial system, for instance, by performing stress tests and scenario analysis. He characterizes NCB as a nuclear plant and a university within the same building. Payment systems operations can be compared to the nuclear plant. Absolutely no errors are permitted in managing the flow of cash money, from printing the money, to regulating its circulation, to the destruction of it at the end of its lifecycle. At the same time, NCB needs to be open. It is of paramount importance that decisions are not based on perceived wisdom, but are open to challenge. In this respect, the environment is more academic in nature. Moreover, for any regulator to remain healthy, there needs to be some degree of transparency that allows criticism. As a consequence, NCB's researchers are allowed to publish all their research, and cooperation with academia is strongly encouraged.

Novozymes (Denmark)

Novozymes is the world leader in bioinnovation, holding more than 6,000 patents. It has been in business since 1939, for many years as a division in a larger company focusing on producing insulin. Following an IPO and demerger in 2000, the company today successfully produces industrial enzymes, microorganisms, and biopharmaceutical ingredients. Enzymes are proteins that are naturally found in all living organisms and act as catalysts in transforming one substance into another, for instance, in breaking down waste. Proteins created by fermenting microorganisms or animal cells provide ingredients for medication produced by the biopharmaceutical industry. In 2008, Novozymes, headquartered in Denmark, reported 8,146 million Danish kroner revenue, which is over U.S.$1.5 billion. With more than 5,000 employees worldwide, the company offers more than 700 products sold in 130 countries.

Most members of the executive team, led by CEO Steen Riisgaard, have a tenure of more than 20 years, and the average staff tenure within the company is 10 years. Other characteristics that would define Novozymes' culture are being very collaborative and group and relationship oriented, and a "no-BS" attitude. You have to know your stuff in order to be taken seriously.

Polycom (United States)

Polycom is the global leader in telepresence, video, and voice solutions. Voice solutions and videoconferencing systems include equipment for audio conferences, ranging from the desktop to the conference room, to enable more productive meetings and allow people to collaborate over large distances. Telepresence solutions represent the top of the range, providing what Polycom calls the "RealPresence Experience," with a natural, "across-the-table" experience where every meeting participant is shown in true-to-life dimensions—just as if you were all in the same room. Polycom, founded in 1990 and having gone public in 1996, has more than 2,500 employees worldwide and revenues of over $1 billion. With Polycom technology, customers can save significantly on travel costs, lower their carbon footprint, and enable global collaboration.

Heidi Melin joined Polycom in September 2007 as senior vice president and chief marketing officer. She is responsible for Polycom's marketing strategy, which includes global branding and corporate identity, field and channel marketing, corporate communications, analyst relations, enterprise solutions, demand generation, and events.

Vopak (Netherlands)

Vopak's history goes back to 1616, when the world-renowned Dutch East Indies Company was flourishing, bringing in coffee, tea, and spices from the Far East and making the Netherlands a rich and powerful nation. The speed of its growth necessitated smooth and effective transshipment and storage infrastructures at the Dutch harbors. Groups of weigh-house porters joined forces to offer the necessary services, including weighing, sorting, and storage. Today, Vopak is the world's largest provider of conditioned storage facilities for bulk liquids. Through 79 terminals in 31 countries, the company covers the world's major shipping lanes for oil products, petrochemicals, biofuels, vegetable oils, and liquefied natural gas. Vopak employs more than 3,500 people, and its revenue for 2008 was €923.5 million.

Jack de Kreij is a member of the executive board since 2003 and the company's chief financial officer. As a former partner at PwC, he specializes in mergers and acquisitions. Ton van Dijk is Vopak's chief information officer. He is an expert in IT architecture and governance and a specialist in lean process improvement.

Dick Berlijn (Netherlands)

General D.L. (Dick) Berlijn began his military career in 1969 at the Royal Military Academy in Breda. In 1973, he began his military pilot training in Canada, where he received his wings in 1975. He then did his conversion training for the NF-5 at Twenthe Air Base in the Netherlands. In 1976, he transferred to Leeuwarden Air Base for conversion to the F-104 Starfighter. He later trained as a weapons instructor. In 1981, he received conversion training for the F-16. From 1983 to 1985, he was operations officer and then commander of the Transition and Conversion Division at Leeuwarden Air Base. In 1986, as a member of the "Ready Team," he monitored 315 Squadron's conversion from the NF-5 to the F-16. In 1987, he was supervisor of the multinational Fighter Weapon Instruction Training (FWIT) in Denmark, a specialist weapon training course for experienced fighter pilots. In 1988, he was stationed at the Tactical Air Command, as head of the Fighter Weapon Branch. From 1989 to 1991, he attended the Advanced Staff Course at the Air Force Staff College. This was followed by a post as head of the Operations and Training Section at the Royal Netherlands Air Force Staff. From August 1992, he was chief of flying operations at Twenthe Air Base. In that capacity, he was tasked with the air base's operational preparations for Operation Deny Flight. From April to October 1993, he was commander of the first F-16 detachment deployed to Italy. In 1994, he became head of the Fighter Operations Division, and then in 1995, deputy chief (Operations) of the Royal Netherlands Air Staff, holding the rank of Air Commodore. In 1997, as deputy chief (Operations) of the Defense Staff, his tasks included heading the Defense Crisis Management Centre. In November 1998, he was appointed commander of the Tactical Air Force, ranked as Major General. On March 24, 2000, he was appointed commander-in-chief of the Royal Netherlands Air Force and on June 24,

2004 he took over as chief of the Defense Staff, and was promoted to general. In 2005 General Berlijn became the First Commander of the Dutch Armed Forces. Currently, Mr. Berlijn holds the position of Senior Board Advisor at Deloitte Consulting, specialized in safety, strategy, and international collaboration.

Decorations

- Orde van Oranje Nassau (Degree of Commander)
- Legion of Merit (Degree of Commander), awarded by the U.S. Secretary of Defense
- Légion d'honneur (Degree of Commander), awarded by the President of the République Française
- Officers' long service medal (25 years)
- NATO Medal (110397)
- Multinational Peace Operations Commemorative Medal, Operation Deny Flight, former Yugoslavia (281093)

Nirmal Singh Hansra (Australia)

Nirmal Singh Hansra, based in Australia, has more than 35 years of experience as a chief financial officer and finance director in various business functions, including R&D, manufacturing, sales and marketing, distribution, and services, across varied industries: IT&T, FMCG, Chemicals, Pharmaceutical, Retail, Agriculture, and Rental Financing. The companies he has worked with and for have operations in Australia, New Zealand, India, Malaysia, Singapore, Japan, South and East Africa, the United Kingdom, and North America. Mr. Hansra has significantly contributed to M&A activity, including preparation of bidders/target statements, cost synergy assessment, business restructure and change management, board response committees, and so on. Today, Mr. Hansra is a business advisor for various firms at the board and executive management level, covering financial and strategic business management as well as setting up or improving performance of audit, investment, and remuneration board committees.

Dr. Edmund Stoiber (Germany)

Dr. Edmund Stoiber is former minister-president of the state of Bavaria, Germany, and former chairman of the German political party, Christian Social Union (CSU).

In 1978, Dr. Stoiber was elected secretary general of the CSU, a post he held until 1982–1983. From 1982 to 1986, he served as Bavarian secretary of state, and then as minister of state until 1988. From 1988 to 1993, he served as minister of the interior in Bavaria. In May 1993, the Bavarian *Landtag* (parliament) elected him as minister-president, a role he would fill until 2007. Currently, Dr. Stoiber is the honorary chairman of the CSU, and chairman of the High Level Expert Group on Administrative Burdens of the European Union. As a keen football (soccer) fan, Dr. Stoiber also serves as co-chairman on the Advisory Council of FC Bayern Munich.

Notes

Chapter 1

1. Takeuchi, H., Osono, E., Shimizu, N., June 2008, "The Contradictions That Drive Toyota's Success," *Harvard Business Review*.
2. Heller, J., 1961, *Catch-22*, Simon & Schuster.
3. Rapoport, A., Chammah, A.M., 1965, *Prisoner's Dilemma: A Study in Conflict and Cooperation*, The University of Michigan Press.
4. Patterson, K., Grenny, J., McMillan, R., Switzler, A., 2002, *Crucial Conversations: Tools for Talking When Stakes Are High*, McGraw-Hill.
5. Kim, Y.S., 2000, *The Natural Philosophy of Chu Hsi (1130–1200)*, Diane Publishing.
6. Seeskin, K., 1987, *Dialogue and Discovery: A Study in Socratic Method*, SUNY Press.
7. Mintzberg, H., 2009, *Managing*, Berrett Koehler.
8. Trompenaars, F., 2003, *Did the Pedestrian Die?*, Capstone.
9. Collins, J.C., Porras, J.I., 1994, *Built to Last*, HarperCollins.

Chapter 2

1. Kaplan R.S., Norton, D.P. 2000, "Having Trouble with Your Strategy? Then Map It," *Harvard Business Review*.
2. Foss, N., 1997, *Resources, Firms, and Strategies: A Reader in the Resource-based Perspective*. Oxford University Press, UK.
3. Drucker, P., September–October 1994, "The Theory of the Business," *Harvard Business Review*.
4. Mintzberg, H., June 1987, "The Strategy Concept: Five Ps for Strategy," *California Management Review*.
5. Porter, M.E., November–December 1996, "What Is Strategy?," *Harvard Business Review*.
6. Bryan, L.L., 2002, *Just-in-Time Strategy for a Turbulent World*, www.mckinseyquarterly.com.
7. Raynor, M.E., 2007, *Strategy Paradox: Why Committing to Success Leads to Failure*, Broadway Business.

8. Trigeorgis, L, 1999, *Real Options and Business Strategy*, Risk Publications, UK.
9. Steen, J., March 1961, "*PS* Puzzlers," *Popular Science*.
10. Wit, B. de, Meyer, R., 2004, *Strategy: Process, Content, Context: An International Perspective*, South-Western College Publications.
11. Porter, M.E., 1980, *Competitive Strategy*, Free Press.
12. Treacy, M., Wiersema, F., 1994, *The Discipline of Market Leaders*, Addison-Wesley.
13. Kim, W.C., Mauborgne, R., 2005, *Blue Ocean Strategy: How to Create Uncontested Market Space and Make Competition Irrelevant*, Harvard Business Press.
14. Mintzberg, H., Lampel, J., Ahlstrand, B., 1998, *Strategy Safari: A Guided Tour through the Wilds of Strategy Management*, Free Press.
15. Porter, M., January 2008, "The Five Competitive Forces that Shape Strategy," *Harvard Business Review*.
16. Walton, M., 1998, *The Deming Management Method*, Perigee Books.
17. Buytendijk, F.A., 2008, *Performance Leadership*, McGraw-Hill.
18. Andel, P. van, 45/1994, "Anatomy of the Unsought Finding. Serendipity: Origin, History, Domains, Traditions, Appearances, Patterns and Programmability," *British Journal for the Philosophy of Science*, UK.
19. Heyden, K. van der, 1996, *Scenarios: The Art of Strategic Conversation*, John Wiley & Sons.
20. Davenport, T.H., Harris, J.G., 2007, *Competing on Analytics: The New Science of Winning*, Harvard Business Press.
21. Lovallo, D.P., Mendonca, L.T., 2007, *Strategy's Strategist, An Interview with Richard Rumelt*, www.mckinseyquarterly.com.
22. Prahalad, C.K., Hamel, G., 1996, *Competing for the Future*, Harvard Business Press.

Chapter 3

1. Kaplan, R.S., Norton, D.P., 1996, *Balanced Scorecard: Translating Strategy into Action*, Harvard Business Press.
2. Bible, L., Kerr, S., Zanini, M., Summer 2006, "The Balanced Scorecard: Here and Back," *Management Accounting Quarterly*.
3. Lawson, R., Hatch, T., Desroches, D., 2007, *Scorecard Best Practices: Design, Implementation, and Evaluation*, John Wiley & Sons.
4. Kaplan, R.S., Norton, D.L., 2000, *Strategy Focused Organization*, Harvard Business Press.
5. Kaplan, R.S., Norton, D.P., 2004, *Strategy Maps: Converting Intangible Assets into Tangible Outcomes*, Harvard Business Press.
6. Buytendijk, F., Hatch, T., Micheli, P., 2009, *Scenario-Based Strategy Maps*, Academy of Management, Chicago.
7. Christensen, C., 1997, *The Innovators Dilemma*, Harvard Business School Press.
8. Schumpeter, J., 1942, *Capitalism, Socialism and Democracy*, Allen & Unwin, UK.
9. Foster, R., Kaplan, S., 2001, *Creative Destruction: Why Companies That Are Built to Last Underperform the Market—and How to Successfully Transform Them*, Doubleday.
10. O'Reilly, C., Tushman, M., April 2004, "The Ambidextrous Organization," *Harvard Business Review*.

11. Atrill, P., 2003, *Financial Management for Non-Specialists*, Prentice Hall, London.
12. Douma, S., Schreuder, H., 2002, "Economic Approaches to Organizations," *Financial Times*, UK.
13. Hansen, S.C., Torok, R.G., 2004, *The Closed Loop: Implementing Activity-Based Planning and Budgeting*, CAM-I and Bookman Publishing.
14. Sull, D., February 2009, "How to Thrive in Turbulent Markets," *Harvard Business Review*.
15. Abernathy, W. J., 1978, *The Productivity Dilemma: Roadblock to Innovation in the Automobile Industry*, Johns Hopkins University Press.
16. March, J.G. 1991/2, "Exploration and exploitation in organizational learning," *Organ. Sci.*
17. Levinthal, D.A., March, J.G., 1993/14, "The Myopia of Learning," *Strategic Management Journal*.
18. Henderson, B., Larco, J. 1999, *Lean Transformation*, Oaklea Press.
19. Brue, G., 2002, *Six Sigma for Managers*. McGraw-Hill Professional.
20. Takeuchi, H., Osono, E., Shimizu, N., June 2008, "The Contradictions That Drive Toyota's Success," *Harvard Business Review*.
21. Brunner, D.J., Staats, B.R., Tushman, M.L, Upton, D.M., September 2008, "Wellsprings of Creation: Perturbation and the Paradox of the Highly Disciplined Organization," Harvard Business School Working Paper.
22. Mintzberg, H., Lampel, J., Ahlstrand, B., 1998, *Strategy Safari: A Guided Tour through the Wilds of Strategy Management*, Free Press.
23. Bell, G., Q3/2001, "Looking Across the Atlantic: Using Ethnographic Methods to Make Sense of Europe," *Intel Technology Journal*.

Chapter 5

1. Branson, R., 2006, *Screw It, Let's Do It: Lessons in Life*, Virgin Books, UK.
2. Peters, T.J., Waterman, R.H., 1982, *In Search of Excellence: Lessons from America's Best-Run Companies*, HarperBusiness.
3. Rosen, S., Murphy, K., Scheinkman, J., 1994/102, "Cattle Cycles," *Journal of Political Economy*.
4. Tapscott, D., 2008, *Grown Up Digital: How the Net Generation Is Changing Your World*, McGraw-Hill.
5. The text on framing decisions is based on Tversky A., and Kahneman, D., 1981/4481, "The Framing of Decisions and the Psychology of Choice," *Science*, and Tversky A., and Kahneman, D., 1986/4, "Rational Choice and the Framing of Decisions," *Journal of Business*.
6. Gardner, H., 2007, *Five Minds for the Future*, Harvard Business Press.
7. Ohmae, K. 1991, *The Mind of the Strategist: The Art of Japanese Business*, McGraw-Hill.

Chapter 6

1. Foster, R.N., 1986, *Innovation: The Attacker's Advantage*, MacMillan.
2. Stein, A., July 2003, "Kodak: The Next Polaroid," CNN Money.

3. Flint, J., March 2009, "Why Rick Wagoner Had to Go," *Forbes*.
4. Heyden, K. van der, 1996, *Scenarios: The Art of Strategic Conversation*, Wiley.
5. Lee, L., June 2004, "Jean Therapy, $23 a Pop," *BusinessWeek*.
6. Murnighan, J., Mowen, J., 2002, *The Art of High-Stakes Decision-Making: Tough Calls in a Speed-Driven World*, John Wiley & Sons.
7. Zadek, S., November 2007, "Inconvenient but True: Good Isn't Always Profitable," *Fortune*.
8. Collison, D.J., Cobb, G., Power, D.M., Stevenson, L.A., 2007, "The Financial Performance of the FTSE4Good Indices," *Journal of Corporate Social Responsibility and Environmental Management*.
9. Blowfield, M., Murray, A., 2008, *Corporate Responsibility: A Critical Introduction*, Oxford University Press.
10. Franklin, D., 2008, "A Special Report on Corporate Social Responsibility, The Next Question: Does CSR Work?," *The Economist*, UK.
11. Franklin, D., 2008, "A Special Report on Corporate Social Responsibility, Just Good Business," *The Economist*, UK.
12. Innovest Strategic Value Advisors, January 2003, "Europe's Largest Pension Fund Buys a Minority Stake in SRI Research Firm," press release.
13. McCarthy, B., Linder, J.C., October 2008, "Managing for High Performance in an Uncertain Economy," Outlook Point of View, Accenture.
14. Durand, R., 2003, "Bancassurance across the Globe Meets with Very Mixed Response," *SCOR Technical Newsletters*.
15. Fowler, G.A., Bryan-Low, C., September 2009, "EBay Sells Skype to Investor Group," *Wall Street Journal*.

Chapter 7

1. Gordon, G., Pressman, I., 1983, *Quantitative Decision-Making for Business*, Prentice-Hall International.
2. Terninko, J., Zusman, A., Zlotin, B., 1998, *Systematic Innovation: An Introduction to TRIZ (Theory of Inventive Problem Solving)*, CRC.
3. White, R.E., 1986/7(3), "Generic Business Strategies, Organizational Context and Performance: An Empirical Investigation." *Strategic Management Journal*.

Chapter 8

1. Tapscott, D., 2008, *Grown Up Digital: How the Net Generation Is Changing Your World*, McGraw-Hill.
2. Komorita, S.S., Parks, C.D., 1996, *Social Dilemmas*, Westview Press.
3. Rossouw, D., Vuuren, Leon van, 2004, *Business Ethics*, Oxford University Press, UK.
4. Rossouw, G.J., 1994/13, "Rational Interaction for Moral Sensitivity: A Postmodern Approach to Moral Decision-making in Business," *Journal of Business Ethics*.

5. Trompenaars, F., Hampden-Turner, C., 1997, *Riding the Waves of Culture*, McGraw-Hill.

6. Ohmae, K. 1991, *The Mind of the Strategist: The Art of Japanese Business*, McGraw-Hill.

7. Goldrath, E., 1986, *The Goal: A Process of Ongoing Improvement*, North River Press.

8. Goldrath, E.M. 1990, *What Is This Thing Called Theory of Constraints and How Should It Be Implemented?*, North River Press.

9. Schragenheim, E., 1999, *Management Dilemmas: The Theory of Constraints Approach to Problem Identification and Solutions*, CRC Press.

10. Johnson, M.W., Christensen, C.M., Kagermann, H., December 2008, "Reinventing Your Business Model," *Harvard Business Review*.

11. Tong, V., October 2007, "Live Nation's $120M Deal Lures Madonna," *Washington Post*.

12. Swash, R., April 2008, "Jay-Z to Sign Deal with Live Nation," *The Guardian*, UK.

13. Haycock, G., February 2007, "Prince's Free Album Causes Storm with Retails," Reuters.

Chapter 9

1. Simon, H.A., 1957, *Administrative Behavior: A Study of Decision-Making Processes in Administrative Organizations*, MacMillan.

2. Myers, S., 1977/5, "Determinants of Corporate Borrowing," *Journal of Financial Economics*.

3. Trigeorgis, L, 1999, *Real Options and Business Strategy*, Risk Publications, UK.

4. Coy, P., June 1999, "Exploiting Uncertainty: The 'Real Options' Revolution in Decision-making," *Business Week*.

5. Adner, R., Levinthal, D.A., 2004, *What Is Not a Real Option: Considering Boundaries for the Application of Real Options to Business Strategy*, Academy of Management Review.

6. Porter, M.E., 1985, *Competitive Advantage: Creating and Sustaining Superior Performance*, Free Press.

7. Luehrmann, T.A., September 1998, "Strategy as a Portfolio of Real Options," *Harvard Business Review*.

8. Beinhocker, E.D., 2006, "The Adaptable Corporation," www.mckinseyquarterly .com.

9. Prahalad, C.K., Hamel, G., 1996, *Competing for the Future*, Harvard Business Press.

10. Schwartz, P., 1996, *The Art of the Long View*, Currency Doubleday.

11. Porter, M.E., 1985, *Competitive Advantage: Creating and Sustaining Superior Performance*, Free Press.

12. Drucker, P., September–October 1994, "The Theory of the Business," *Harvard Business Review*.

13. Kaplan, R.S., Norton, D.P., 2004, *Strategy Maps: Converting Intangible Assets into Tangible Outcomes*, Harvard Business Press.

14. Othman, R. 2007/3, "Enhancing the Effectiveness of the Balanced Scorecard with Scenario Planning," *International Journal of Productivity and Performance Management*.
15. Treacy, M., Wiersema, F., 1994, *The Discipline of Market Leaders*, Addison-Wesley.
16. Leach, P. 2006, *Why Can't You Just Give Me the Number?*, Probabilistic Publishing, Texas/Florida.

Chapter 10

1. Collins, J., 2001, *Good to Great: Why Some Companies Make the Leap, And Others Don't*, Collins Business, USA; and Collins, J.C., Porras, J.I., 1994, *Built to Last*, HarperCollins.
2. Peters, T.J., Waterman, R.H., 1982, *In Search of Excellence: Lessons from America's Best-Run Companies*, HarperBusiness.
3. Waal, A. de, 2007, *High-Performance Organizations*, Mainpress, Netherlands.
4. Buytendijk, F.A., 2005, "CPM Helps Build the High-Performance Organization," www.gartner.com.
5. According to TRIZ, a methodology for innovation and problem solving, as described in M.J. Hicks, *Problem Solving and Decision Making*, Cengage Learning Business Press, 2004.
6. World Commission on Environment and Development, 1987, *Our Common Future, Report of the World Commission on Environment and Development*, published as Annex to General Assembly document A/42/427, Development and International Co-operation: Environment.
7. International Standards Organization (ISO), 2002, "Strategic Advisory Group on Corporate Social Responsibility: Preliminary Working Definition of Organizational Social Responsibility," International Organization for Standardization, Switzerland.
8. Commission Green Paper, 2001, "Promoting a European Framework for Corporate Social Responsibility."
9. Friedman, M., 1962, *Capitalism and Freedom*, University of Chicago Press.
10. Drucker, P.F. 1977, *People and Performance: The Best of Peter Drucker on Management*, Butterworth-Heinemann.
11. Porter, M.E., Kramer, M.R., December 2006, "Strategy & Society: The Link between Competitive Advantage and Corporate Social Responsibility," *Harvard Business Review*.
12. Mintzberg, H., 1983/4, "The Case for Corporate Social Responsibility," *Journal of Business Strategy*.
13. Freeman, R.E., 1984, *Strategic Management: A Stakeholder Approach*, Pitman.
14. Crane, A., Matten, D., 2007, *Business Ethics*, Oxford University Press, UK.
15. Malone, T.W., 2004, *The Future of Work: How the New Order of Business Will Shape Your Organization, Your Management Style, and Your Life*, Harvard Business Press.
16. Buytendijk, F.A., 2008, *Performance Leadership*, McGraw-Hill.
17. Neely, A., Adams, C., Kennerley, M., 2002, *The Performance Prism: The Scorecard for Measuring and Managing Business Success*, FT Press, UK.

18. Kotler, P., 2003, *Marketing Insights from A to Z: 80 Concepts Every Manager Needs to Know*, John Wiley & Sons.
19. Kim, W.C., Mauborgne, R., 2009, "How Strategy Shapes Structure," *Harvard Business Review*.
20. Gilmore, J.H., Pine II, B.J., 2007, *Authenticity: What Consumers Really Want*, Harvard Business Press.

About the Author

Frank Buytendijk is one of the world's most recognized authorities in business intelligence and performance management. This professional background gives Frank a strong strategic perspective across many domains in business and IT. He is a world-class speaker at conferences all over the world, and is known for his out-of-the-box thinking and provocative style. With 20 years of experience, Frank has worked as an implementation consultant, project manager, management consultant, business manager, industry analyst and strategist. Frank has a background as Research VP at Gartner and currently holds the position of Vice President and Fellow at one of the largest software vendors in the world. Frank is also a visiting fellow at Cranfield University School of Management. Frank has authored more than a hundred papers and articles, and is author of various books, including *Performance Leadership* (McGraw-Hill, 2008).

For more information, please visit www.frankbuytendijk.com.

Index